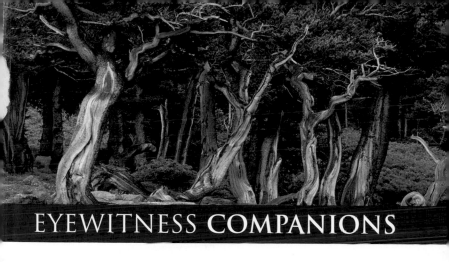

EYEWITNESS **COMPANIONS**

Trees

COLIN RIDSDALE
JOHN WHITE
CAROL USHER

Foreword by
DAVID MABBERLEY

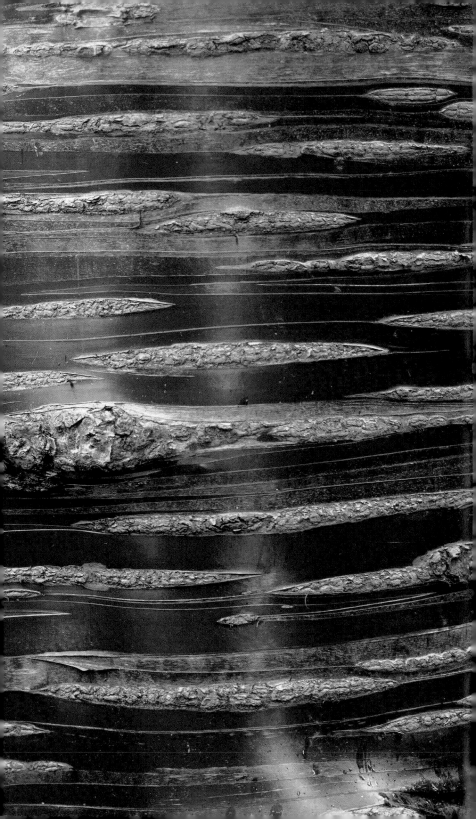

LONDON, NEW YORK,
MUNICH, MELBOURNE, DELHI

Senior Art Editor	Ina Stradins
Senior Editor	Angeles Gavira Guerrero
Art Editor	Vanessa Marr
Project Editor	Cathy Meeus
Designers	Kavita Dutta, Shefali Upadhyay, Romi Chakraborty, Arunesh Talapatra, Enosh Francis
Editors	Dipali Singh, Glenda Fernandes, Rohan Sinha, Aekta Jerath, Mary Lindsay
Managing Art Editor	Phil Ormerod
Managing Editor	Liz Wheeler
Art Director	Bryn Walls
Reference Publisher	Jonathan Metcalf
DTP Coordinator	Pankaj Sharma
DTP Designers	John Goldsmid, Balwant Singh, Sunil Sharma
Production Controller	Kevin Ward
Illustrators	Gill Tomblin, Ann Winterbotham

First American Edition, 2005
Published in the United States by
DK Publishing, Inc.
375 Hudson Street, New York, New York 10014

05 06 07 08 09   10 9 8 7 6 5 4 3 2 1

A Cataloging-in-Publication record for this book is available from the Library of Congress.

ISBN-10: 0-7566-1359-0
ISBN-13: 978-0-75661-359-4

Color reproduction by Colourscan, Singapore
Printed and bound in Hong Kong, China by L Rex

Discover more at
www.dk.com

Foreword 10

WHAT IS A TREE?
12

CONTENTS

"THE FOREST IS A PECULIAR ORGANISM OF
UNLIMITED KINDNESS AND BENEVOLENCE THAT
MAKES NO DEMAND FOR ITS SUSTENANCE AND
EXTENDS GENEROUSLY THE PRODUCTS OF ITS LIFE
ACTIVITY: IT AFFORDS PROTECTION TO ALL BEINGS,
OFFERING SHADE EVEN TO THE AXMAN WHO
DESTROYS IT." *The Buddha*

FOREWORD

In every society, trees provide food in the form of fruits and nuts, flavorings, and even edible flowers and leaves. Trees are the source of pharmaceuticals, as well as building timber and firewood. Their protective bark provides not only medicines but also resins, barkcloth, and cork. Their heartwood and water-transport systems produce long-lasting wood that is used to make furniture and the pulp for all modern books and newspapers. Trees provide the bases for the perfume industry.

As a whole, forests harbor 75 percent of the world's biodiversity. Trees intercept rainfall and gently release it in watersheds; they absorb carbon dioxide and replenish the air with oxygen. Trees are planted to restore degraded landscapes and provide forage for hungry animals. They protect coastlines and riverbanks. Some act as important shade trees and windbreaks; many others are grown as ornamentals.

The original vegetation of much of the world was dominated by trees, and our ancestors were tree-living primates. Trees were the sources of food and medicine long before there was human consciousness. They still feature strongly in our human psyche: the forbidding forests of fairy tales, sacred groves, the Tree of Knowledge, and the Tree of Life—in Christianity, Jesus's cross is often called "the Tree." We have a great fascination with the tallest and oldest trees, which span generations of human lives. Their majestic gigantism is as attractive as that of the dinosaurs.

Perhaps even more importantly, trees have provided the building materials and fuel for most civilizations, either as wood or fossilized as coal. More trees are used for fuel than construction—indeed, the North American peoples thought that the first European settlers could only have left their country because they had run out of firewood.

Brought up in the English countryside before it was so mercilessly pressed into intensive agriculture, I was privileged, as a boy, to wander through woodlands and along hedgerows, learning for myself about the trees and the animals that they sheltered. Standing in a tropical rainforest, among the redwoods of California, the giant eucalyptus of southwestern Australia, or even the relic pine forests of Scotland, inspires an awe that few other experiences can.

Not merely for economic reasons, then, should we do all we can to conserve these bases of civilization, trees, but because we rely on them so much for our spiritual welfare, too.

SWAMP CYPRESS
The buttresses of this deciduous conifer rise from the freshwater swamps of the southeastern United States. The bald cypress (*Taxodium distichum*) displays rich, orange-brown colors in fall.

DAVID MABBERLEY
University of Washington, Seattle;
Universiteit Leiden, Netherlands;
University of Western Sydney & Royal
Botanic Gardens Sydney, Australia

WHAT IS A TREE?

Tree Classification

The definition of a tree accepted by science and the forestry industry is: "A woody plant (arboreal perennial) usually with a single columnar stem capable of reaching six meters [21 feet] in height." Less than 21 ft (6 m) of potential height is regarded as a shrub.

This definition is not absolute; gardeners contest the height threshold, some preferring to use 17 ft (5 m) as their cutoff and others choosing a threshold of 13 ft (3 m). It is likely that bonsai enthusiasts would entirely dismiss any figures suggested. Horticultural selections of dwarf conifers also fall into a gray area usually called "dwarf trees."

BOTANICAL CLASSIFICATION

Classification is the process of arranging plant groups into an order. This helps with the identification of individual species and indicates natural relationships between groups. Attempts to classify plants were made by the ancient Greeks and Romans, including Theophrastus in the 3rd century BCE. and Pliny the Elder before 79 CE. Their methods relied on sometimes very long descriptions instead of succinct names.

Over the centuries, several other systems were proposed. The two-part scientific naming system still in use today (see right) was devised by Karl von Linné (known as Linnaeus) a Swedish botanist who published his *Species Plantarum* in 1753. Linnaeus used a classification system known as artificial

SPORE TREES   **SEED TREES**

MAJOR DIVISIONS
This chart indicates the major groups and subgroups of trees described in this book. It does not imply any kind of evolutionary order. Trees are not equally divided between groups. The spore trees, the most primitive, are represented by only one living genus, although they were far more plentiful in prehistoric times. Seed trees include the most numerous group: the dicotyledons.

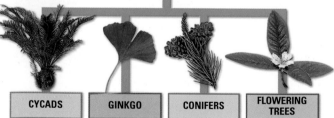

CYCADS   **GINKGO**   **CONIFERS**   **FLOWERING TREES**

SEED TREES
This varied group includes the primitive cycads and ginkgo as well as conifers and the diversity of tree types found among the flowering trees.

FLOWERING TREES
Each of these categories of flowering trees includes a number of families that share certain features, such as fruit type or leaf arrangement.

PRIMITIVE ANGIOSPERMS   **MONOCOTYLEDONS**   **DICOTYLEDONS**

THE NORDMAN FIR IN CONTEXT

In the Linnaean system, all species are classified within their major grouping by family and then by genus. Each species may include one or more subspecies. This example shows the classification of the Nordmann fir (subspecies *borisii-regis*).

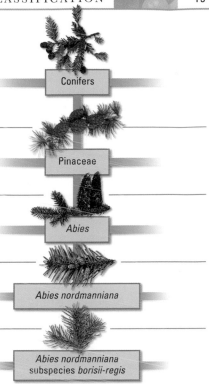

Conifers

FAMILY

A family contains one or more related genera. The family name is always capitalized in roman type.

Pinaceae

GENUS

A genus contains one or more species, and its name forms the first part of the species name. It is capitalized in italic type.

Abies

SPECIES

The species is the basic unit of classification. The name is made up of the genus and species names in italic type.

Abies nordmanniana

SUBSPECIES

Some species have subspecies that may differ in a minor way from the main species. The name has three elements.

Abies nordmanniana
subspecies *borisii-regis*

classification, which places plants into groups such as families and genera based on the establishment of a few shared defining characters (characteristics). Other classification systems place plants into an evolutionary order based on fossil records and comparative anatomy. This book is arranged in the system accepted by the International Union for the Conservation of Nature (IUCN). The principal source is Kubitzki's *Families and Genera of Vascular Plants*. According to this system, trees fall into two main groupings: spore trees and seed trees. Seed trees are further divided between cycads, ginkgo, conifers (gymnosperms), and flowering trees (angiosperms). Flowering trees have three subdivisions: primitive angiosperms, monocotyledons and dicotyledons.

A MULTIPLICITY OF FORMS

The basic definition of a tree encompasses an astonishing variety of plant forms, from the grass-tree (below, left) to the boojum (below, center) and the beech (below, right).

Tree Evolution

Plant life has existed on Earth for millions of years, with records of the first land plants dating from the Silurian period (350–320 million years ago). The huge success of trees in evolutionary terms is due to their ability to adapt to a wide variety of environments.

The earliest trees were conifers, which arose in the Permian period (220–195 million years ago), but it was not until toward the end of the Cretaceous period (140–70 million years ago) that forest vegetation had evolved into tree types that we would recognize today. By this time, forests contained trees that were similar to planetree, magnolia, poplar, and fig. Such flowering plants were better equipped to spread to new areas than earlier flora. This spread was dictated by geographical and climatic changes. Another advantage of flowering trees was their association with pollinating insects such as bees; this enabled the plants to colonize a wide diversity of new sites.

PREHISTORIC FOREST
Prehistoric forests were dominated by tree ferns and giant horsetails creating areas of dense vegetation, as here in the Yarra Ranges National Park, Australia.

Evergreen trees appear. Scale trees, such as *Lepidodendron*, form forests with Calamites, which resembled modern bamboos and creepers.

First land plants, such as *Cooksonia*, appear.

GEOLOGICAL PERIOD	Silurian	Devonian	Carboniferous	Permian
MILLION YEARS AGO	350–320	320–275	275–220	220–195

Seed ferns and horsetails develop stiff stems. Reproduction is by spores dispersed by the wind.

Conifers develop and shade out most horsetails but coexist with seed ferns.

COOKSONIA

LEPIDODENDRON

CYCADS
This ancient family of tropical and subtropical plants is represented by about 100 living species.

GINKGOS
Only one living species (maidenhair tree) remains of this once extensive group of primitive plants.

TREE FERNS
Part of the Cycad family, these ferns from the Southern Hemisphere grow up to 33 ft (10 m) tall.

TREE MIGRATION

Trees respond to changes in conditions on Earth by adapting their size and shape morphologically or by "moving." A tree population moves by successfully seeding in the direction of the most favorable conditions. In this way, modern trees have survived ice ages and global warming or global cooling for millions of years.

CONTINUING EVOLUTION

Tree evolution is a continuing process. Today there are species that are particularly unstable and prone to cross-breeding with near relatives. However, the resulting progeny are occasionally better suited to prevailing conditions than the original tree and are therefore more likely to survive and reproduce.

COAL

Coal is carbon from forest swamps of the Carboniferous period. Regular subsidence caused the forest to be flooded by fresh or salt water. Eventually mudstone, shale, or limestone sediments accumulated, compressing the remnants of forest and peat to form coal. In some areas, a long sequence of inundation and forest regeneration occurred, causing "coal measures"— thin alternating bands of coal and rock. The layers below coal seams frequently contain fragments of tree roots.

COAL

MINING FOR COAL

		Conditions not favorable for tree growth until late in the period. Tree ferns (such as *Dicroidium*), cycads, and conifers are able to survive.		Flowering plants (angiosperms), such as the birchlike *Betulites*, begin to appear. Most modern tree families have evolved by this time.		Grassland replaces large areas of forest. Forested swamps lay down brown coal (lignite). Modern trees have changed little since this period.

ARAUCARIA

Triassic	Jurassic	Cretaceous	Eocene	Oligocene
195–170	170–140	140–70	70–45	45–35

Cycads and conifers flourish. Maidenhair trees (*Ginkgo* and *Baiera*) and *Araucaria* conifers appear.

Flowering trees dominate. Palms appear. The deciduous conifer dawn redwood is first noted.

BETULITES

DICROIDIUM

Tree Structure

Like all living organisms, a tree is a complex structure composed of millions of cells, each with a distinct function. Unlike animals, however, trees are unable to move around to find food, so they make their own using sunlight and obtain water from the soil via their roots.

Trees need a reliable supply of essential nutrients for growth, reproduction, and immunity. They are distinct from many other plants in that they are designed for longevity. Most trees have the potential to live for decades and, in some cases, hundreds of years, and need to adapt themselves accordingly. Each year, trees add a new layer of growth to their existing frames. To support this extra bulk, stiff wood is made in the stem and branches. Spreading roots develop to provide anchorage. These are subdivided into thousands of rootlets for maximum water- and mineral-absorbing capacity. In many species, flowers, followed by seeded fruits, are the means of reproduction.

PARTS OF A TREE

All trees have the same basic components of roots, trunk, branches, leaves, and flowers but there is huge variation between species.

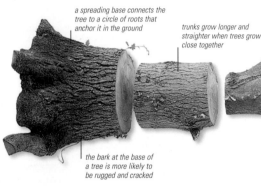

a spreading base connects the tree to a circle of roots that anchor it in the ground

trunks grow longer and straighter when trees grow close together

bark becomes smoother higher up the tree

the bark at the base of a tree is more likely to be rugged and cracked

branches remain at the same height above ground as a tree grows, becoming thicker each year

ROOTS

The roots of all trees anchor the tree into the ground so it is well supported and can grow upright, and enable it to seek out water and minerals to sustain growth and reproduction. Contrary to popular belief, root systems do not mirror the branches of a tree. They seldom reach very deep down into subsoil or bedrock; however, they do extend sideways well beyond the tree canopy.

TRUNK AND BARK

The trunk holds the tree upright so that the foliage can reach the light. Tissues within the wood conduct water and nutrients to the leaves, and sugars to all parts of the tree. The central heartwood confers strength and stiffness. Bark, which may be smooth, rough, or fissured, is the distinctive outer covering of the trunk that protects against the elements and invasion by insects, animals, and disease.

FISSURED BARK

corky layer

deep cracks

ROUGH BARK

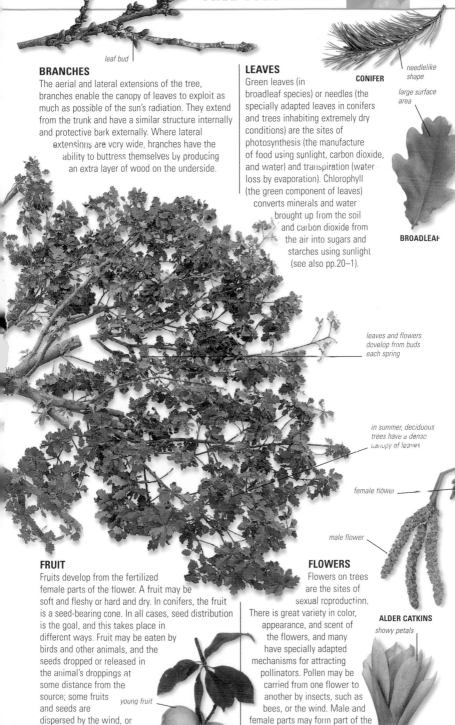

leaf bud

BRANCHES

The aerial and lateral extensions of the tree, branches enable the canopy of leaves to exploit as much as possible of the sun's radiation. They extend from the trunk and have a similar structure internally and protective bark externally. Where lateral extensions are very wide, branches have the ability to buttress themselves by producing an extra layer of wood on the underside.

LEAVES

Green leaves (in broadleaf species) or needles (the specially adapted leaves in conifers and trees inhabiting extremely dry conditions) are the sites of photosynthesis (the manufacture of food using sunlight, carbon dioxide, and water) and transpiration (water loss by evaporation). Chlorophyll (the green component of leaves) converts minerals and water brought up from the soil and carbon dioxide from the air into sugars and starches using sunlight (see also pp.20–1).

CONIFER

needlelike shape

large surface area

BROADLEAF

leaves and flowers develop from buds each spring

in summer, deciduous trees have a dense canopy of leaves

female flower

male flower

FRUIT

Fruits develop from the fertilized female parts of the flower. A fruit may be soft and fleshy or hard and dry. In conifers, the fruit is a seed-bearing cone. In all cases, seed distribution is the goal, and this takes place in different ways. Fruit may be eaten by birds and other animals, and the seeds dropped or released in the animal's droppings at some distance from the source; some fruits and seeds are dispersed by the wind, or by becoming attached to an animal's fur.

young fruit

PEACHES

FLOWERS

Flowers on trees are the sites of sexual reproduction. There is great variety in color, appearance, and scent of the flowers, and many have specially adapted mechanisms for attracting pollinators. Pollen may be carried from one flower to another by insects, such as bees, or the wind. Male and female parts may form part of the same flower, or they may be borne separately.

ALDER CATKINS

showy petals

MAGNOLIA

How Trees Work

Growth and reproduction are a tree's most important functions, and to achieve this end, the tree needs a constant supply of food and water that must be circulated to all parts of its structure. This is a complex process, the main component of which is photosynthesis.

Three fundamental stimuli govern tree growth: geotropism (response to gravity) makes shoots grow up and roots go downward; phototropism (response to light) affects the direction of foliage growth and keeps roots away from light; hydrotropism (response to water in the ground) affects the direction and extent of root growth.

HOW TREES MAKE FOOD

The manufacturing of food for a tree—photosynthesis—takes place within the leaves. The end products are carbohydrates (starch and glucose) and cellulose formed from hydrogen, oxygen, and carbon derived from the air and minerals from the soil. Sunlight provides the energy for this process. Photosynthesis can only take place in the presence of chlorophyll,

a green pigment found within structures called chloroplasts in the leaf cells. The carbohydrates are transported to all parts of the tree. On arrival at the root tips, the sugar content builds up in the cells until it is greater than in the surrounding soil. To maintain a state of equilibrium, water

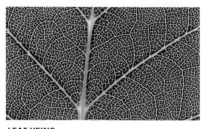

LEAF VEINS
A network of veins (sometimes called nerves) on the underside of a leaf transports the products of photosynthesis to and from all parts of the tree.

HOW PHOTOSYNTHESIS WORKS

The leaf is the main site of photosynthesis, which is the process by which carbon dioxide and hydrogen are converted into carbohydrates to feed the tree and the waste product oxygen is released into the atmosphere.

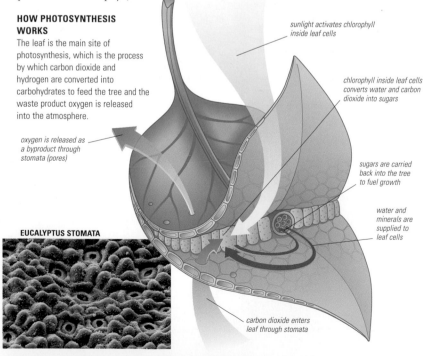

sunlight activates chlorophyll inside leaf cells

chlorophyll inside leaf cells converts water and carbon dioxide into sugars

oxygen is released as a byproduct through stomata (pores)

sugars are carried back into the tree to fuel growth

water and minerals are supplied to leaf cells

EUCALYPTUS STOMATA

carbon dioxide enters leaf through stomata

TREE CIRCULATION

The transportation of nutrients and water between leaves and roots is a complex process in a tree. The main components of the system (shown schematically below) are xylem vessels, which transport water and mineral salts, and phloem vessels, which carry mainly sugars. These vessels are situated in the veins of leaves and in the growing sections of the wood of the trunk and branches.

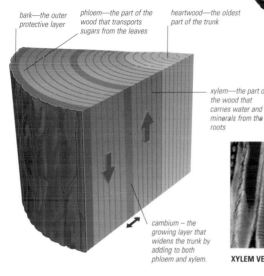

bark—the outer protective layer

phloem—the part of the wood that transports sugars from the leaves

heartwood—the oldest part of the trunk

xylem—the part of the wood that carries water and minerals from the roots

cambium – the growing layer that widens the trunk by adding to both phloem and xylem.

TREE RINGS

Each band in a cut trunk represents a new layer of xylem laid down annually during the growing season.

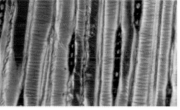

XYLEM VESSELS IN A PINE BRANCH

passes through cell walls into the root. The liquid is taken up by the tree, aided by a partial vacuum caused by the loss of excess water (transpiration) from foliage. Eventually the mineral-rich water reaches the leaves and is used in the food-manufacturing process.

USING EARTH AND AIR

A tree requires mineral salts, which are obtained by the roots in solution from the soil. Minerals go up through the xylem in the trunk (see Tree Circulation, above).

Excess water is expelled through pores on the surface of the leaf (stomata) and on young shoots (lenticels). These pores open or close in response to humidity and drying winds to maintain constant water pressure within the tree. The most important of the mineral salts is nitrogen. Leaves absorb hydrogen, carbon, and oxygen from the air, but nitrogen cannot be absorbed in this way. Lightning storms cause nitrogen and oxygen to combine and dissolve in rain to form nitrous and nitric acids. In the soil, these combine with mineral salts and ammonia to form nitrites and nitrates, a process called the nitrogen cycle. A few plant species have nitrifying bacteria on their roots that convert nitrogen in the air into an absorbable form. Nutrients are recycled when dead leaves fall and rot, eventually being taken up again by the root system.

GNARLED BARK

The outermost layer of the trunk is composed of dead cells that impart a distinctive appearance. Bark is primarily protective, but it also contains tiny pores that allow gases to flow in and out.

Tree Reproduction

As in most other plants, many trees reproduce in three stages—pollen release, fertilization, and seed dispersal. Since trees are static, many devices have evolved over the years to increase the chances of successful reproduction. Trees also have other means of propagation.

POLLINATION

Most trees are either gymnosperms (conifers) or angiosperms (flowering plants). Conifers have separate, male and female flowers on the same tree; these are wind-pollinated. The male flowers are small conelike structures of bracts and stamens that produce vast clouds of pollen in early spring. The female flowers are miniature versions of the mature cones they will eventually become. Angiosperms have an elaborate array of flower types, some designed for wind pollination and others with fragrant petals and nectar to attract insects or other creatures. In some species, trees are exclusively male or female (dioecious). In others, both male and female flowers appear on the same tree; they may be combined (hermaphrodite) or they may be separate (monoecious).

DIOECIOUS

An example of a dioecious tree, holly (*Ilex aquifolium*) is either exclusively male or, as in this case, female, which produces berries.

MONOECIOUS

The majority of conifers have both male and female flowers on the same tree, as in the Scotch pine (*Pinus sylvestris*).

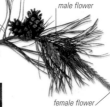

male flower

female flower

HERMAPHRODITE

Apple (*Malus*) blossoms are hermaphroditic, with male and female parts.

BEE ON BLOSSOM

While the bee penetrates the petals for nectar, pollen sticks to the insect and is transferred to the next flower.

BIRD DISPERSAL
In addition to receiving nutritional value from the berry, the feeding bird inadvertently spreads the seed.

WATER DISPERSAL
One of the largest and heaviest seeds, the coconut has evolved to travel hundreds of miles by water

WIND DISPERSAL
When temperature and humidity are just right, the cone opens to release seeds that are carried by the wind.

SEED DISPERSAL

Conifer seeds are usually dispersed by the wind. Cones open in response to heat and humidity, releasing the winged seeds over a long period to ensure that some of it has a chance of survival in ideal conditions. Some pines have seeds that stay in the cone until it drops to the ground and is carried away by an animal. Other conifers benefit from forest fires. The cones survive the heat of the fire, then open to shed seed some hours later when the ash-enriched ground has cooled. Broadleaved trees employ a range of seed-distribution techniques. Some fruits have to be ingested by birds or animals before they will grow. Others are carried away and buried by animals or birds and may be abandoned or forgotten, allowing them to germinate. Winged seeds (keys) are carried away from the mother tree. Some, such as alder, are able to float in water. Many large seeds also float; some, such as the coconut, can travel great distances across oceans.

SELF-PROPAGATION

Some trees have the ability to layer—that is, root into the soil when a branch rests on the ground. This is useful for trees prone to lightning strikes; the parent is destroyed but a ring of clones survives. Suckering is another successful survival technique. Surface roots send up new stems at a distance from the parent, eventually forming new trees. A few wetland trees propagate by breaking up. The crack willow (*Salix fragilis*) drops twigs, which eventually stick in wet mud and grow. Some forms of this species no longer reproduce sexually.

SUCKERING
With new shoots constantly springing up from the root system, this grove of aspens (below) is in fact composed of multiple stems of a single parent tree.

LAYERING
The lower branches of some trees can take root if they make contact with the soil. The red mangrove (*Rhizophora mangle*), pictured above, provides an extreme example of this.

Coniferous Forests

Conifers were once the dominant group of trees on the Earth but suffered from competition from broadleaved evergreens, which flourished in temperate and warm climates. Conifer forests now dominate only in cold, dry, mountainous regions.

SURVIVING THE COLD

Primitive conifers could not compete for light with the large, flat leaves of the new broadleaf species. They could grow tall, reaching above the canopy, but in so doing they provided shelter and incentive for the broadleaves to catch up. However, conifers had an advantage in that their narrow, often waxy foliage was good for conserving moisture. The only way for them to survive was to move by seeding into colder, drier areas. So conifers moved north toward the polar region and up into the mountains.

CONIFER NEEDLES

Cones of tamarack (*Larix laricina*) on a long branchlet with needlelike leaves adapted for wintry conditions.

BLACK FOREST

Densely packed plantations of conifers characterize temperate conifer forests such as the Black Forest region in Germany, pictured here.

CONIFERS TODAY

In the cold Arctic tundra, the forest consists of thin, narrow-crowned spruces and low, bushy junipers. On mountains, dwarf pines hug the tree line, stunted by snow and wind. In the vast wastes of Siberia and Canada, growth is slow, but trees remain vertical with short

SURVIVAL THROUGH THE SEASONS

Massive forests of fir, spruce, and pine trees follow the winding path of the majestic Rocky Mountains in North America. They are able to survive the harsh winter conditions as far north as Alaska.

branches to shed snow easily. Dense forests of pine and silver fir (*Abies alba*) occur in the German Black Forest, the Caucasus, and Asia. Pine forests thrive in the northwestern US and along the Pacific coast.

Conifers are genetically programmed to a particular climate. They must grow actively for about two months a year to survive, and many hardy species need a cold spell to rest, which ripens and stiffens the wood. In the south, Alpine trees fail by growing during brief warm winter spells, only to be cut back by late frosts. Southern trees moved north start growing too late and do not complete their growth cycle before the winter.

ACID RAIN

Oxides of nitrogen and sulfur, produced by burning coal and oil, combine with raindrops to form solutions of nitric and sulfuric acids. In high concentrations, these acids can kill plants and animals and raise acid levels in soil and water. Conifer forests in Scandinavia have been particularly affected by acid rain.

ACID RAIN DAMAGE

FORESTS WORLDWIDE

THE AMERICAS

A huge belt of forest runs from Alaska to Labrador. Species of redwood (*Sequoia*) populate conifer forests of the western US. The monkey puzzle tree (*Araucaria araucana*) is a conifer species that occurs in the wild in Argentina and Chile.

ASIA

Vast areas of Russia are covered by dense spruce and pine forests, mainly Siberian spruce (*Picea obovata*) The characteristic conifer species of Japan are the Japanese cedar (*Cryptomeria japonica*) and Japanese larch (*Larix kaempferi*).

SEQUOIA

EUROPE

Northern Europe is home to vast pine and spruce forests. Conifers extend south into the broadleaf zone—for example, Maritime Pine (*Pinus pinaster*) close to the Mediterranean.

Temperate Broadleaf Forests

Temperate broadleaved trees evolved from tropical species. During dry periods, certain species on the fringes of tropical forests eventually became deciduous, that is, dropped their leaves in response to lack of rain as a strategy for survival.

BROADLEAVES WORLDWIDE

Since they first appeared, broadleaf trees have developed survival tactics, including dropping leaves. Some evergreen species evolved alternative ways of conserving moisture, either by developing a waxy coating on the foliage (eucalyptus and hollies) or by reducing their surface area. Mixed deciduous woodland often has an understory of evergreens, including boxwood and holly, that absorb enough light during the winter months, when the leaves are off the larger trees, to survive. The zone of temperate broadleaf forest occupies the eastern US, and Europe from Britain to Belarus and Russia.

BEECH FOREST
Where beech predominates in a forest, it tends to shade out competitor species of trees so that eventually only mature beech trees survive.

MAPLE LEAVES

In fall, chemical changes in leaves as they are about to be shed produce a rich palette of warm colors.

Another large area of this type of forest exists in China and Japan. In the Southern Hemisphere, the zone includes temperate rainforest in Argentina and Chile, southern areas of Australia, and part of New Zealand's South Island.

FORESTS PRESERVED FOR GAME

In many parts of the world, particularly in northern European countries, tracts of broadleaf woodland have been preserved specifically as hunting forests and havens for game, such as deer and wild boar. Traditionally, pigs were kept in the woods and fattened on beech "mast" and acorns before being slaughtered.

ELK IN A FOREST CLEARING

BROADLEAVES AT HIGH ALTITUDE

In some tropical areas, isolated temperate broadleaved trees grow in the cooler conditions at high altitude. In southern Australia, eucalyptus forests typically consist of slender trees up to 200 ft (60 m) tall, and the forest is a light, airy environment because the leaves hang down and turn edgeways on to the sun, keeping them cool but letting the light through.

AUTUMN GLORY

In New England, acre upon acre of mixed deciduous woodlands of maple, hickory, hornbeam, and aspen produce a fine display of fall color, which heralds the changing of the seasons every year.

FOREST TYPES

BEECH FOREST

Beech forest occupies warm temperate zones and is demanding of light. It suppresses other trees.

BIRCH–ALDER FOREST

Found in cold and poor soil conditions. Birch exists across the Northern Hemisphere up to the Arctic tundra. Alder colonizes wetland by making its own nitrogen fertilizer.

EUCALYPTUS FOREST

South of the tropical zone in Australia, cold-tolerant species form dense forests. In Tasmania, some tolerate snow.

OAK FOREST

Many forests evolve into oak, with different oak species in America, Europe, and Asia. Other trees coexist, creating a rich and diverse ecosystem.

SOUTHERN BEECH FOREST

In Chile and Argentina, southern beech (*Nothofagus* sp.) forms dense forests. Smaller forests occur in New Zealand.

Tropical Broadleaf Forests

One of the most diverse categories, tropical broadleaf forests are found in all tropical habitats, except rainforest and barren lands. The tree species that populate such forests have adapted in many different ways to a wide range of habitats and climates.

TROPICAL BROADLEAF FOREST AREAS

CONTINENTAL TROPICAL FOREST

This type of forest is found in hot, dry places such as Australia and Africa.

MONSOON WOODLAND

Found in India, Myanmar, Laos, Thailand, Cambodia, Sumatra, and Java.

OCEANIC TROPICAL FOREST

These coastal forests are found in the Pacific Islands and northeastern Australia.

RIVERINE FOREST

Found in deep river valleys where there is waterfall spray and high humidity.

SUBTROPICAL RAINFOREST

Found in Florida, the Brazilian Highlands, and the Great Divide in Australia.

THORN FOREST

Found in east Brazil, Paraguay, and coastal Texas and Mexico.

DIVERSE CONDITIONS

The climate that encourages growth of tropical broadleaves is similar to that of tropical rainforests. The difference is that a dry season occurs for part of the year, which interrupts growth and forces trees into a dormant phase. Deciduous species shed leaves in response; evergreen trees enter a rest period as seen in the wood by discernible rings of fast and slow growth.

Classification of this type of forest is difficult because there are many transitional areas, particularly along the cooler fringes of a tropical zone or where forest meets the sea. Oceanic tropical forests are mainly evergreen, forming an incomplete canopy, with further levels of vegetation including a shrub layer and ground cover. Lianas and epiphytes are frequent. Sea mist contributes to alleviating the freshwater deficit. Red mangrove (*Rhizophora mangle*) swamps rapidly build up a humid jungle of stems and roots.

SPARSE AFRICAN FOREST

In inhospitable parts of the world where extreme heat and dry conditions prevail, tree life is sporadic, with only a few species, such as acacia, able to survive.

GIRAFFE BROWSING ON ACACIAS

DENSE TROPICAL EUCALYPTUS FOREST
Tight packing and flammable leaves make eucalyptus prone to forest fires, but they have a built-in response. hidden buds in the stump regrow after the fire is out.

SURVIVING DROUGHT

Continental tropical forests have a very dry season that affects survival and natural selection. Many trees have small leaves protected by dense hairs. Others have drastically reduced their leaf area to conserve moisture. An example is the beefwood (*Casuarina equisetifolia*), which resembles a horsetail with slender-jointed branches and scalelike leaves. Tropical forms of eucalyptus often grow alongside this species.

Monsoon woodland is a type of tropical forest that grows in tropical climates characterized by periods of very high rainfall. Typical species include ebony (*Diospyros ebenum*) and sago palm (*Metroxylon sago*). Riverine forests occur in humid valleys where rainfall is less excessive.

Subtropical rainforest occurs at high elevation often above tracts of actual rainforest (see pp.32–3).

The mainly deciduous thorn forest occurs between dense tree cover and semi-desert in tropical zones. It is hot and dry for long periods. Adequate moisture is maintained in the soil and trees derive protection from their close proximity to one another. Species that thrive in these areas include carob (*Ceratonia siliqua*) and baobab (*Adansonia digitata*).

MOUNTAIN GUM LEAVES
The pale, gray-green waxy leaves of this species are an adaptation to prevent excess heat and moisture loss.

WILDLIFE IN EUCALYPTUS FOREST

Tropical forms of eucalyptus are among the most successful of trees, with over 500 species and 150 varieties known. Almost all of these can be found in Australia, where their aromatic leaves provide the staple diet for koalas. Eucalyptus leaves are not very nutritious, but these tree-dwelling marsupials have a low energy output, spending up to 18 hours a day resting in the branches.

KOALA EATING EUCALYPTUS LEAVES

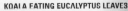

Tropical Rainforests

Luxuriant tropical rainforest is a diverse evergreen plant community that exists in parts of the equatorial zone where there are conditions of high humidity and consistently warm temperatures. There is no dry season, and growth of plants is continuous throughout the year.

UNIQUE ECOSYSTEM

An astonishing variety of plants live in the rainforest, all with an ability to grow rapidly, an essential ingredient in the battle for light and survival. Rainforest trees typically have long, branch-free

stems and small leafy tops packed into a continuous green canopy. Beneath this are smaller trees and shade-tolerant shrubs. Numerous climbing plants, such as lianas, cling to trees, and orchids and ferns flourish on the dark forest floor. The rainforest habitat is perpetuated from within as well as by the climate. Reducing its size or making holes in it by felling trees changes the microclimate, at great cost to the diverse species it supports.

SOUTH AMERICAN RAINFOREST

Larger than all the other rainforests combined, the Amazon basin rainforest (below and left) is home to almost half the world's bird species. Its trees release vast amounts of oxygen into the atmosphere.

TEAK
In the rainforest, species such as teak (*Tectona grandis*) grow to great heights to reach the light.

MAHOGANY
Mahogany trees (*Swietenia* spp.) growing close together in the rainforest have few lower branches.

HOW A RAINFOREST WORKS

Transpiration of moisture from the trees supplements the natural rainfall in the forest. Massive quantities of life-giving oxygen are manufactured by the trees as a byproduct of photosynthesis and pumped into the atmosphere. The whole ecosystem is also a huge storeroom of fixed carbon. Although moisture is plentiful, rainforest soils tend to be poor. Evergreen foliage produces little leaf mold, and the very high rainfall saturates unprotected soil so that nutrients not locked up in plants are soon leached away.

ORCHID
Orchids often share the rainforest, some growing on moist bark instead of soil.

AROUND THE WORLD

AFRICA
Equatorial rainforest occupies much of the Congo Basin and the Guinea coast. There are isolated areas in Zambia, near the Indian Ocean, and in eastern Madagascar.

INDIAN SUBCONTINENT
The western seaboard of India and Sri Lanka is tropical rainforest in the strict sense. Similar monsoon jungle and equatorial broadleaf forest obscure its eastern limits. Concentrations of rainforest also occur in Bangladesh.

SOUTH AMERICA
The world's largest area of rainforest occupies the Amazon Basin, extending from the Atlantic coast to the foothills of the Andes. It merges into savanna in the north and in the south, tropical broadleaf forest and grassland.

SOUTHEAST ASIA
Much of this area once supported rainforest, particularly Sumatra, Borneo, the Celebes, and the Philippines. In Myanmar, teak (*Tectona grandis*) is still harvested commercially. It is sustainable only if replanted or allowed to regenerate.

RUBBER PLANTATION

Rainforests provide many of the raw materials for industry, including plants for the pharmaceutical industry and rubber. The rubber tree (*Hevea brasiliensis*) was first found in the Amazon rainforest; vast plantations now exist in India, Indonesia, Malaysia, and other equatorial regions. Latex is the sap of the tree, and careful cutting of the bark (known as "tapping") releases the latex without causing damage. An individual tree can produce latex in viable quantities for up to 30 years.

RUBBER TIRE   **TAPPING RUBBER**

Barren Lands

Many situations exist in which trees survive against all the odds, and it is remarkable how they can adapt to hostile places. Lands may be barren for many reasons, including temperature extremes, boggy ground, and wind and salt near the sea.

TREE PIONEERS

Some groups of trees are specially adapted as pioneers, opening the way for others. Attributes of such trees include early maturity, massive seed production, rapid growth, and a relatively short life span. For example, the lodgepole pine (*Pinus contorta*) produces its first cones and fertile seed in just six years, and some poplars grow 6½ ft (2 m) a year. The ability to survive in close proximity to one another is another attribute of pioneer species such as the birch, which often grows in dense thickets, producing few branches and small, bushy tops. The birch plantation starts to decline and break up after only

DESERT TREES

Cacti show an extreme adaptation to a dry habitat. Their fleshy trunks conserve water, while their leaves have been reduced to spikes to reduce water loss.

ADAPTED FOR THE HEAT

The drooping leaves of many eucalyptus species have evolved to turn edgeways to minimize the area exposed to the heat of the sun.

40–60 years, usually giving way to more robust species, such as oak, that require shelter as seedlings. Alder is an ideal wetland pioneer, able to seed in sedge beds and other boggy places.

EXTREMES OF TEMPERATURE

Barren land often occurs where extremes of heat or cold provide a challenge to survival. In cold regions such as the Arctic sub-tundra, mountain snowlines, and bleak moorland, a number of hardy tree species exist just inside the limits of survival, waiting for a chance to venture into new, treeless territory. The trigger may be a run of slightly warmer winters or the arrival of rudimentary shelter. Even damage on hills by avalanche or erosion may provide an opportunity for seeding. Shelter is usually in the form of hardy alpine shrubs such as dwarf willows, dwarf birch (*Betula nana*), or shrubby junipers. Once established, these species provide additional shelter for larger woody plants, and a progression to scrub and eventually forest occurs. In hot conditions, migration into treeless semi-desert is triggered by a climatic anomaly, such as freak rainfall or temporary cooling. The activities of burrowing animals may also provide opportunities for seeds of acacia, thorn, or palm to germinate. Tree survival in hot conditions often depends on establishing a tight group that will provide mutual shelter from the sun. All desert trees rely on deep roots to seek out groundwater and on nighttime condensation being trapped and dripping from the foliage.

ADAPTED TO COLD
In cold climates, the tree species that survive tend to grow slowly and have small, hard needles. Chances of survival increase where trees grow close together.

CLINGING ON
Some trees require little soil, surviving in rock fissures and damp, peaty cavities. Here, an acacia is clinging to the edge of the Waimea Canyon, Kauai Island.

TREES BY THE SEA

In coastal areas, sea water leaching into the ground can make the land inhospitable to trees; most are killed by excessive soil salinity. Some plants, however, are salt-resistant and rapidly move back into bare ground. Salt spray is limiting but not usually fatal. Young growth may be killed each year, so trees take on a sculpted appearance, leaning away from the sea. As in other hostile conditions, trees survive by making use of available shelter.

STONY GROUND
Frankincense trees (*Boswellia sacra*) survive in stony deserts because small amounts of moisture condense between the hot surface and cold subsoil.

Identifying Trees

Many people can easily identify the trees that are common in the area in which they live. However, there are times—for example, when traveling or when confronted with an unfamiliar species—when it is useful to be able to identify a tree in a more systematic way.

FIELD WORK

Reliable identification depends on thorough observation. Gather as much information as possible in the form of notes, sketches, photographs and, with permission, small samples of foliage, including a flower and fruit, even if it is old material picked up from the ground. As well as the items described in the panel below, a useful piece of equipment for field work is a pair of binoculars to see features that are out of reach. Many types of binoculars work as a powerful hand lens if used backward.

You will also find it useful to acquire a detailed guide to the trees of the area in which you are interested. Some guides, known as keys, are designed to identify trees by a process of elimination. Trees are divided into groups according to certain distinguishing characters. Smaller groups are then subdivided until finally the plant, or group to which it

VARIABLE HABIT
Each tree species has a characteristic overall shape when it grows unimpeded. However, the habit can be dramatically different if the tree is, for example, growing in close proximity to others, as can be seen in these photographs of beech trees alone (above) and in a forest (left).

belongs, can be identified. It is important to always use a local key that refers to the region you are in. Photographs and illustrations are a valuable aid at every stage of the identification process.

TAKING FIELD NOTES

When you go out on a "tree spotting" trip, you will find it helpful to take a few items of equipment to aid identification. You will need a notebook, pencil, and a selection of colored pencils to record your observations in words and pictures. You don't need to be an accomplished artist to make useful visual notes and sketches. A magnifying glass will enable you to see details on leaves, such as hairs and veins. With wax crayons and plain paper, you can take rubbings of bark texture. If you intend to bring samples of fallen leaves or fruit home, be sure to have a store of labels and bags to put them in. Finally, bring a camera to take photographs of the tree.

A TREE FILE
Detailed notes, sketches, photographs, bark rubbings, and samples of leaves and fruit should enable you to identify all but the most unusual trees.

...RVATION

...a tree that you are
...nize immediately, it is
...llow the process of
identification systematically. Observe and
take notes on each aspect of the tree's
physical characteristics: bark, leaves, fruit,
and flowers (see below). Take note, too, of
the tree's size and habit (overall shape),
although this is not necessarily a defining
feature (see Variable Habit, opposite).
Other important information to record
could include the tree's location and the
type of habitat in which it is growing—

for example, open park...
mountainside, or dense f...
too, other tree species grov...

Many tree enthusiasts de...
satisfaction from keeping the...
of interesting trees they have se...
photographs, sketches, and bark r...
can all contribute to a fascinating r...
of "meetings" with trees. A record or...
associated birds, insects, and other wild...
is also of interest. You might consider
observing several trees close to your
home through the seasons and over
a number of years.

LEAVES

Observation of a leaf should include
taking note of its type, how it is
arranged on the shoot, its overall shape,
whether the leaf margins are smooth,
lobed, or toothed, and what color they
are above and beneath. Use a
magnifying glass to observe fine hairs
and veining. (See Glossary for more
information on leaf types.)

toothed
margin

clustered
arrangement

bright green
coloration

NEEDLES   **SIMPLE**   **COMPOUND**

BARK

The bark of a tree often changes with
age. Nevertheless, it is an important
feature to observe. Note the color and
the texture, whether it is smooth, flaking
or peeling, or fissured. Make a bark
rubbing with wax crayon for your
records. You should also look for any
resin visible from previous cuts in the
bark. Do not make such cuts yourself.

FISSURED   **SMOOTH**   **FLAKING**

FLOWERS

The color and shape of the flower are
the most obvious features, but be sure to
also look at their arrangement—whether
they are solitary blooms or appear in a
more complex inflorescence (see also
Glossary). Some species have male
and female flowers on the same tree.
Others have male and female flowers
on different trees.

CLUSTER   **SOLITARY**   **INFLORESCENCE**

FRUIT

Fruits appear after flowers and will only
rarely be seen together. They may be
several different types. Take note of the
external color, shape, and size. Then, if
possible, open one and observe the
number and arrangement of seeds within
the fruit. Be aware that fruit often changes
significantly in size and color as it ripens
on the tree.

DRUPE   **CONE**   **POD**

LIVING WITH
TREES

Early People and Trees

More than ten million years ago, our apelike ancestors lived in trees,
which provided their major needs of safety, food, and warmth.
By five million years ago, our human ancestors walked on the ground.
But we have still relied on trees through every phase of our prehistory.

Since humans first evolved from apelike mammals, trees and forests have provided us with food, warmth, protection from the elements, and safety from predators. Trees were a source of plentiful and varied food, from succulent shoots to leaves, fruits, nuts, and berries. Many Neanderthal sites from 100,000 years ago are still littered with tree seeds and husks. Woods were also home to animals to hunt, from squirrels to deer and wild boar.

WOOD FOR FIRE

Early people probably noticed a wildfire's warmth, saw how the flames kept large predators at bay, and even tasted how the heat cooked carcasses. Early evidence for controlled fires at a specific site, using collected wood, comes from the charred animal bones and fossil ash layers at "Dragon Bone Hill," Zhoukoudian, near Beijing, China. These hearths date back more than 400,000 years. They were tended by representatives of the now-extinct human species *Homo erectus*. By 100,000 years ago, the also-extinct Neanderthal people were using wood-fueled fires at various sites around Europe, to help keep them warm in the intense cold of the last great Ice Age.

LIVING ALOFT
Our closest living cousins, the chimpanzees, still rely on trees for most of their requirements.

TREES FOR TRANSPORT
Dugout canoes (like this modern Dutch example) may date back over 8,500 years.

TREES FOR SHELTER

Prehistoric humans probably sheltered in woods, since conditions among the trees were preferable to the harsh sun or windy blizzards of open country. Some 400,000 years ago near Bilzingsleben, Germany, patterns of preserved holes suggest upright posts for specially built wooden shelters—again,

DEER-HUNT WITH WOOD BOWS AND ARROWS
This painting from Cavalls Cave near Valltorta, Spain, dates back 12,000 years. Luckily, pigments of prehistoric art last longer than most wooden objects they depict.

probably the handiwork of *Homo erectus*. By 60,000 years ago, Neanderthal people may have constructed hutlike shelters in Moldova. From 30,000 years ago, Grimaldis and Cro-Magnons—European groups of our own species, *Homo sapiens*—made more complex dwellings from wood, mammoth tusks, and animal skins, at sites such as Dolni Vestonice, in the Czech Republic.

WOODEN WEAPONS

Before the Stone Age, ancient humans probably used branches to smash and stab. But unlike stone, wood decays. So evidence for wooden weapons and utensils comes mostly from associated stone artifacts such as ax-heads, spear-tips, or arrow-heads, and prehistoric art. *Homo erectus* may have thrown spears some 400,000 years ago near Schoningen, Germany. Nearby in Lehringen, the Mousterian tool culture of Neanderthal people probably included wooden spears. Early *Homo sapiens* left evidence of wooden spears 80,000 years ago at Mount Carmel, Israel. The notched spear-thrower or *atlatl*, for greater power and distance, dates from over 20,000 years ago; it may have led to the bow and arrow. Stone arrowheads were known in Africa before 25,000 years ago, with European versions from 12,000 years ago. Danish bows of yew and elm date to 10,000 years ago. A frozen traveler, "Otzi the Iceman," who died 5,300 years ago in the European Alps, had 14 wooden arrows in his quiver.

ANASAZI AX
This Aztec tool, almost 1,000 years old, has its original wooden shaft and willow twine binding.

ATLATL
Wooden spear-throwers probably preceded the bow and arrow.

FLINT-HEADED ADZ
A stone held in a wooden shaft was a basic tool for early humans.

Tree Myths and Spirits

Trees were the largest and oldest living things known to many early peoples. Their size and their importance in terms of providing shelter, sustenance, and a wide variety of materials have earned trees a prominent place in the world's myths and legends.

SPIRIT HOMES

Although ancient storytellers sometimes spoke of trees as spirits, in most mythologies trees are the homes of spirits. From North America to Africa, these spirits protect the trees they inhabit—they are said to attack anyone who tries to harm a tree or cut it down. If treated properly, tree spirits are usually seen as helpful to humans, but forests can be dark and intimidating places, and this is reflected in stories, common in Africa, of forest spirits that trap the unwary in their branches or eat human flesh.

Large baobabs are said to be home to many spirits. People are expected to warn these spirits well in advance—often in writing—before felling a baobab. The notice gives the spirits the chance to find another tree. If people need to cut down a tree for the timber, this has to be done with the correct respect and ritual. Repeating the appropriate spell or chant before felling a tree will bring good fortune to any objects that are made from the wood. In a similar way, a shaman must observe the correct rituals when cutting wood

YGGDRASIL
The great ash tree of Norse mythology, Yggdrasil, was believed to support the world. Its branches and roots provided structure and protection.

and carving it to make a drum. Only then will the drum speak with the tree spirit's voice.

The ancient Greeks believed that each tree had its spirit, or hamadryad, who watched over the tree and tried to stop people from cutting it down. Hamadryads, like the trees they inhabited, could live for hundreds of years, and a hamadryad only perished when her tree met its death. In Japanese folklore, many trees are said to have spirits. One story tells how the spirit of

THE ENDURING BAOBAB
The capacity of the towering African baobab to survive lightning strikes contributes to its link with the supernatural.

VOICE OF THE TREE
In Africa, people say that trees are the homes of powerful spirits. A shaman's drum is usually made from wood, and he hopes that the spirit of the tree speaks when he plays his instrument.

a plum tree defended a peasant who tried to stop a nobleman from transplanting the tree. When the nobleman drew his sword on the peasant, the tree moved so that the blow hit one of her branches, which then fell on the nobleman's head.

THE POWER OF ANCIENT TREES

Trees that are unusually tall and old have always been given special respect and status. Especially ancient trees, such as some yews in English churchyards, are particularly revered and are said to "ward off evil spirits." The "world tree" of Norse mythology, the ash called Yggdrasil, was

SPRUCE TREE MYTH

Some native peoples of the North American subarctic have myths of the Distant Time, when living things had a human form. Among these people were widows who pinched their skin and cried when told that their husbands had died. These women were believed to have become spruce trees, whose coarse, pinched bark was the result of this repeated pinching.

SPRUCE TREES IN WINTER

so huge that it linked together the entire Norse cosmos. The tree spread its canopy over the whole world and the sky, while its roots extended into the underworld. Stags grazed on its branches, a wise eagle lived in its canopy, and a squirrel carried messages between the eagle and the underworld. A sacred spring bubbled among its roots.

PRAYING BENEATH A BO-TREE

A Hindu devotee of Vishnu prays beneath a bo-tree (or bodhi tree) in Sarnath's Deer Park. Both Hindus and Buddhists have special reverence for the bo-tree, which Hindus regard as the eternal tree of life, and under which the Buddha achieved enlightenment.

Trees for Sustenance

Early humans depended on natural woodlands for foods such as fruit and nuts, later learning to cultivate trees for these foodstuffs. In the modern world, vast businesses are based on edible tree products, from fruit and nuts to crops, such as coffee, that have to be processed.

FROM TREE TO TABLE

Fruit and nuts from trees are harvested worldwide: from hot climates come the date, papaya, pomegranate, olive, lychee, mango, avocado, coconut, pistachio, and Brazil nut, among many others. Citrus fruits (lemons, oranges, among others) are an important group grown mainly in southern Europe and North Africa.

Cooler climes produce apples, pears, plums, damsons, cherries, walnuts, chestnuts, and almonds. Peaches, apricots, and figs are found in temperate regions.

Growing fruit and nuts commercially is a precise science. Orchards must be correctly managed, and the right type of plants must be grown and, if grafted, put on the right rootstock. Irrigation and protection from extremes of weather are important considerations. Pests, diseases, and competition from grass or weeds must be anticipated and controlled before damage occurs. Pruning to control tree growth and improve crop yield is critical.

APPLE ORCHARD
With hundreds of varieties and rich in fiber and vitamin C, the apple is a deservedly popular fruit. Orchard trees (below) are often specially selected for small size to make the job of harvesting the crop (left) easier.

COCONUT
A giant among nuts, the versatile coconut provides a rich food source for humans and animals alike.

COFFEE BEANS
Coffee undergoes a long process of production before it can be roasted, ground, and savored as a drink.

ALMOND
Grown in cool climes, the nut of the almond tree can be eaten raw, cooked, or made into confectionery.

PROCESSED CROPS

Many fruits and nuts that are eaten raw may be processed into other products to extend their life. Pineapple is canned, juiced, and pulped. Apples and oranges are turned into juice. Plums and apricots are made into jam, canned, or bottled. Coconut is shredded, creamed, or made into milk, and olives and many nuts are pressed to extract edible oils.

Other crops, notably coffee and cocoa, are transformed totally before they are fit for consumption. Coffee and cocoa beans are harvested by hand, and dried or roasted. The beans are then sold to manufacturers around the world, to be turned into a vast array of edible products and beverages.

HARVESTING COCOA BEANS

Cocoa beans are found in the seed pods of the cocoa tree (*Theobroma cacao*). The pods are harvested at the peak of ripeness, split open, and the beans removed for fermentation and drying, before being made into chocolate.

SHELLING COCOA PODS

Trees for Wood and Building

In previous centuries, people depended entirely on wood to build fences, boats, dwellings, and furniture. Easy availability, sustainability, and variety made it a reliable choice. Although now replaced by other materials for many purposes, wood is still a valuable resource.

Wood is a sustainable commodity. Produced year by year in the stems of trees, it is made by the tree itself from nutrients from the soil and plant food manufactured in the leaves. Each type of tree produces wood with different qualities, making it useful for various functions. Some woods, such as oak, are hard and strong; others, such as yew and ash, are soft and flexible; poplar has fire retardant qualities; and many others are sought out for their color or grain.

WOOD TYPES

SOFTWOOD

Softwoods come from coniferous trees. They have a more primitive cellular structure than hardwoods and often contain aromatic resins.

CEDAR

Softwoods can actually be heavier than hardwoods. Some are used mainly for construction (cedar, pine, or larch, for example), others for paper or board manufacture (spruce, fir, hemlock, among others).

HARDWOOD

Timber from deciduous or evergreen broadleaved trees is called hardwood. The term does not refer to the physical hardness of wood but is a classification based on complex cell structures.

BEECH

Hardwoods range from very hard ebony to very soft balsa and are used mainly for building or furniture-making.

WOODEN DWELLING
In some parts of the world, a simple shelter made from cut branches provides an effective refuge from the elements for one or more families and their animals.

PRACTICAL USES

In former times, people relied on wood for shelters and boats. Often, thin rods of coppice wood (trees repeatedly cut back to produce material of a particular size) were used to build a basic shelter and confine domestic livestock. Early houses and barns tended to be built with small timbers squared up with an adz, or large cruck frames produced by splitting a whole tree trunk in half. Saw technology lagged far behind the ax, adz, or splitting wedge, and therefore sawn wood was rarely used.

Wood was usually processed in the forest to avoid the problems of hauling heavy timbers great distances on poor roads. Choosing the right shape of tree or limb for a particular job was an important consideration, no more so than in shipbuilding, where naturally curved timbers were selected for frames and "knees" to support decks.

With the industrial age sawn wood came into its own. Balks of timber were used for grand houses, sea defenses, wharves, mill machinery, railroad ties, and industrial buildings of every sort. Round wood was used extensively in coal mines to reinforce shafts and tunnels and for telephone and electricity transmission poles.

Today, wood in a building may be a reconstituted constituent of manufactured board or glued laminated beams. Wood supplies now are much depleted and, increasingly, timber comes from carefully managed plantations rather than natural forests.

WOOD-FRAMED BOAT
Where handmade boats are still produced, naturally curved timbers are preferred for the frames because of their superior strength and durability.

FURNITURE
Wood has been much prized over the centuries for making fine furniture.

WOOD-FRAMED HOUSE
Wood-frame construction is the most common method of house-building in the United States. Wooden elements may be reconstituted or laminated for extra strength.

Trees for Paper and Pulp

Wasps have been making paper for millions of years, but for humans, it started in the 3rd century BCE in ancient Egypt. The Chinese were the first to use wood for paper. Their skills reached the Middle East in the 8th century CE, and Europe 300 years later.

WOOD PRODUCTS

ETHANOL

Volatile ethanol is a traditional fuel derived from wood. It is prepared by fermentation of sugars, but the process requires substantial amounts of energy.

ETHANOL BURNING

MODERN WOOD FUEL

Modern use of wood for fuel involves efficient self-feeding combusters, boilers, and heat exchangers that burn wood chips from sustainable low-grade woodland or sawmill waste. Such wood-fuel heating is environmentally friendly, clean, and cost-effective.

BIOMASS

Some species, such as poplar, willow, and eucalyptus, can be grown like an agricultural crop, cut every two or three years. The end product is wood chips that are suitable for fuel and other purposes such as mulching.

FIBERBOARD

FIBERBOARD

Pressed wood chips and pulp mixed with adhesives and hardeners produce various types of fiberboard for insulation, flooring, interior surfaces, and domestic cabinetry and shelving.

TRADITIONAL HANDMADE PAPER

Contemporary traditional papermaking techniques involve pouring prepared liquid pulp onto a mesh of finely woven cloth set in a wooden frame the size of the intended sheet. The water drains through, leaving a flat film of fibers. Thickness of paper can be adjusted by adding more or less pulp. A second framed mesh (the deckle) is pressed onto the surface of the pulp, expelling more moisture. Soon, the fibers form a sheet that is turned upside down onto damp felt to dry. Color, scent, and herbs can be added to the pulp. Various methods of pressing the paper are used to produce different surfaces.

INDUSTRIAL PROCESS

In 1840, Friedrich Keller invented an industrial process, still in use today, for reducing logs into paper pulp. Softwood made up of long fibers, such as spruce and poplar, is particularly suitable for making paper. It is sometimes used with hardwood, such as oak, to make paper for a particular purpose or quality.

Modern factory papermaking is a remarkable process that starts with vats of liquid pulp at one end (the wet end) of the milling machine and finishes with dry rolls of paper at the other end (the dry end). Pulp is usually made of waste, which is wood not reserved for lumber; it is chopped into chips that are broken down by steam and chemicals into a semi-liquid "soup" of fibers. A pump sprays a thin layer of liquid paper pulp onto a moving wire screen, which may be up to 20 ft (6 m) wide, traveling at 60 mph (95km/h). By the time pulp reaches the end of the screen, it has partly solidified, and the damp "paper" is fed onto the first of many pressing and heated drying rollers. Finally, rolls of paper, some around 16 ft (5 m) wide and weighing many tons, are removed from the machine. The process is continuous, with new rolls being started without breaking the cycle. Papermaking is a highly skilled and precisely coordinated job.

HANDMADE PAPER
Coloring and flowers can be added to the pulp to create special effects.

LOGGING
Trees are felled, floated downriver, and processed on a vast scale at this lumber mill in Sabah, Borneo.

OTHER PULP PRODUCTS

Wood pulp is naturally brown and has to be bleached to produce paper for printing. The brown pulp can be used to make cardboard, boxes, or brown paper. This and other packaging is made in much the same way as paper. Posterboard is produced in individual sheets. Wet pulp is molded to make shaped packaging.

Medium-density fiberboard (MDF) and hardboard are pressed from hot pulp made from finely ground wood. Chipboard and thick reconstituted

boards are pressed from coarse material bound by adhesive. These products require relatively low-quality raw materials and can incorporate preservatives and insect repellent.

PAPER FOR PRINTING
Every day around the world, massive amounts of paper are used to print newspapers. Paper quality does not have to be high, so recycled paper is used, which helps to conserve resources.

...ucts from Trees

...r vital role in producing wood, paper, and
...are the sources of a wide variety of other products
...textiles to medicines. Each product is harvested from
...r part of the tree: bark, sap, leaves, flowers, or fruit.

...D USES

...ore the advent of the modern
...pharmaceutical industry, most medicines
came from trees and other plants. Today,
many trees are still exploited for their
medicinal products, such as quinine from
the bark of the chinchona tree (*Cinchona
officinalis*), which is sometimes used to
treat malaria. There are also many
species still to be discovered that have
potential medicinal value, particularly
among the rich flora of the rainforests.
It is important that these species are

allowed to flourish—they may hold the
key to conquering many diseases. Many
poisons and mind-altering drugs, such as
khat (*Catha edulis*), also come from trees.

All trees contain long, tensile fibers to
give them strength and the ability to bend
in the wind. These capabilities have been
harnessed to make a range of everyday
items such as cloth, rope, and baskets.

Rubber, cork, various resins, and
tannin all come from the bark of trees,
and many natural dyes are made from
leaves, flowers, or crushed seeds. Trees
are also the sources of many highly
valued volatile oils that are used in
perfumes, aromatherapy, and cooking;
the oils may be extracted from the bark,
leaves, flowers, or fruit.

WILLOW

Many types of willow trees (particularly *Salix purpurea*)
have bark that is rich in salicin, a chemical that is the
active ingredient of the painkiller aspirin.

SELECTED TREE PRODUCTS

Products from trees range from hard-wearing materials to delicate volatile oils. In most cases, a much larger quantity of raw material is harvested compared to the end product. Cork and fibrous matter are exceptions in that extraction is not required, so the picked materials roughly equal the final wares.

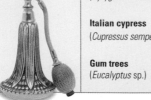

FIBER	**Kapok tree** (*Ceiba pentandra*)	Seed pods are the source of kapok fiber
	Little-leaf linden (*Tilia cordata*)	Inner bark used for rope and coarse fiber
	Raffia palm (*Raphia farinifera*)	Twine for weaving and agricultural use
CORK	**Cork oak** (*Quercus suber*)	Bark provides wine corks and flooring
LATEX, GUM	**Rubber tree** (*Hevea brasiliensis*)	Sap (latex) is the raw ingredient of rubber
	Mastic tree (*Pistacia lentiscus*)	Resin used for gum, varnish, medicines
TANNIN AND PRESERVATIVES	**Oaks** (*Quercus* sp.)	Tannin from bark for preserving leather
DYE	**Annatto** (*Bixa orellana*)	Coloring for food, cosmetics, fabric
	Henna (*Lawsonia inermis*)	Coloring for hair and skin decoration
RESIN, VARNISH, TURPENTINE	**Maritime pine** (*Pinus pinaster*)	Resin used for varnishes and turpentine
MEDICINAL	**Willows** (*Salix* sp.)	Original source of chemical in aspirin
	Loquat (*Eriobotrya japonica*)	Leaf extract provides antibacterial agents
	Maidenhair tree (*Ginkgo biloba*)	Extracts used to improve mental function
AROMATIC OIL	**Clove** (*Syzygium aromaticum*)	Oil for flavoring and toothache relief
	Italian cypress (*Cupressus sempervirens*)	Oil used in perfumes and to repel insects
	Gum trees (*Eucalyptus* sp.)	Oil used in aromatherapy and inhalations

rees for Amenity and Ornament

or thousands of years, trees have been planted to bring pleasure.
A rich history of gardening exists in China and Japan, particularly
near temples. In the West, the first gardens were cultivated in North
Africa, the Mediterranean area, and Mesopotamia before 2000 BCE.

DESIGNING WITH TREES

Humans seem to have a need to surround
themselves with trees, and this is
especially important in the artificial
environment of a modern city. Planting
trees in a city or landscape involves
careful planning because results may
not be achieved for
over 50 years.
It involves an
understanding of
how trees evolve.
They grow larger,
change with the
seasons, and rapidly
fill up spaces. The
extended time scale
also means the
original purpose of the planted area may
change—for example, an area planned as
a park may be developed for housing.

THE RIGHT SPECIES

Care is vital when choosing tree species to
avoid the need for lopping and felling,
and to discourage unhealthy or dangerous
trees from growing. It is vital to know the
growth rate and potential size and shape
of every species that is to be considered
in the plan. Various questions should be
asked—for example, is the tree broad,
narrow, spreading, weeping, columnar,
shrubby, evergreen, or deciduous? Does it
have any particular soil preference? Is it
tolerant of shade, strong sunlight, wind,
or pollution, either of the air or soil? Tree
breeding, especially in the United States,
has produced various cultivated forms of
trees that have been developed to fulfill
special requirements, particularly narrow-
crowned trees that are suitable for lining
streets. A species of Chinese pear (*Pyrus
calleryana*) has provided a rich resource for
experiment, yielding not only a narrow
profile tree well suited to the urban
environment, but also a range of

attractive fall foliage colors in individual
cultivars, such as 'Redspire', 'Trinity', and
'Autumn Blaze'.

The nature of the site will impose
limits on the types of tree that can be
planted. Grazing animals, conservation
constraints, recreation needs, landscape

STREET TREES
Palms are ideal street
trees in warm countries;
they cast shade, have
clear stems, and do not
drop slippery leaves or
block streetlights.

enhancement, shade, and screening traffic require trees with different kinds of tenacity. Regular maintenance is essential to ensure that beauty, function, and longevity can be prolonged.

CITY TREES

The urban environment is harsh and the lifespan of a city tree is short compared to the same species in the country. Screening, one of the main uses of trees in a city, is best achieved by mass planting, but this may not be appropriate where people feel threatened in dark, confined places. Thickly planted trunks may also form a litter trap.

CENTRAL PARK, NEW YORK

Tree-filled parks in the center of major cities not only provide much needed leisure space, but also create a "green lung" that helps to improve air quality in areas of high pollution.

JAPANESE GARDEN

The Japanese are masters of garden design. They are famous for thoughtful planting of trees to provide a good succession of spring blossoms and fall foliage.

TREES IN GARDENS

Garden trees can form an eye-catching focus or a pleasing background. Size is crucial; small yards need small trees, and some species should not be planted near houses because of the risk of damage from invasive roots. Dense foliage can be used to advantage, providing shade and blocking unattractive views. You can create striking contrasts and accents by planting trees with copper or red foliage. Features such as glossy leaves, an unusual undersurface color, or colored bark can add interest in a garden, as can trees with conspicuous flowers, although tree blossoms are often short-lived.

BONSAI TREES

The ornamental value of trees has been taken to the extreme in the Japanese art of bonsai, in which miniature versions of trees are cultivated. Maple and juniper are commonly grown species. The art of bonsai lies in producing aesthetically appealing shapes by prescribed techniques of growing, pruning, and training, and by choosing a base or container that perfectly complements the tree. More art than horticulture, bonsai is a very popular pastime.

BONSAI LARCH AND PINE TREES

...ng and Caring for Trees

...of planting a tree is the final and least difficult stage in a
...s that involves consideration of many factors ranging from the
...n to the type of tree. Assessing the physical attributes of the site,
...n as soil type and position, is also a key element.

CHOOSING AND PLANTING A TREE

Every tree has ecological and physical needs that should, ideally, match the location. Exposure, drainage, soil type, drought, and disease must all be considered. In addition, there are problems of whether the tree is likely to block light, break into sewers or septic systems, grow into overhead power lines, or damage cables, walls, or foundations. Expert advice on the choice of tree is essential. Having chosen the species, the next consideration is the optimum time

for planting. Temperate trees should be planted in the dormant season, evergreens shortly before they start to grow in spring. Prepare the site by removing rubble or diseased roots. The ground surrounding the tree should be treated or covered to stop weeds and grass from growing. Plastic mulch mats work well and can be disguised with composted wood chips. Only add fertilizer to deficient soil. Do not add uncomposted mulch—this can cause oxygen and nitrogen deficiencies.

PLANTING A TREE

The hole should be freshly dug so it does not dry out, flood, or lose beneficial soil organisms. Keep the tree in the shade, roots covered, until you are ready to plant. When you are finished planting, support the tree with a stake.

1 Place the tree to be planted in the center of the chosen site and mark out a circle about 3 ft (1 m) in diameter.

2 Dig a hole in the marked area; mix the soil with well-rotted organic compost before partly refilling the hole. Water if dry.

3 Remove the tree from the pot and gently ease the compacted roots apart and remove any that are damaged.

4 Drive a short stake off-center and put the tree next to it; the root collar should be level with the ground. Backfill with soil.

PRUNING A BRANCH
Using a sharp saw, pruners, or loppers, cut unwanted branches or competing leading shoots close to the collar. Do not cut into the trunk.

PRUNING CONSIDERATIONS

In general, once a tree is established, it requires minimal maintenance. Pruning should be kept to a minimum in the early years, bearing in mind that every scrap of green top growth is needed to feed the tree. However, dead or diseased twigs can be safely cut off. Once the tree is more mature, pruning and training can begin, especially by removing competing leading shoots and wayward branches that may eventually turn into weak, dangerous forks. Wound painting is not recommended unless there is a serious risk of infection locally from airborne diseases.

PEST AND DISEASE CONTROL

Pest and disease damage is best prevented right from the start by a good choice of species. A tree that is not naturally suited to its site is always more vulnerable than one that is. Protection from air pollution, salt spray, and wind can best be achieved by choosing a hardy species and a protected site. Browsing animals have to be kept out with tree shelters or fencing. Squirrels and small rodents can be a difficult problem that may require professional control. Avoid watering if at all possible in order to promote root growth, but if it is essential, water liberally and continue watering until the end of the growing season. It is preferable to use rain water that has collected in a barrel instead of city water, which contains many chemicals that are potentially harmful to a growing tree.

SPOTTING PROBLEMS

HOLES IN LEAVES

This damage is often caused by sawfly. The larvae will strip whole branches. Holes in leaves can also be caused by weevils and fungal or bacterial canker.

WEBBER MOTHS

Leaf damage along with the appearance of a dense white webbing over the affected leaves and shoots may be the result of infestation by the caterpillars of various moths. Mild cases can be treated by careful pruning. In more serious cases, it may be necessary to use chemical pesticides.

RUST DAMAGE

Summer foliage covered with orange-colored crusts is usually the result of fungal disease. If the tree is small enough, it can be treated with a commercial fungicide following the instructions on the label.

BARK DAMAGE

Splits in the bark may be caused by drought and made worse by irregular watering. Bark damage can also be caused by rodents or by diseases such as stem canker.

Forest Practice

The aim of a well-run commercial forest is to produce timber, while also conserving wildlife and providing amenities. For success, the long process depends on careful planning in the early stages and expert management throughout the life of the forest plantation.

Forest management begins with the selection of new sites or suitable existing woodlands for regeneration. Preparation of the ground may involve clearing and draining, cultivating bare sections, and fencing the area to keep out animals. Vehicle access may need upgrading, but often not until it is time to harvest.

TREE SHELTERS
Plastic tubes called tree shelters are used to protect young trees from attack by rodents and sometimes deer. They are removed once the trees are well established.

COMMERCIAL PLANTING

Forest nurseries grow seedlings in raised beds, and these are dug up and transplanted after a year. These young trees grow to around 12 in (30 cm) tall in two to three years depending on the species. This technique encourages a dense root system and a well-balanced plant. Hardwoods with long taproots, such as oak, often have the main root shortened to promote fibrous growth; this improves the tree's survival chances. Planting is still generally done by hand, except in open sites, such as farm woodlands, where an adapted agricultural planting machine may be used. To plant a tree, a slot is cut in the ground and opened up by a transverse slot and some leverage with the spade. The tree is lowered into the hole, then firmed in with a boot. After the first year or two, failed trees are replaced. Planting takes place at the start and end of winter in order to avoid periods of severe weather, particularly frost.

COPPICING
This ancient and sustainable system of woodland management involves harvesting the shoots from an established root system every 7–15 years.

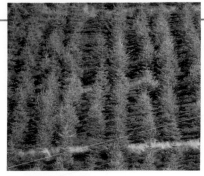

GROWING IN ROWS
Managed forests are usually planted in neat rows that allow for easy access for forest-maintenance work, as in this plantation of young conifers in Scotland.

FOREST MAINTENANCE

Young plantations survive best where competition from natural vegetation is minimal. This is achieved by hand-weeding, herbicides, or the use of tree shelters. Pest control may be required since young trees are vulnerable to attack from rodents and insects. Fertilizer may be applied if the soil shows deficiencies. In order to produce single-trunked, straight trees, some pruning, training, and sometimes staking may be necessary.

Thinning may be carried out either for the benefit of the remaining trees or to produce small trunks for a particular market. Mixed forests can also be thinned to favor particular species, usually those best suited to the site. Silvicultural thinning is a painstaking process that looks at the situation and prospects of every tree and marks those for removal. A more common and cheaper option is to remove single lines of trees; usually one in four. The advantage is that machines can easily access the site to cut and remove the trees. A disadvantage is that this thinning method results in the indiscriminate removal of healthy and unhealthy trees.

FELLING

Final felling may involve total clearance with machinery. Continuous-cover forestry is a more aesthetic method in which some trees are left until new ones planted in between become established. Natural regeneration, if of good quality, may be encouraged. Commercial management of natural forests usually works in this way.

Coppicing is a form of forest management in which a single species is regularly cleared from small areas of a larger wood. It may also involve frequent removal of underbrush from a forest of a slower-growing species. This is a sustainable system that provides a regular supply of timber.

PLANTING IN COSTA RICA
Environmentalists and farmers work together planting trees by hand as part of a reforestation program in the Puriscal region, Costa Rica.

Trees and the Environment

A delicate and complex balance exists between the environment and trees and, at the most basic level, one cannot survive without the other. Environmental problems impact on the health of trees, and if large numbers of trees die or are removed, the environment suffers.

THE CARBON CYCLE

Central to the relationship between trees and the environment is the carbon cycle (see facing page). Carbon exists in the atmosphere in the form of carbon dioxide. Leaves absorb this during photosynthesis (see page 20). A byproduct of this process is oxygen, which is released into the air. Animals take in oxygen and release carbon dioxide when they breathe. They also release carbon when their dead bodies decompose. Another source of carbon in the air is from burning fuels such as wood, oil, and coal. The net result is an increase in atmospheric carbon above the amount that can be reabsorbed, and the equilibrium is upset.

SOIL STABILIZATION
In the African state of Niger, trees are planted to form wind breaks as part of a project to stabilize sand dunes.

ENVIRONMENTAL CHANGES

Pollution and climatic changes are the factors most likely to endanger tree species. First, chemicals released by industry and other human activities are polluting the atmosphere. In some areas, this pollution goes beyond the tolerance of native trees; sulfur dioxide poisoning is an extreme example. In some polluted areas, however, trees have benefited in the short term because insect predators and fungal diseases tend to succumb first, allowing the trees to grow more vigorously. But there may also be other, undesirable effects, such as the loss of immunity to disease.

The major climatic change is global warming—heating up of the planet by polluting (greenhouse) gases: carbon dioxide, nitrous oxide, and methane. Many modern trees that have evolved with a particular climate will have to adapt, migrate, or perish. The last substantial rise in global temperature was about 6,000 years ago. If human activities force the temperature up this high again, trees will be affected. Conifers, such as juniper and spruce, and broadleaved species of birch and beech will become extinct or will need to migrate to higher and cooler regions. Eucalyptus and fan palms will colonize new areas. Fungi, bacteria, and insects will also evolve and could unleash epidemics of disease and infestation on an unprecedented scale.

RAINFOREST DEFORESTATION

The destruction of huge areas of rainforest, most seriously in South America (far right), is going to cause untold problems for humankind. Short-sighted commercial interests risk depriving the world of many plant and animal species, and destroying the planet's largest living "lung."

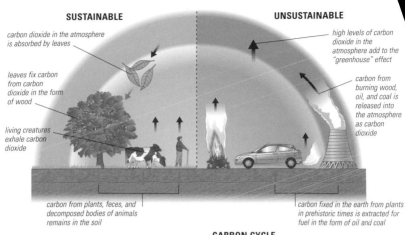

SUSTAINABLE

carbon dioxide in the atmosphere is absorbed by leaves

leaves fix carbon from carbon dioxide in the form of wood

living creatures exhale carbon dioxide

carbon from plants, feces, and decomposed bodies of animals remains in the soil

UNSUSTAINABLE

high levels of carbon dioxide in the atmosphere add to the "greenhouse" effect

carbon from burning wood, oil, and coal is released into the atmosphere as carbon dioxide

carbon fixed in the earth from plants in prehistoric times is extracted for fuel in the form of oil and coal

BENEFICIAL EFFECTS OF TREES

The presence of trees around us is something we often take for granted, failing to appreciate the many vital functions that they perform. Tree roots provide infinitely better erosion control than any artificial substitute. Not only do the roots stop soil from being washed away, but the trunk and branches above ground can trap silt and debris until the ground level rises above the flood plain. Salt-tolerant species such as mangroves can even do this close to the sea. Shelter

CARBON CYCLE

The diagram above shows the contrast between sustainable carbon levels in which emissions roughly equal absorption, and unsustainable, where carbon release far exceeds the ability of trees to absorb it.

from wind is another benefit provided by trees. Shelterbelts of trees can modify a microclimate so that crops and domestic animals can be raised on land that was once too bleak to use. In the southern United States, magnolias are used to protect homes; often, the lower branches are layered to increase stability.

Tree Conservation

Trees and forests are vulnerable. A tree may take hundreds of years to grow to maturity and be replaced, but only a few hours to be destroyed. Technology has produced an arsenal of lethal weapons that have increased the ease with which trees can be removed.

Trees have been exploited for thousands of years, and some people feel that as long as communities rely on logging and societies demand the products, the forestry industry cannot be abandoned. Commercial pressures can certainly help to maintain certain tree species, but this is not always possible in the case of rare trees that grow only slowly. However, unless sustainable forest management strategies are implemented, certain types of forestry will die out because the resource will be gone.

NATURAL THREATS

Although many individual species of trees are threatened with extinction due to overexploitation, trees in general are not threatened to the same degree. Species that we know and rely on may go, but others will take their place. Volcanoes, asteroids, continental drift, sea-level fluctuations, and ice ages have failed to exterminate trees completely. Trees have a long history of survival, but they have to evolve. Where there is bare earth or a great tree is cut down, scores of new seedlings will move in. An oak may go, but ash, elder, and birch will replace it.

RED-FAN PARROT
Habitat loss threatens this vulnerable South American species.

EDEN PROJECT
Carved out of an abandoned clay pit in Cornwall, England, the Eden Project comprises a series of domes in which a botanic garden and conservation center flourishes.

GENE POLLUTION
In some cases, new alien introductions will accidentally cross-breed with native trees until no pure progeny exist. Goat willow (*Salix caprea*), pictured above, is a species that has been affected by this phenomenon.

HABITAT CONSERVATION

Conserving tree habitats is one of the cornerstones of any conservation program. When a forest is cut down, the plant and animal community is modified and partly destroyed. Animals leave and the biological and genetic diversity of the site is altered. Any change to a natural habitat will divert it from its evolutionary path. It will become a different kind of habitat. In areas where the landscape is "artificial," past human activities are considered a valid biological contribution. If "alien" species were planted 300 years ago and they have hybridized with native plants, the aliens are considered indigenous.

ARBORETUMS AND SEED BANKS

Saving today's trees is the business of botanical gardens and arboretums, and seed banks play a vital role in preserving our tree heritage. However, it is doubtful if many saved trees will ever be returned to the wild; there may not even be a habitat to return to. There is also a danger that new trees released into an existing habitat might endanger resident species. Many rescued plants stand the best chance of survival in an artificial plantation containing as many diverse individuals as possible. Biodiversity is essential for vigorous trees and to avoid threats from disease and predators.

ENDANGERED SPECIES

DIOSPYROS EBENUM

In demand for its ⸺ this species is threat⸺ overexploitation.

ARAUCARIA ARAUCANA

The genetic diversity of this species has been severely depleted by overharvesting.

SORBUS LEYANA

This whitebeam was at one time reduced to only nine specimens in Wales, UK.

DENDROSICYOS SOCOTRANUS

The cucumber tree is threatened by human activity and climatic changes.

CUCUMBER TREE

MILLENNIUM SEED BANK

Part of Britain's Royal Botanic Gardens, Kew, and based in West Sussex, the Millennium Seed Bank is an international plant conservation program and center. This global initiative aims to safeguard the future of 24,000 plant species in an effort to prevent them from worldwide extinction. Started in 2000, the program has already secured the future of most of the UK's flowering plants. The seed bank also aims to provide a world-class resource facility.

SEED STORAGE

TREES OF
THE WORLD

SPORE TREES

Spore trees belong to the families Cyatheaceae and Dicksoniaceae and are also known as tree ferns. They are the most primitive trees, reproducing by means of spores, which form tiny plants that produce sperm or eggs. The fertilized eggs then grow into new ferns.

Spore trees are natives of tropical rainforests, where they may exceed 65 ft (20 m) in height. Persistent roots that form a dense buttress support the stem, which is rarely branched. Spore trees do not form wood. Instead, the tall trunks of tree ferns are strengthened by deposits of a material called lignin. The trunk supports a crown of pinnate leaves that may reach 13 ft (4 m) in length. During every growing season, some adult ferns form two types of fronds; sterile fronds that lack sporangia (spore sacs) and fertile fronds that bear sporangia. In some species, fronds formed by a juvenile fern are very different from those formed when the same plant reaches maturity.

A YOUNG FROND UNCURLS

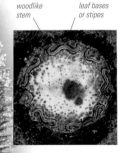

woodlike stem

leaf bases or stipes

STEM CROSS-SECTION
The fronds of the black tree fern (*Cyathea medularis*) are attached to the stem by leaf bases, seen here arranged around the stem.

Dicksonia antarctica

Tasmanian Fern

HEIGHT up to 50 ft (15 m)
TYPE Evergreen
OCCURRENCE Australia
(S.E. Queensland, New South Wales,
Victoria coast, Tasmania)

The Tasmanian fern is very slow-growing, but can live for up to 400 years. It grows at a rate of about 1½–2 in (3.5–5 cm) per year and does not start producing spores until it is at least 20 years old. A thick mass of brown fibrous roots forms on the trunk, which is covered with soft brown hairs on top, and large fronds form a spreading canopy. In the wild, this species thrives in damp places and is usually found in moist gullies and sheltered forests. However, it is also tolerant of frost and drought. The pith can be eaten, either cooked or raw, and is a very good source of starch. **BARK** Dark brown, with leaf scars. **LEAF** Dark green, roughly textured, arching fronds, about 9¾ ft (3 m) long, with tiny pointed leaflets, frond stalks very hairy at the base. **FLOWER** Flowerless. **FRUIT** Small round groups of spore capsules or sporangia (sori).

frond
stalk

reddish
brown
hairs

bark covered
with roots
and old leaf
bases

frond
segments

BARK

FROND BUD

SEED TREES

Seed trees are vascular plants (plants with a circulatory system) that transport water and nutrients by means of tissue called xylem and phloem. Seed plants first appeared some 350 million years ago. They were plants with fernlike leaves that bore seeds on their leaves.

P roducing seed bypasses the need to have water in the environment for fertilization to occur, because the pollen, which contains the male germ cells, is transported to the female parts by wind or insects, so the sperm does not have to swim to the egg. Another advantage of seeds is that they have an outer layer that protects the embryo and incorporates a food reserve for it.

ADAPTED FOR SURVIVAL
The enormous range of adaptations of seed trees has helped them to colonize all parts of Earth.

GROUPS OF SEED TREES

Seed trees can be divided into gymnosperms and angiosperms. Cycads, ginkgo, and conifers are all woody gymnosperms. All of these produce seeds that are covered by a seed coat, but are not true fruits. The angiosperms (flowering trees) are the largest and most diverse group. They all produce seeds within a fruit. Angiosperm flowers may have some or all of four structures: a stalk; a perianth (petals and sepals); stamens (male pollen-bearing structures) and/or carpels (female ovule-bearing structures). Gymnosperm "flowers" never have a perianth or bear ovules or pollen on the same plant. They are wind-pollinated. Angiosperm flowers have more means of becoming pollinated (wind, insects, birds, and bats). Many angiosperms have evolved alongside the insects that pollinate them.

JAPANESE MAPLE
Flowering trees have a wide variety of seed dispersal methods. The seed of this maple is enclosed in a winged key.

CYCAD SEED CONES
Female cycads are fertilized by free-swimming sperm that are carried by wind from a male plant.

seed cone of a female cycad

YCADS

cads are woody plants that produce seeds and resemble ferns and alms. They are, however, unique and unrelated to any other group of living plants. Cycads were at their peak some 150 million years ago in the Jurassic period. Today there are around 185 species of cycads in 11 genera, native to warm, subtropical regions.

The main roots of cycads are thickened and fleshy. All species also produce upright-growing, branched roots, known as coralloid roots. These roots contain symbiotic blue-green algae, which can fix nitrogen from the atmosphere. The woody stems of cycads may grow entirely below ground or emerge from the ground to form a trunklike structure. The leaves of most species are pinnate and often develop a palmlike crown. A plant is either male or female. Cycads reproduce by producing cones. Woody growths on the cones, called sporophylls, bear the sexual parts.

new shoots

FOSSIL CYCAD FROND
A frond of the fossil cycad *Nilssonia compta* from the Jurassic period, approximately 180 million years ago.

FIRE ADAPTED
Shoots that will develop into palmlike fronds emerge from the top of a *Cycas media* following a forest fire.

old leaves

Cycas circinalis

False Sago

HEIGHT up to 16 ft (5 m)
TYPE Deciduous
OCCURRENCE India (Karnataka, Kerala, Tamil Nadu, Maharashtra)

The false sago (not to be confused with the sago palm) occurs in dense, dry, scrubby woodland in hilly areas and sheds its foliage in extremely dry seasons. It is valued for its beauty and is widely planted as an ornamental. Its trunk contains an edible, starchy material.
BARK Brown, covered in old leaf bases.
LEAF Pinnate, glossy bright green, 5–8 ft (1.5–2.5 m) long, with 170 opposite leaflets, flat, on hairy stalks.
FLOWER Males: narrowly ovoid,

FOLIAGE

orange pollen cones, covered in matted woolly hairs; females: cones arranged in a ring around the shoot tips.
FRUIT Yellow, nearly round seeds that can float.

featherlike leaves

female cone

CAROLUS LINNAEUS

Carolus Linnaeus (Karl von Linné; 1707–1778) was a Swedish physician and botanist who introduced the taxonomic system for grouping and categorizing organisms. He established *Cycas circinalis* as a single species, but his description was based on earlier work that covered at least three distinct species.

GINKGO

The ginkgos are a group of seed trees that appeared about 250 million years ago and reached their maximum diversity 100 million years ago. By about 40 million years later, the number of species in this group had been reduced to a single, very variable species known as *Gingko adiantoides*, which is similar to the only species of ginkgo in existence today, *Ginkgo biloba* (maidenhair tree).

parallel veins

golden coloration in fall

LEAF SHAPE
The bright green leaves of the maidenhair tree (*Ginkgo biloba*) have a distinctive two-lobed shape with a deep cleft in the center.

Often thought of as a "living fossil," *Ginkgo biloba* is a large woody tree, with branched stems and small simple leaves. There is considerable doubt that any ginkgo trees still exist outside cultivation, although specimens in the wild have been reported in eastern China. This plant might only exist today because of the efforts of Buddhist monks in Japan and China. They adopted *Ginkgo biloba* as a sacred tree and cultivated it in their temple gardens. Subsequently, its worldwide popularity as a garden tree has secured its survival. It is a highly adaptable plant, growing in almost any temperate or Mediterranean climate. It is also unusually resistant to pollution and pests. These attributes have made ginkgos very popular in cities. The females are not as sought-after as the male trees for yards or street trees because of the unpleasant smell of their seeds.

MALE FLOWERS
Male ginkgo flowers produce pollen containing motile (free-swimming) sperm that are among the largest in the plant kingdom. Fertilization is usually by wind pollination.

Ginkgo biloba

Maidenhair Tree

HEIGHT up to 100 ft (30 m)
TYPE Deciduous
OCCURRENCE E China

A primitive and ancient species, the maidenhair tree is held sacred by Buddhists and it is often seen around Buddhist temples. It symbolizes longevity, hope, and unity, and is now widely cultivated around the world, especially in the US. Its wood does not decay quickly, is fire-resistant, and has a fine grain and silky shine. It is used for carving, furniture, chessboards, and tubs for brewing "saké," among other items. The leaves and seeds are used in herbal medicine. The rotting fruit has a particularly unpleasant odor. **BARK** Pale brown, roughening into corky fissures.

LEAVES | cleft between lobes

LEAF Fan-shaped, bright green turning golden yellow in the fall, two-lobed, notched; with parallel veins, dividing into two, about 3¼ in (8 cm) wide.
FLOWER Males and females on separate trees; males: in small green catkins, females: in pairs, stalked, small, green, and round. **FRUIT** Greenish yellow plum-like fruit with a fleshy coating, and edible kernel.

FRUIT
— silvery bloom

up to 1½ in (4 cm) long

SEEDS

MEDICINAL LEAVES

People in China began using the seeds of this species for medicinal purposes over 1,000 years ago. Its leaves have traditionally been used for treating circulatory and respiratory ailments. In the West, in recent years, ginkgo has become popular as a natural remedy to improve mental performance and boost short-term memory.

GINKGO SUPPLEMENTS

GINKGO
The ginkgo's unusual fanlike leaf shape, with two lobes (hence its species name *biloba*) and parallel venation, is easily identified. The leaves are used in traditional Chinese medicine to treat a variety of ailments, including high cholesterol and angina.

CONIFERS

The conifers are so called because they bear seed in distinctive cones. They first appeared in the fossil record in the Permian period over 200 million years ago, and they are still abundant today. There are seven families of living conifers, containing over 600 species. They are widely distributed, dominating forest habitats in the earth's colder, drier regions in which other trees cannot survive.

The leaves of conifers vary widely. In many conifer genera, such as spruce (*Picea*), fir (*Abies*), and pine (*Pinus*), the leaves are long and narrow, and are called "needles." In others, the leaves are very small and scalelike—for example, junipers (*Juniperus*), incense cedar (*Calodcedrus*), and cypresses (*Cupressus*). Conifer leaves are usually covered in a waxy layer, and the stomata (tiny pores) lie beneath the leaf surface. These leaf characteristics prevent water loss and help conifers resist drought. In most conifers, the leaves develop on long shoots, and are arranged spirally and alternately.

Conifers produce distinct male and female cones on the same or separate trees. These function as flowers. Female cones tend to be much larger than

FEMALE CONES AND MALE FLOWERS
Male lodgepole pine (*Pinus contorta)* flowers (right) appear on the same tree as females. The female develops into a seed-bearing cone (left).

males. Male conifer flowers may appear in the leaf axils or on new shoots. They usually wither away after the pollinating period has ended.

Conifers are wind-pollinated. After pollination, the scales of the female cone close tightly, until the developed seeds are released from the mature cones (now serving as the fruit). In the "closed-cone pines," the heat produced by a forest fire is usually needed to liberate the seeds. The Taxaceae (yew family) do not have cones: each seed is enclosed in a fleshy coating, known as an aril.

SCALELIKE LEAVES
Some conifers such as the Hinoki cypress (*Chamaecyparis obtusa*) have leaves that resemble scales instead of needles.

leaves arranged in flattened sprays

GIANT CONIFERS
Conifers are known for attaining enormous heights. Giants of the conifer world include giant sequoia (*Sequoiadendron giganteum*), pictured right, and the grand fir (*Abies grandis*), which may reach a height of 200 ft (60 m).

Abies alba

Silver Fir

HEIGHT up to 150 ft (46 m)
TYPE Evergreen
OCCURRENCE C. Europe

The branches at the top of this tree often divide, giving it a "stork's nest" appearance. Its resin is a constituent of turpentine. **BARK** Gray, smooth, cracking with age. **LEAF** Flat needles, dark green above with two silver bands below. **FLOWER** Males: yellow, grouped on undersides of shoots; females: green. **FRUIT** Erect, cylindrical brown cone.

FLOWERS

needle ½–1¼ in
(1.5–3 cm) long　　**LEAVES**

Abioo grandis

Grand Fir

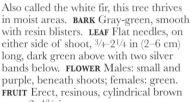

HEIGHT up to 240 ft (75 m)
TYPE Evergreen
OCCURRENCE W. North America

Also called the white fir, this tree thrives in moist areas. **BARK** Gray-green, smooth with resin blisters. **LEAF** Flat needles, on either side of shoot, ¾–2¼ in (2–6 cm) long, dark green above with two silver bands below. **FLOWER** Males: small and purple, beneath shoots; females: green. **FRUIT** Erect, resinous, cylindrical brown cone, 2–4¾ in (5–12 cm) long.

Abies nordmanniana

Nordmann Fir

HEIGHT up to 150 ft (46 m)
TYPE Evergreen
OCCURRENCE N.E. Turkey, W. Caucasus

This popular Christmas tree, also known as the Caucasian fir, has thick foliage and a conical shape. **BARK** Gray, smooth, but developing fissures with age. **LEAF** Flat, notched needles, shiny dark green above, two silver lines beneath. **FLOWER** In separate clusters. Males: red; females: yellow-green. **FRUIT** Erect, greenish brown cone.

needle ¾–1¼ in
(2–3 cm) long

male flower
clusters

LEAVES AND FLOWERS

Abies koreana

Korean Fir

HEIGHT 30–60 ft (9–18 m)
TYPE Evergreen
OCCURRENCE Korea

This fir is shrubby or broadly pyramidal. **BARK** Purple-gray, smooth, with resin blisters, furrowed in plates. **LEAF** Narrow, notched needles, in dense spirals, ½–2 in (1.5–5 cm) long, green above, underside keeled with blue-green lines. **FLOWER** Males: broad, oval, red to yellow or green, tinted with violet-brown; females: rounded, blue-gray. **FRUIT** Cone, ripens to dark violet; red-brown bracts.

YOUNG CONES

Abies procera

Noble Fir

HEIGHT up to 165 ft (50 m)
TYPE Evergreen
OCCURRENCE W. North America

Tolerant of wind, snow, and poor soil,
this tree has light but strong timber,
which is used for interiors. **BARK** Silver-
gray, smooth, cracking on older trees.
LEAF Flat needles with rounded tips, blue-
green on both sides. **FLOWER** Males: deep
red, beneath shoot; females: yellow, above
shoot. **FRUIT** Erect, barrel-shaped cone,
4³/₄–10 in (12–25 cm) long.

needle ³/₈–1¹/₂ in
(1–3.5 cm) long

LEAVES

Cedrus atlantica

Atlas Cedar

HEIGHT up to 200 ft (60 m)
TYPE Evergreen
OCCURRENCE North Africa

The Atlas cedar has a stout trunk and its
branches are angled upward. The blue
form, *Cedrus atlantica* 'Glauca', has blue-
white needles and is planted as an
ornamental in parks. **BARK** Silver-gray,
becoming grooved with age. **LEAF** Green
or blue-green needles, ³/₈–1¹/₄ in (1–3 cm)
long, arranged in tufts. **FLOWER** Males:
pinkish; females: bright green.
FRUIT Egg-shaped cones, 2–3¹/₄ in
(5–8 cm) long, with hollowed tips.

Cedrus deodara

Deodar Cedar

HEIGHT up to 200 ft (60 m)
TYPE Evergreen
OCCURRENCE Himalayas

Like the Atlas cedar, this tree has a stout
trunk with a triangular crown, but with
downswept branches, and a drooping
leading shoot. Its oil was once used to
treat skin diseases. **BARK** Gray-brown and
smooth when young, rough and grooved
when mature. **LEAF** Pale green needles,
up to 2 in (5 cm) long, in tufts of   **CONE**
about 15–20 on spur shoots.
FLOWER Males: yellowish,
in clusters, often curving;
females: greenish, in upright
clusters, **FRUIT** Erect,
barrel-shaped cones that   to 4³/₄ in
turn brown as they ripen.   (12 cm) long

LEAVES WITH YOUNG CONES

Cedrus libani

Cedar of Lebanon

HEIGHT up to 130 ft (40 m)
TYPE Evergreen
OCCURRENCE Middle East

A slow-growing tree, this cedar has a conical shape when young. When mature, it has a massive trunk and large, tiered branches with dense foliage. It is very long-lived; those in the Taurus Mountains in Turkey are up to 1,000 years old. There are over 18 references to this tree in the Bible and the timber is said to have been used to construct King Solomon's Temple. It is now used for veneers or drawer linings.

EMBLEM TREE

Some cultures hold the Cedar of Lebanon in special esteem. The green cedar, symbolizing immortality and fortitude, is placed in the middle of the Lebanese flag. Between two horizontal red stripes, the tree stands out against a white background that is reminiscent of snow on the mountains of Lebanon.

LEBANESE FLAG

BARK Red-brown, finely fissured between shallow ridges. **LEAF** Dark green needles, borne singly on long shoots and in tufts of about 10–20 on short side shoots. **FLOWER** Males: yellow-brown when open, up to 2¼ in (6 cm) long; females: bright green with purple tinge, 2¾–6 in (7–15 cm) long. **FRUIT** Erect, barrel-shaped cones with rounded tops, ripening from purple to pink-brown.

cone 2¾–6 in (7–15 cm) long

needle ¾–1¼ in (2–3 cm) long

LONG SHOOT WITH CONE

spreading branches

Larix decidua

European Larch

HEIGHT up to 125 ft (38 m)
TYPE Deciduous
OCCURRENCE C. Europe

European larch is one of the first trees to burst into leaf in spring. Its timber is strong and durable. **BARK** Gray-brown, cracking with age. **LEAF** Flat, soft needles, blunt or short-pointed tips, bright green. **FLOWER** Males yellow; females pink-red. **FRUIT** Brown, egg-shaped cones, with smooth scales and visible bracts.

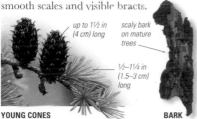

up to 1½ in (4 cm) long

scaly bark on mature trees

½–1¼ in (1.5–3 cm) long

YOUNG CONES   **BARK**

Larix kaempferi

Japanese Larch

HEIGHT up to 115 ft (35 m)
TYPE Deciduous
OCCURRENCE Japan

Also known as the money pine, this tree is used in Japan for bonsai. It is a popular species for timber because it grows faster than other larches and is more disease-resistant. **BARK** Red-brown, cracking with age. **LEAF** Flat, soft needles with blunt or short-pointed tips, blue-green with two gray-white bands on underside, mostly in rosettes of 30–40. **FLOWER** In clusters. Males yellow; females green-yellow. **FRUIT** Small brown cones, with hidden bracts.

needle to 1½ in (4 cm) long

upright cone 1¼ in (3 cm) long

CONE

Larix laricina

Tamarack

HEIGHT up to 80 ft (25 m)
TYPE Deciduous
OCCURRENCE North America

needle ⅜–1 in (1–2.5 cm) long

LEAVES AND CONE

cone ⅜–¾ in (1–2 cm) long

Mostly found on upland, loamy soils, this hardy tree also grows in cold, poorly drained areas like sphagnum bogs. Its wood is used for fenceposts and railroad ties, and for building boats. **BARK** Red-brown, scaly, and thin. **LEAF** Flat, soft needles with blunt or short-pointed tips, light blue-green, turning yellow in fall. **FLOWER** Males: yellowish and very small; females: deep red, small. **FRUIT** Small, egg-shaped cones, with rounded, overlapping scales, rose-red turning to pale brown.

CEDAR OF LEBANON
Over the centuries, forests of cedar of Lebanon
(*Cedrus libani*) have been depleted as a result of
felling. However, this tree is a popular specimen
planting in many temperate parklands, such as this
garden in Sussex, England.

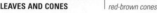
Picea abies

Norway Spruce

HEIGHT up to 130 ft (40 m)
TYPE Evergreen
OCCURRENCE N., C., and E. Europe

The wood of this popular Christmas tree is used for building work, packing cases, paper pulp, and for making sounding boards and posts for violins. **BARK** Orange-brown, turning gray-brown with age and developing small scales. **LEAF** Stiff, prickly, four-sided needles, dark green on all sides. **FLOWER** In separate, upright clusters. Males: red; females: dark red. **FRUIT** Pendent cylindrical cones have scales that are notched at the tip, 4³/₄–6¹/₂ in (12–16 cm) long, tapered at each end, like a cigar.

LEAVES

needle ³/₈–³/₄ in (1–2 cm) long

LEAVES AND CONES | red-brown cones

Picea sitchensis

Sitka Spruce

HEIGHT up to 260 ft (80 m)
TYPE Evergreen
OCCURRENCE North America

Named after the Sitka Sound in Alaska, this tree thrives in moist conditions, and is found only within 50 miles (80 km) of the coast. Its strong but light wood is used for pulp. **BARK** Gray, becoming purple-gray and peeling with age. **LEAF** Thin, sharp needles, dark green and shiny above, two broad white bands below. **FLOWER** In clusters. Males: red; females: green-purple. **FRUIT** Pendent, slightly tapered, pale brown cones.

needle ³/₄–1¹/₄ in (2–3 cm) long

cone 2³/₄–3¹/₄ in (7–8 cm) long

LEAVES AND FRUIT

Pinus banksiana

Jack Pine

HEIGHT up to 90 ft (27 m)
TYPE Evergreen
OCCURRENCE North America

This species is the northernmost pine in the world. It grows on poor, dry soil and depends on fire to release the seeds from its cone. **BARK** Orange-red to red-brown, scaly. **LEAF** Twisted, yellow-green needles, with fine lines on both surfaces, in pairs. **FLOWER** Males: orange to yellow; females: green yellow. **FRUIT** Cones, lance-shaped, pale brown, ripening after two years.

cone 1½–2 in (3.5–5 cm) long

needle ¾–2 in (2–5 cm) long

CONES AND LEAVES

Pinus pinea

Italian Stone Pine

HEIGHT up to 80 ft (25 m)
TYPE Evergreen
OCCURRENCE S. Europe

cone 3¼–4¾ in (8–12 cm) long

needle 14–7 in (0–18 cm) long

LEAVES AND FLOWERS

male flower cluster

CONE

This pine has a broad, domed crown, a tall, bare trunk, and branches that radiate upward. **BARK** Pale brown, cracking into long, flat plates. **LEAF** Needles, in pairs, gray-green, with fine lines on each side. **FLOWER** Golden males and green females in separate clusters at the ends of shoots. **FRUIT** Cones, ripening from green to brown, containing edible "pine nuts."

Pinus parviflora

Japanese White Pine

HEIGHT up to 65 ft (20 m)
TYPE Evergreen
OCCURRENCE Japan and Korea

A common ornamental, this pine has a wide, low crown and a massive, straight trunk, which sometimes splits into two or more branches. **BARK** Smooth, gray, becoming rough and fissured, peeling off into scales. **LEAF** Twisted needles, triangular in cross-section, dark green above, pale green beneath, borne densely around shoot in fives. **FLOWER** Males: clustered around shoot; females: at end of shoot, pink-purple. **FRUIT** Cones, 2–3 in (6–8 cm) long, ripen from green to purple.

yellow or brown male flowers

needle 1¼–2¼ in (3–6 cm) long

LEAVES AND FLOWERS

Pinus pinaster

Maritime Pine

HEIGHT up to 100 ft (30 m)
TYPE Evergreen
OCCURRENCE W. Mediterranean, N.W. Africa

This pine thrives on sandy soil and was used to reclaim sand dunes in southern France. **BARK** Dark with red, brown, black, and buff tones; thick, scaly, and fissured. **LEAF** Needles, usually in pairs, green to yellow green, with fine lines. **FLOWER** Males: yellow, at base of shoots; females: red, in clusters at the ends of shoots. **FRUIT** Long, oval, glossy brown cones, in small clusters.

needle 4¾–10 in (12–25 cm) long

cone 3½–7 in (9–18 cm) long

LEAVES AND CONES

ITALIAN STONE PINE

The broad, domed crown and graceful, slender trunks of the Italian stone pine (*Pinus pinea*) are a characteristic feature of many Mediterranean landscapes. However, prized for its edible nuts, it has also been widely planted elsewhere.

Pinus cembra

Swiss Stone Pine

HEIGHT up to 70 ft (22 m)
TYPE Evergreen
OCCURRENCE Europe, Russia (Urals, Siberia)

needles
2–3¼ in
(5–8 cm)
long

LEAVES

This tree grows at higher altitudes than any other pines. **BARK** Pale brown, with resin blisters when young. **LEAF** Stiff needles, in fives, shiny green above, whitish beneath. **FLOWER** In clusters. Males: yellow; females: red. **FRUIT** Erect, egg-shaped cones.

Pinus caribaea

Caribbean Pitch Pine

HEIGHT up to 100 ft (30 m)
TYPE Evergreen
OCCURRENCE Caribbean Islands, Mexico, Nicaragua

This invasive pine forms dense stands. **BARK** Gray, forming plates. **LEAF** Needles, in bundles of 3–5. **FLOWER** In clusters. Males: stalkless; females: conical. **FRUIT** Pale brown or reddish cone.

yellow-green
needles
6–10 in
(15–25 cm)
long

LEAVES

Pinus contorta

Lodgepole Pine

HEIGHT up to 165 ft (50 m)
TYPE Evergreen
OCCURRENCE North America

The cones of this pine stay closed for years, opening up only in the heat of forest fires. **BARK** Red- or yellow-brown; old trees have deep fissures and dark scales. **LEAF** Needles in pairs, 1½–2 in (4–5 cm) long, blue-green turning yellow-green in winter. **FLOWER** Males: yellow; females: green. **FRUIT** Elongated brown cone.

LEAVES AND CONES   cone to 2 in (5 cm) long

Pinus longaeva

Bristlecone Pine

HEIGHT up to 50 ft (16 m)
TYPE Evergreen
OCCURRENCE North America

The largest tree in the subalpine zone, this pine can be very long-lived. The oldest specimen is the 4,789-year-old "Methuselah" tree in the White Mountains of California. **BARK** Red-brown, fissured. **LEAF** Deep yellow-green, needles in fives. **FLOWER** Males: purple-red; females: purple. **FRUIT** Red-brown, drooping cone, 2¼–3½ in (6–9 cm) long.

LEAVES AND FLOWERS

purple-red
male flowers

needle ⅝–1¼ in
(1.5–3.5 cm) long

Austrian Pine

HEIGHT up to 165 ft (50 m)
TYPE Evergreen
OCCURRENCE W. Mediterranean mountains

With its straight trunk, thick bark, and slender branches, this pine is a useful source of timber. It needs plenty of light. **BARK** Gray, thick. **LEAF** Twisted, slender, rigid, dark green needles in pairs, 4–6 in (10–15 cm) long, with pointed tips. **FLOWER** Males: ⅜–⅝ in (1–1.5 cm) long, yellow, in clusters at base of shoots; females: red, at shoot tips. **FRUIT** Cone, 2–3¼ in (5–8 cm) long, green, ripening to gray- or yellow-buff, falling intact from the tree when ripe.

Mexican Pine

HEIGHT up to 100 ft (30 m)
TYPE Evergreen
OCCURRENCE Mexico

needles 6–10 in (15–25 cm) long   cone 2¾–4 in (7–10 cm) long   **LEAVES AND CONES**

The Mexican pine prefers acid soil and plenty of moisture. Its timber is used for pulp. **BARK** Red-orange, becoming grey-brown and vertically ridged. **LEAF** Pale green to yellow-green needles, in threes or fives. **FLOWER** Males and females on same plant; females appearing a year later than males. **FRUIT** Brown or yellow-brown cones in groups of 3–6.

Eastern White Pine

HEIGHT up to 215 ft (65 m)
TYPE Evergreen
OCCURRENCE E. North America

Also called the Weymouth pine, this tree was once extensively logged to construct ships' masts. **BARK** Gray, becoming furrowed with purple-tinged rectangular plates. **LEAF** Needles, in bundles of five. **FLOWER** Males: yellow, in clusters at the base of shoots; females: pinkish, in pairs at the end of shoots. **FRUIT** Banana-shaped, pale brown cones, in clusters.

LEAVES AND CONES   cone 3¼–8 in (8–20 cm) long   needle 2¼–4 in (6–10 cm) long

Chir Pine

HEIGHT up to 180 ft (55 m)
TYPE Evergreen
OCCURRENCE Himalayas

The timber of this tree is a rich source of resin. **BARK** Dark red to brown, resinous, thick, scaly, fissured. **LEAF** Needles, in bundles of three, 8–12 in (20–30 cm) long. **FLOWER** Males and females on same plant. **FRUIT** Elongated cones, 4–8 in (10–20 cm) long.

BRISTLECONE PINE
Bristlecone pines (*Pinus longaeva*) are typically found in barren landscapes such as this on the slopes of Mount Washington, Nevada. The wood of this pine decays extremely slowly; some wood on the ground may be over 10,000 years old.

Pinus sylvestris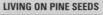

Scotch Pine

HEIGHT up to 130 ft (40 m)
TYPE Evergreen
OCCURRENCE Europe, N. Asia

The Scotch pine is one of only three conifers native to the British Isles, although it is distributed in many other parts of the world. It grows well on poor sandy soil, and it tolerates a remarkably wide range of climatic conditions, from the warm summers of southern Europe, to the bitterly cold winters of Siberia.

LIVING ON PINE SEEDS

The Scottish crossbill, an endangered species, is restricted to the highlands of Scotland, and depends heavily on Scotch pine seeds for its food. Its curved mandibles cross over when the bill is closed, enabling the bird to pry open pine cones and get at the seeds. The female is dull greenish, while the male is bright orange-red in color.

CROSSBILL

LEAVES, FLOWERS, AND CONES

male flower

female flowers

cone 1¼–2¾ in (3–7 cm) long

Its wood is strong, yet easily worked, and is used to make saw logs, veneers, and telephone poles. **BARK** Red-brown, turning purple-gray, with deep fissures. **LEAF** Blue-green twisted needles, 2–3 in (5–7.5 cm) long, in pairs, with white waxy lines on both surfaces. **FLOWER** Males: yellow, in clusters at the base of shoots; females: crimson, in pairs at the ends of shoots. **FRUIT** Small egg-shaped cones, with broad scales, each ending in a raised peak; glossy green, ripening to brown in the second fall.

Pinus wallichiana
Bhutan Pine

HEIGHT up to 160 ft (50 m)
TYPE Evergreen
OCCURRENCE Himalayas

The hard, durable wood of this conifer is used for buildings and to make tea chests. **BARK** Orange or pink-brown, cracks with age. **LEAF** Needles in fives, 6–8 in (15–20 cm) long, green on top, bluish white lines below. **FLOWER** Males: yellow, in clusters; females: green-yellow in groups of up to six. **FRUIT** Long cones, mature from green to pale brown.

wide-tipped scales

LEAVES AND CONE

Pseudotsuga menziesii
Douglas Fir

HEIGHT up to 325 ft (100 m)
TYPE Evergreen
OCCURRENCE North America

female flowers in clusters

cone 2–3¼ in (5–8 cm) long

Named after plant collector David Douglas, this tall fir is valued for its fine timber. **BARK** Dark gray or purple, fissured. **LEAF** Soft, green needles; two white bands beneath. **FLOWER** Males: yellow, beneath shoots; females: red, on shoot tips. **FRUIT** Pendent cone, pale brown.

CONE

three-pronged bracts

Tsuga canadensis
Eastern Hemlock

HEIGHT 100 ft (30 m)
TYPE Evergreen
OCCURRENCE E. North America

Cultivated as an ornamental, with many bushy dwarf forms, the eastern hemlock grows well on chalky soil. Its timber is used for pulp. **BARK** Gray, ridged, flaking. **LEAF** Twisted needles on yellow stalks, in three ranks, minute teeth on edges, especially near tip; dark green above, narrow silvery bands beneath; fruity smell when crushed. **FLOWER** Males yellow; females green. **FRUIT** Small, oval cones on short stalks.

LEAVES AND CONES

needle to ¾ in (2 cm) long

cone ⅝–1 in (1.5–2.5 cm) long

Tsuga heterophylla
Western Hemlock

HEIGHT up to 200 ft (60 m)
TYPE Evergreen
OCCURRENCE W. North America

The wood of this hemlock is used for building and making boxes. The bark has a high tannin content. **BARK** Red-brown, turning purple-brown, flaking. **LEAF** Blunt-tipped needles, dark green above, with two blue-white bands below; unpleasant smell when crushed. **FLOWER** Reddish; males: under shoot, turn pale yellow when pollen is shed; females: at shoot tips. **FRUIT** Small bronze green to brown oval cones, with rounded scales.

Agathis australis

Kauri

HEIGHT up to 160 ft (50 m)
TYPE Evergreen
OCCURRENCE New Zealand

This tree has a rounded, flat crown when it grows above the forest canopy. The Maoris used its wood for making canoes. **BARK** Sheds thick flakes. **LEAF** Alternate, straplike. **FLOWER** Clustered. Males: cylindrical; females: spherical, gray-green. **FRUIT** Cone.

thick green foliage

BARK | gray to purple mottled bark

Agathis robusta

Queensland Kauri

HEIGHT up to 160 ft (50 m)
TYPE Evergreen
OCCURRENCE Australia (Queensland)

This tree grows on the margins of rainforests. **BARK** Orange- to gray-brown, smooth to flaky. **LEAF** Stiff, linear to elliptic adult leaves, 2–5 in (5–13 cm) long. **FLOWER** Males cylindrical; females pear-shaped. **FRUIT** Cones, 4–6 in (9–15 cm) long, that release winged seeds.

Araucaria bidwillii

Bunya-bunya

HEIGHT up to 160 ft (50 m)
TYPE Evergreen
OCCURRENCE Australia (S.E. and N. Queensland)

Sacred to Aboriginals, this tree is valued for its large, hard-shelled, edible nuts. **BARK** Dark brown to black. **LEAF** Oval adult leaves, overlapping on branchlets. **FLOWER** Males cylindrical, females round. **FRUIT** Huge cone, weighing 5½ lb (10 kg), dark green, with 50–100 seeds.

Araucaria columnaris

Cook Pine

HEIGHT up to 200 ft (60 m)
TYPE Evergreen
OCCURRENCE South New Caledonia, Loyalty Islands

This tree is also known as the coral pine. **BARK** Dark brown to black. **LEAF** Needle-like juveniles; adults more triangular. **FLOWER** Male cone: single, oblong, 8 in (20 cm) long; females: 4–6 in (10–15 cm) long. **FRUIT** Large, egg-shaped seed cone.

conical crown

Araucaria araucana

Monkey Puzzle

HEIGHT 100–130 ft (30–40 m)
TYPE Evergreen
OCCURRENCE S. Chile, S.W. Argentina

This species is now protected in the wild, and is mainly used as a popular ornamental in cool temperate regions. **BARK** Gray-brown and resinous. It is smooth and marked by rings from old branch scars. **LEAF** Scalelike, persisting for 10–15 years, even on the trunk, broadly triangular, 5/16–1 in (0.8–2.5 cm) wide, shiny green on both sides, with sharp spines.

FLOWER Male cones are erect, yellow-brown, 2³/4–6 in (7–15 cm) long and 2 in (5 cm) wide, with 20 whorled scales that have outward-curving points; female cones are globelike, green, 4–7 in (10–18 cm) long and 3¹/4–6 in (8–15 cm) wide. **FRUIT** Spherical seed cone has overlapping spiny bracts, ripen to brown in 2–3 years.

rounded crown

developing flower cluster

leaf with sharp spines

old male flower

THE PEHUENCHE

The Pehuenche people of Chile consume the seeds of the monkey puzzle tree as a staple food. The nuts are rich in nutrients and delicious when cooked. These seeds are also used as animal fodder. The tree is important in the harvest and fertility ceremonies of the Pehuenche people.

MONKEY PUZZLE
This ancient stand of monkey puzzle trees (*Araucaria araucana*) is in the Malacahuello National Reserve, Chile. Trees of the *Araucaria* family are now found only in the Southern Hemisphere, although they were once widespread in the Northern Hemisphere as well.

Moreton Bay Pine

HEIGHT up to 200 ft (60 m)
TYPE Evergreen
OCCURRENCE Australia (N. Queensland to New South Wales), W. New Guinea

This conifer is used as an ornamental and plantation tree in Australia. The quality of its white to light brown timber is excellent, especially for plywood. **BARK** Gray-brown, rough, with horizontal bands; flakes in fine circular bands. **LEAF** Juvenile leaves arranged spirally on branches, gray-green to green, with smooth edges; adult leaves overlapping on branches, keeled on both sides, scalelike, 5/16–3/4 in (0.8–2 cm) long. **FLOWER** Males: cylindrical, 3/4–1 1/4 in (2–3 cm) long; females: more oval, 3 1/4–4 in (8–10 cm) long. **FRUIT** Oval cone up to 4 in (10 cm) long, releases seeds with narrow wings when mature.

Klinki Pine

HEIGHT up to 275 ft (85 m)
TYPE Evergreen
OCCURRENCE Papua New Guinea

A pyramidal tree when young, the Klinki pine becomes flat-topped with age. It is an endangered species. **BARK** Dark brown, resinous, flakes in corky plates. **LEAF** Juvenile leaves awl-shaped; adult leaves lanceolate, 2 1/4–6 in (6–15 cm) long, flat. **FLOWER** Males: narrow, cylindrical; females: oval. **FRUIT** Oval cone up to 8 in (20 cm) long.

Norfolk Island Pine

HEIGHT 165–230 ft (50–70 m)
TYPE Evergreen
OCCURRENCE Norfolk Island (east of Australia)

This ornamental tree has branchlets in whorls of 4–7. **BARK** Gray-brown. **LEAF** Awl-shaped juvenile leaves; scalelike mature leaves. **FLOWER** Males: in clusters, 1 1/2 in (4 cm) long, yellow-brown or reddish; females: broader than long, with triangular scales and a bract. **FRUIT** Cone, releasing winged seeds.

bright green mature leaves

Podocarpus macrophyllus
Yew Plum Pine

HEIGHT up to 50 ft (15 m)
TYPE Evergreen
OCCURRENCE China, Japan

The fruit of the yew plum pine has a fleshy, footlike base, giving rise to the genus name, *Podocarpus*, which means "foot" and "fruit" in Greek. **BARK** Gray, red, and brown, long flakes. **LEAF** Alternate, lanceolate, green above, gray-green below. **FLOWER** Males: in conelike catkins, 1¼ in (3 cm) long; females: solitary. **FRUIT** Round green or purplish cone, ⅜ in (1 cm) wide, with an outer fleshy layer.

Cephalotaxus harringtonia
Plum Yew

HEIGHT up to 40 ft (12 m)
TYPE Evergreen
OCCURRENCE China, Japan

Used as an ornamental, this spreading tree can be shrubby. It grows at altitudes up to 3,000 ft (900 m). **BARK** Grayish, flakes in strips. **LEAF** Needles in two rows, curving upward to a V-shaped trough, glossy green above, two light bands beneath.
FLOWER Yellow; females larger than males. **FRUIT** Oval, plumlike cone.
FEMALE FLOWERS

male flowers

yellow flowers

LEAVES

Sciadopitys verticillata
Umbrella Pine

HEIGHT 65–100 ft (20–30 m)
TYPE Evergreen
OCCURRENCE Japan

An attractive ornamental, this tree is sacred in Japan. Its wood is water-resistant. **BARK** Red-brown, thick, soft, and stringy. **LEAF** Brown scale leaves on stem; fleshy needles in clusters of 10–30 at shoot nodes, glossy green above. **FLOWER** Males: yellow, in dense clusters; females: oval, green, solitary. **FRUIT** Fragile cone, ripens to brown; orange-brown seeds.

CONE   **LEAVES AND FLOWERS**

1½–2½ in (3.5–6.5 cm) long

male flower

Taxus brevifolia
California Yew

HEIGHT up to 65 ft (20 m)
TYPE Evergreen
OCCURRENCE North America (N.W. Pacific coast)

This yew was used by American Indians to make weapons and implements. Its foliage, seeds, and bark are poisonous but are also a source of taxol, an anticancer drug. **BARK** Scaly, purplish brown outer scales and reddish purple inner scales. **LEAF** Whorled, linear, ⁵⁄₁₆–1½ in (0.8–3.5 cm) long, green, two yellow-green bands beneath. **FLOWER** Males: pale yellow; females: tiny green globes. **FRUIT** Oval seed in fleshy red coating.

Taxus baccata

English Yew

HEIGHT up to 80 ft (25 m)
TYPE Evergreen
OCCURRENCE Europe, W. Asia

The English yew tree has poisonous bark, leaves, and seeds. It is a symbol of eternal life in several religious traditions, perhaps because it is evergreen, exceptionally long-lived, and resistant to decay, thus uniting death (by poison) to eternal life. It thrives on chalky soil.
BARK Smooth, red-brown with patchy flakes that reveal purple-red underbark.
LEAF Needles, in two ranks on horizontal branches but in spirals on upright shoots, linear, glossy dark green above with two gray-green bands below, ridged midrib.
FLOWER Catkins, males and females on separate trees. Males: spherical, beneath shoots; females: like tiny buds, near shoot ends. **FRUIT** Aril enclosing a single brown seed.

THE LONGBOW

The close-grained wood of the yew has elastic properties and was valued for making longbows in the Middle Ages. The English used these bows, capable of piercing armor, to defeat French forces in the Battle of Agincourt in 1415. Yew wood was in such demand for bow-making that local supplies were soon exhausted.

needle ⅜–1¼ in (1–3 cm) long

bright red ripe fruit

RIPE AND UNRIPE FRUIT

pale yellow male flowers

MALE FLOWER CLUSTERS

yellow fruit

T. BACCATA 'LUTEA'

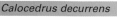

Torreya californica

California Nutmeg

HEIGHT up to 65 ft (20 m)
TYPE Evergreen
OCCURRENCE United States (California)

This prickly tree thrives in moist places. Its leaves exude a strong odor when crushed. **BARK** Gray to gray-brown. **LEAF** Needles, shiny green above, two white grooves beneath. **FLOWER** Males: yellowish white; females: green. **FRUIT** Seed in fleshy aril.

vertical fissures

spherical male flowers

FLOWERS AND LEAVES   **BARK**

Calocedrus decurrens

Incense Cedar

HEIGHT 60–150 ft (18–46 m)
TYPE Evergreen
OCCURRENCE W. United States, Mexico

This tree is named for its aromatic leaves. **BARK** Pale reddish brown. **LEAF** Shiny green and scalelike, in flattened, vertical sprays. **FLOWER** Males red-brown to pale brown; females red to golden brown. **FRUIT** Cone, with up to four seeds.

mature open cone

leaf to ⅛ in (3 mm) long

BRANCH WITH CONES

Chamaecyparis lawsoniana

Port Orford Cedar

HEIGHT up to 165 ft (50 m)
TYPE Evergreen
OCCURRENCE United States (S.W. Oregon to N.W. California)

Cultivated as an ornamental, this tree is also valued for its versatile timber **BARK** Reddish brown, stringy. **LEAF** Tiny, overlapping scales in sprays, in four ranks, dark green above, paler beneath. **FLOWER** Males: red to purple with red pollen sacs; females: green, budlike. **FRUIT** Cones, dull purple to red-brown, with 8–10 scales in pairs, each scale containing 2–4 seeds.

leaf 1/16–⅛ in (2–3 mm) long

cone 5/16–4¾ in (8–12 mm) wide

BRANCH WITH RIPE CONES

Chamaecyparis pisifera

Japanese False Cypress

HEIGHT up to 65 ft (20 m)
TYPE Evergreen
OCCURRENCE Japan

This ornamental tree is especially valued for its timber in Japan. **BARK** Reddish brown, vertical strips. **LEAF** Sharp-tipped scales, glossy green above, white marks beneath. **FLOWER** Males pale brown; females green. **FRUIT** Cone.

BARK

Cryptomeria Japonica

Japanese Cedar

HEIGHT up to 165 ft (50 m)
TYPE Evergreen
OCCURRENCE Japan, China

In Japan, this is the most important timber tree and is widely planted around temples. **BARK** Reddish brown to dark gray, peeling in strips. **LEAF** Pale green needles in spirals. **FLOWER** Males: plum-red, in racemes; females: green, rosette-like, in groups of 1–6. **FRUIT** Spherical cone.

cone ripens to brown

RIPE CONE

male flowers 3/16 in (5 mm) long

Cupressus lusitanica

Mexican Cypress

HEIGHT up to 100 ft (30 m)
TYPE Evergreen
OCCURRENCE Mexico, Guatemala, Honduras

This narrowly conical tree has an open, sometimes weeping, habit. **BARK** Reddish or grayish brown, thick. **LEAF** In four ranks, bluish green. **FLOWER** In clusters; males yellow-brown; females blue-white. **FRUIT** Cone.

LEAVES AND CONES

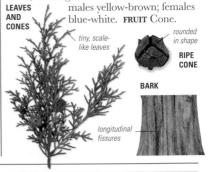

tiny, scale-like leaves

rounded in shape

RIPE CONE

BARK

longitudinal fissures

Cupressus macrocarpa

Monterey Cypress

HEIGHT up to 100 ft (30 m)
TYPE Evergreen
OCCURRENCE United States (California)

This unusual tree is a rarity in the wild, where it is stunted. It often grows tall in cultivation. **BARK** Yellowish brown. **LEAF** Scalelike, in sprays. **FLOWER** Males: yellow, egg-shaped; females: green, oblong. **FRUIT** Spherical cone.

gray-brown when ripe

MATURE CONES

Cupressus sempervirens

Italian Cypress

HEIGHT up to 100 ft (30 m)
TYPE Evergreen
OCCURRENCE Mediterranean region

A common ornamental, planted around the world, this tree grows well on alkaline and acid soil. Its wood is durable and easily worked. **BARK** Gray, smooth, turning gray-brown and furrowed with age. **LEAF** Scalelike, tiny, less than 1/24 in (1 mm) long, dull green. **FLOWER** Males yellow-brown; females green. **FRUIT** Short-stalked, glossy brown to gray cone, with 8–14 wavy edged scales in pairs, brown seeds.

cone 3/4–1/4 in (2–3 cm) long

FOLIAGE AND CONES

x *Cupressocyparis leylandii*

Leyland Cypress

HEIGHT up to 130 ft (40 m)
TYPE Evergreen
OCCURRENCE Britain

Widely planted as garden hedges and screening, this fast-growing conifer is a hybrid between the Nootka cypress (*Chamaecyparis nootkatensis*) and the Monterey cypress (*Cupressus macrocarpa*), trees from different genera. The first seedlings were planted in Britain by C. J. Leyland, after whom this tree was named. This species has ascending, nearly vertical branches. **BARK** Reddish brown, with shallow fissures. **LEAF** Densely packed, overlapping on shoots, scalelike, in sprays, up to 1/16 in (2 mm) long; green, yellow, or grayish **FLOWER** Both in clusters at the tips of shoots; males yellow and females green. **FRUIT** Spherical cone, with four scales in pairs.

cone 3/4 in (2 cm) wide

LEAVES AND YOUNG CONES

Juniperus communis

Common Juniper

HEIGHT up to 20 ft (6 m)
TYPE Evergreen
OCCURRENCE North America, Europe

conical crown

1/4–1 1/32 in (6–9 mm) wide

RIPE FRUIT

needles 3/16–3/4 in (0.5–2 cm) long

sharp tips

Juniper oil was used with cedar oil by the ancient Egyptians for embalming. The berrylike fruits were used medicinally in medieval times, and are still used to flavor gin. When crushed, the leaves smell of apple or gin. **BARK** Red-brown, with papery sheets that peel in strips. **LEAF** Flattened, awl-shaped needles, in whorls of three; concave, blue-green above, with a broad, waxy band; pale gray beneath, with a blunt keel. **FLOWER** Males and females on separate plants. Males yellow; females green, budlike in leaf axils. **FRUIT** Spherical, fleshy berrylike cone, taking three years to ripen from green to blue to black.

Eastern Red Cedar

HEIGHT up to 60 ft (18 m)
TYPE Evergreen
OCCURRENCE E. North America

conical to columnar habit

Also called the pencil cedar because its wood was used to make pencils, this tree has a slender profile and is the tallest of the junipers. Its wood is light, soft, and aromatic. It is durable and resists attack by insects. For this reason it has been used to make mothproof linings for cupboards. **BARK** Reddish to grayish brown, peeling vertically. **LEAF** Juvenile leaves: needlelike, up to 1/4 in (6 mm) long, in threes at shoot tips; mature leaves: scalelike, 1/32–1/8 in (1–3 mm) long, overlapping, below shoot tips. **FLOWER** Yellow males and green females on separate shoots. **FRUIT** Smooth, oval cone, ripens to violet-brown.

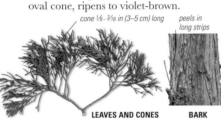

cone 1/8–3/16 in (3–5 cm) long   *peels in long strips*

LEAVES AND CONES   **BARK**

conical habit

Dawn Redwood

HEIGHT up to 150 ft (45 m)
TYPE Deciduous
OCCURRENCE China

This tree was only known from fossil records until specimens were found in China in 1941. **BARK** Peels vertically in stringy flakes. **LEAF** Soft, needlelike, flat, borne on deciduous branchlets; bright green at first, turning dark green, and later red-brown in fall. **FLOWER** Males: catkinlike in pairs on stalks, yellow, tiny, oval; females: in hanging clusters, green, rounded. **FRUIT** Pendent cones, turning woody and dark brown when ripe.

leaf up to 1 in (2.5 cm) long

LEAVES

orange-brown

unripe cone

BARK   **FRUIT**

Sequoia sempervirens

California Redwood

HEIGHT up to 360 ft (110 m)
TYPE Evergreen
OCCURRENCE U.S. (S.W. Oregon, N.W. California)

The world's tallest tree, the California redwood can live for over 2,000 years. It is named after a Cherokee Indian, Sequoyah. **BARK** Red-brown, tough, fibrous, deeply furrowed with broad, scaly ridges. **LEAF** Sharp-pointed needles, shiny dark green above with two white bands beneath. **FLOWER** In separate clusters on the same tree; males: yellow-brown, rounded; females: red-brown, budlike. **FRUIT** Diamond-shaped seed cone.

SHOOTS WITH FLOWERS — flowers at ends of shoots

Sequoiadendron giganteum

Giant Sequoia

HEIGHT up to 300 ft (90 m)
TYPE Evergreen
OCCURRENCE United States (California)

The largest tree in the world, although not the tallest, this conifer can weigh up to 2,000 tons. In the Sierra Nevada, it has a lifespan of up to 3,000 years. **BARK** Up to 20 in (50 cm) thick, fibrous, with ridges **LEAF** Sharp-pointed, scalelike, 3/16–5/16 in (5–8 mm) long, gray-green. **FLOWER** Males: pale green, round to oval, at tips of shoots; females: green, oval, at stem tips. **FRUIT** Barrel-shaped pendent cone.

red–brown

male flower buds

LEAVES AND BUDS

2–3¼ in (5–8 cm) long

BARK

UNRIPE CONE

GIANT SEQUIOA
These giant sequioas (*Sequoiadendron giganteum*), photographed at the Jedediah Smith State Park in California, are among the world's tallest trees. Their lofty canopy casts dense shade, but shafts of sunlight penetrate gaps where trees have died.

Platycladus orientalis

Chinese Arborvitae

HEIGHT up to 65 ft (20 m)
TYPE Evergreen
OCCURRENCE China, Korea, E. Russia

This usually shrubby tree has several main branches emerging from the base. It has been extensively cultivated in the past in its native regions. It is long-lived; some trees in China are believed to be over 1,000 years old. **BARK** Red-brown to pale gray-brown, thin, flaking in long strips. **LEAF** Scalelike, with blunt tips, overlapping in four ranks on shoots. **FLOWER** Males and females on the same tree. Males: yellow-green, oval, 1/16–1/8 in (2–3 mm) long; females: at end of shoots, blue-green, round, 1/8 in (3 mm) wide. **FRUIT** Cones, red-brown when ripe, flat, thick, woody, with 6–8 scales; seeds wingless, gray to purple-brown, with ridges.

SHOOT   cone to 3/4 in (2 cm) long

conical habit

Taxodium distichum

Bald Cypress

HEIGHT up to 160 ft (50 m)
TYPE Deciduous
OCCURRENCE S.E. United States

Freshwater swamps are this tree's native habitat. **BARK** Pale brown, furrowed, stringy, peeling at base. **LEAF** Alternate, 80–100 in two ranks on each branchlet; slender, short, flattened. **FLOWER** Males: yellow, in hanging catkins; females: green, in small clusters on the same plant as males. **FRUIT** Rounded cone with small spines, green ripening to purple.

FOLIAGE

Tetraclinis articulata

Arar Tree

HEIGHT up to 50 ft (15 m)
TYPE Evergreen
OCCURRENCE S.E. Spain, Morocco, Malta, Algeria, Tunisia

This medium-sized conifer is tolerant of hot conditions, and is often seen on dry, rocky hillsides. It is renowned for its resin and "thuya burls," outgrowths formed on the roots of the tree due to fungal infection. These are golden red and are highly valued in Morocco. The wood is aromatic, heavy, and oily, turns well, and has a high shine. **BARK** Peeling in long, slender strips. **LEAF** Scale leaves in whorls of four on vertical, dull green branchlets, with horizontal bands. **FLOWER** Males yellow and females green; inconspicuous. **FRUIT** Cones with two pairs of smooth scales containing eight red-brown seeds.

unripe cone

FRUIT

Thuja occidentalis

Arborvitae

HEIGHT up to 65 ft (20 m)
TYPE Evergreen
OCCURRENCE E. North America

leaf 1/16–3/16 in
(2–5 mm) long

**FLATTENED
LEAF SPRAY**

scalelike
leaves

Found in swampy areas, this conical,
multi-stemmed tree is grown as an
ornamental. **BARK** Red-brown, fissured.
LEAF In four ranks, dark green above,
yellow-green beneath, apple-scented.
FLOWER Males: red-brown, on shoot tips;
females: green or purple, on tips of
branchlets. **FRUIT** Oval brown cone.

Thuja plicata

Western Red Cedar

HEIGHT up to 165 ft (50 m)
TYPE Evergreen
OCCURRENCE W. North America

This tree is valued for its soft, durable
wood. **BARK** Red- or gray-brown, fibrous.
LEAF Scalelike, in four ranks, dark green
above, pale beneath. **FLOWER** Males red;
females yellow-green. **FRUIT** Oval cone.

open cones on branchlet

Thujopsis dolobrata

Hiba Arborvitae

HEIGHT up to 50 ft (15 m)
TYPE Evergreen
OCCURRENCE Japan

Also known as false arborvitae, the Hiba
is one of the five sacred trees of Japan.
BARK Red-brown, peeling in strips.
LEAF Scalelike, 1/8–1/4 in (4–7 mm) long
and 1/16 in (2 mm) wide, shiny, broad patch
beneath. **FLOWER** Males: cylindrical,
blackish green; females:
blue-gray. **FRUIT** Oval
cone, with 6–8 scales.

**LEAVES
AND
CONES**

white patch on
underside of leaf

dense,
pyramidal
habit

Xanthocyparis nootkatensis

Yellow Cedar

HEIGHT up to 130 ft (40 m)
TYPE Evergreen
OCCURRENCE W. North America

This tree is well-adapted to its snowy
habitat with its hanging foliage that allows
heavy snow to slide off. **BARK** Grayish
brown, fissured irregularly. **LEAF** Scalelike,
dark green above, yellow-green beneath,
overlapping. in four
ranks, thick.
FLOWER Males
gray-brown;
females green.
FRUIT Dark
red-brown,
waxy cone,
with 4–6
scales.

drooping
branches

BALD CYPRESS
This large tree grows in the freshwater swamps of the southeastern United States. In its natural habitat, oxygen is scarce in the water. Bald cypress (*Taxodium distichum*) thrives because it pushes up aerial roots from its root system.

FLOWERING TREES

Flowering trees belong to the angiosperm group of plants. They first appeared about 100 million years ago in the Cretaceous period. They are diverse in form and habitat—from spreading oaks in temperate forests to leafless, desert-loving cacti. This diversity, alongside other factors, could account for their undoubted success.

The term "angiosperm" is derived from the Greek for "vessel" (*angeion*) and "seed" (*sperma*) and refers to the fact that all the trees in this group produce seeds, which are enclosed in a "vessel," known as a carpel, to form a fruit. Although commonly called flowering plants, the fact that all angiosperms have flowers is not the main distinction between them and the gymnosperms.

A major difference between angiosperms and gymnosperms such as conifers is the origin of the food source for the seed. In angiosperms, two sperm are released from the pollen tube. One fertilizes the egg, the other enters the central cell, which develops into a structure known as the endosperm. This provides nourishment for the seed

FROM FLOWERS TO FRUIT
Angiosperms all produce fruit, but some species such as the Sweet Orange (*Citrus sinensis*) and have been selectively cultivated for the sweet edible pulp that surrounds the seeds.

after germination. In gymnosperms, the tissue that surrounds the egg nourishes the seed before it is fertilized. Angiosperm seeds are enclosed in fruits. The fruits can be dry or succulent. Dry fruits take the form of follicles, capsules, or pods. Succulent fruits include berries, drupes, or pomes. There are three types of angiosperms: primitive angiosperms (page 112), monocotyledons (page 123), and dicotyledons (page 141).

VENATION
The leaves of angiosperms are veined: those of monocotyledons have parallel venation; those of dicotyledons have a branching network of veins.

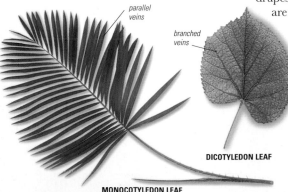

parallel veins

branched veins

DICOTYLEDON LEAF

MONOCOTYLEDON LEAF

JACARANDA IN BLOSSOM
A colorful and often fragrant display of flowers serves the vital purpose of attracting pollinating insects, birds, or bats.

PRIMITIVE ANGIOSPERMS

This small group represents the earliest flowering trees.

These angiosperms first appeared in the Cretaceous Period. Primitive angiosperms are often evergreen and woody, and may have their often simple, leathery leaves arranged in a spiral or alternately, as in nutmeg (*Myristica fragrans*). Some plants in this group have no vessels in the xylem. Many are aromatic, such as pond apple (*Annona glabra*) and Winter's bark (*Drimys winteri*).

The flowers of the primitive angiosperms are showy and tend to be radially symmetrical with petals and sepals that are difficult to differentiate (called tepals). The evolution of flowering plants closely paralleled that of insects. "Primitive" flowers, like those of magnolia trees, are often pollinated by "primitive" insects such as beetles.

PRIMITIVE FLOWER
Southern magnolia (*Magnolia grandiflora*) flowers are typical of this group in that they have tepals and many stamens.

numerous stamens

large tepals

Illicium verum

Star Anise

HEIGHT up to 26 ft (8 m)
TYPE Evergreen
OCCURRENCE S. China, Vietnam

This aromatic tree is valued for the oil obtained from its fruit. This is mainly used as a culinary spice and has medicinal properties. **BARK** White to gray. **LEAF** Alternate, lanceolate, glossy dark green above, dull paler green beneath. **FLOWER** Pale yellow, with more than 15 strap-shaped petals. **FRUIT** Star-shaped, with 5–10 rust-colored seed pods containing hard seeds.

LEAVES
untoothed margins

FRUIT
boat-shaped seed pods
glossy brown seeds

Canella winterana

Wild Cinnamon

HEIGHT up to 33 ft (10 m)
TYPE Evergreen
OCCURRENCE S. US (Florida)

A salt-tolerant species, wild cinnamon is used as an ornamental for its showy flowers. It has rich, dense foliage, which provides pleasant shade. The trunk grows straight up through the center of the canopy and develops thin branches that grow no more than 4 ft (1.2 m) long. The aromatic inner bark and leaves are used in tonics and condiments. The leaves are also used as a medicinal tea. The berries are peppery when dried and crushed. **BARK** Gray-brown. **LEAF** Opposite, olive green, thick, obovate, up to 8 in (20 cm) long. **FLOWER** Red to purple and white. **FRUIT** Bright red, round, fleshy berry, less than 3/8 in (1 cm) wide.

FLOWERS

yellow stamens

purplish buds

Drimys winteri

unripe fruit

whitish green underside

FLOWERING TREE

LEAVES AND FRUIT

Winter's Bark

HEIGHT up to 50 ft (15 m)
TYPE Evergreen
OCCURRENCE Argentina, Chile

This tree is named after Captain William Winter, who sailed with the English seaman Sir Francis Drake in the 16th century. The bark is used to treat digestive ailments. The leaves have a peppery odor when crushed. **BARK** Reddish brown, smooth, aromatic. **LEAF** Alternate, oval, leathery, up to 8 in (20 cm) long, bright glossy green above, paler beneath. **FLOWER** In clusters of up to 10 on branch tips; 5–7 white to cream petals, red sepals. **FRUIT** Small, round, green seed pod, ripening to purple-black, in clusters at the ends of long stalks; black seeds.

flowers in branched clusters

FLOWERS

Myristica fragrans

Nutmeg

HEIGHT up to 60 ft (18 m)
TYPE Evergreen
OCCURRENCE Molucca Islands
(otherwise known as Spice Islands)

The spices nutmeg and mace are both produced by this tree. Middle Eastern traders brought these products to southern Europe in the 6th century. By the 12th century, these spices were well known throughout Europe. The Portuguese found nutmeg trees in the Molucca Islands and dominated the trade until the Dutch gained ascendency in the 17th century. **BARK** Grayish; exudes yellow juice. **LEAF** Alternate, oval, pointed, dark green, shiny above, 3/4–2 3/4 in (2–7 cm) wide, leaf stalks 3/8 in (1 cm) long. **FLOWER** Pale yellow, waxy, fleshy, and bell-shaped; usually unisexual with

2 1/4–3 1/2 in (6–9 cm) long

FRUIT AND LEAVES

2–6 in (5–15 cm) long

BARK

smooth texture

LEAF

male and female flowers found on different trees; males, up to 3/16–7/32 in (5–7 mm) long, are in groups of one to ten; females, up to 3/8 in (1 cm) long are in groups of three. **FRUIT** Drupe, which is similar to an apricot, fleshy, yellow, and smooth, with a longitudinal ridge. When ripe, it splits in half, revealing a purplish brown oval seed (nutmeg), 3/4–1 1/4 in (2–3 cm) long encased in a red covering (mace).

A VERSATILE SPICE

Nutmeg, a spice with a sweet smell, comes from the hard seeds of the nutmeg fruit. It is used to flavor cakes, puddings, and some drinks. The oil is used to make perfume and to flavor tobacco. The nutmeg also contains a thick, yellow fat called nutmeg butter, used to make candles, and is an important ingredient in salves and medicines. Medicinally, nutmeg has been used for thousands of years for headaches and fever, and as a digestive aid and aphrodisiac.

NUTMEG AND MACE

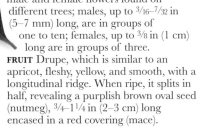

Liriodendron tulipifera

Tuliptree

HEIGHT up to 100 ft (30 m)
TYPE Deciduous
OCCURRENCE E. United States

This tree has a pyramidal crown with a straight trunk. **BARK** Pale gray-green with white grooves or patches. **LEAF** Alternate, palmately veined, and four-lobed. **FLOWER** Showy, with six petals, pale green at the edge and deep orange at the center. **FRUIT** Conelike group of woody, one-seeded fruit with one wing.

LEAVES WITH FLOWER

flower 1½–2 in (4–5 cm) wide

leaf 4–8 in (10–20 cm) long

Magnolia champaca

Champak

HEIGHT up to 110 ft (33 m)
TYPE Evergreen
OCCURRENCE S.E. Asia, India

Essentially a timber tree, the champak is also grown in India as an ornamental, where its flowers are used for adornment. The aromatic orange blooms appear nearly year-round. Essential oil extracted from the flowers is used in expensive perfumes. **BARK** Pale gray, smooth, ¾ in (2 cm) thick. **LEAF** Alternate, lanceolate, glossy above and dull beneath with a ¾–1¼-in (2–3-cm) leaf stalk. **FLOWER** Yellow with three sepals, six strap-shaped petals, and an elongated receptacle. There is also a white variety. **FRUIT** Oval, greenish, with angular seeds.

FRUIT

CROSS-SECTION OF FRUIT

LEAF

fleshy seed covering

5–10 in (13–25 cm) long

Magnolia grandiflora

Southern Magnolia

HEIGHT up to 90 ft (27 m)
TYPE Evergreen
OCCURRENCE US coast (from North Carolina to Florida and east to Texas)

This magnolia is the state flower of Mississippi and Louisiana. Its timber is sometimes used for veneers. **BARK** Brown to gray, thin, smooth, later developing scales. **LEAF** Alternate, pinnately veined, leathery, dark glossy above, with a rusty, velvety underside. **FLOWER** Showy, fragrant white flowers, 8–12 in (20–30 cm) wide. **FRUIT** Bright red, kidney-shaped seeds that hang from a red-brown cone-like structure that is 2–4 in (5–10 cm) long.

LEAVES WITH BUD

leaf 15–8 in (3–20 cm) long

immature fruit receptacle

Annona cherimola

Cherimoya

HEIGHT up to 30 ft (9 m)
TYPE Deciduous
OCCURRENCE Central America

The fleshy, creamy fruit of this tree is considered a delicacy. **BARK** Gray-brown, smooth. **LEAF** Alternate, oval to lanceolate, 3–6 in (7.5–15 cm) long. **FLOWER** Stalked, three green outer petals, three pinkish inner petals. **FRUIT** Pale green, spotted berry, with black, glossy seeds.

FRUIT 4–8 in (10–20 cm) long

Annona muricata

Soursop

HEIGHT up to 30 ft (9 m)
TYPE Evergreen
OCCURRENCE South America, Caribbean, introduced in S.E. Asia

LEAVES

glossy dark green

2¼–8 in (6–20 cm) long

All parts of this tree are used for traditional remedies. **BARK** Red-brown. **LEAF** Alternate, oval to elliptical, pointed at ends. **FLOWER** Single, three yellow-green outer petals, three pale yellow inner petals. **FRUIT** Heart-shaped berry, 4–12 in (10–30 cm) long.

Annona glabra

red inner base

SOLITARY FLOWER

Pond Apple

HEIGHT up to 50 ft (15 m)
TYPE Semi-deciduous
OCCURRENCE Americas, W. Africa

The pond apple is one of the few trees that is equally at home on riverbanks, in freshwater wetlands, and in brackish coastal mud. Its fruit and seeds both float—a feature that helps to make it a highly invasive species in some parts of the tropics. **BARK** Gray and flaky. **LEAF** Alternate, 3–5 in (7.5–12.5 cm) long, leathery, bright green above and paler below, aromatic. **FLOWER** Solitary, 1 in (2.5 cm) wide, creamy white to pale yellow, with three leathery outer petals and three smaller inner petals. **FRUIT** Berry that looks like a green apple, broad at the base; aromatic and fleshy when mature, containing about 140 pumpkinlike seeds.

3–5 in (7.5–12.5 cm) long   **RIPE FRUIT**   oval to elliptical leaf

Asimina triloba

Pawpaw

HEIGHT up to 40 ft (12 m)
TYPE Deciduous
OCCURRENCE North America

Valued for its fleshy, nutritious fruit, this tree is also known as papaw. The fruit has a short shelf-life, but does not require toxic chemicals for cultivation because it contains a natural insecticide. **BARK** Gray-brown, smooth, with wartlike lenticels. **LEAF** Alternate, pale green, oval to kite-shaped, 2–3 in (5–7.5 cm) wide. **FLOWER** Bell-shaped, 2–3 in (5–7.5 cm) wide, with six petals, appearing slightly before or with the leaves. **FRUIT** Green berry that resembles a banana, ripening to yellow and brown.

leaf 5–11 in (12.5–27.5 cm) long

YOUNG FRUIT WITH LEAVES

purplish brown petals

FLOWER

fruit 2¼–4 in (6–10 cm) long

RIPE FRUIT

Cananga odorata

Ylang-ylang

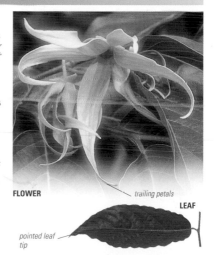

HEIGHT up to 70 ft (21 m)
TYPE Evergreen
OCCURRENCE Indonesia, Malaysia

Also called the perfume tree, the ylang-ylang is famous for the fragrant oil made from its flowers. The oil is used in perfumes and in aromatherapy; it is said to have a calming effect. Coco Chanel introduced Chanel No. 5, a cologne redolent of the scent of this tree, in 1923. Various parts of the tree are used in traditional medicine to treat malaria and fevers. **BARK** Pale gray. **LEAF** Alternate, oval, green. **FLOWER** Fragrant, in dense clusters in leaf axils, with six narrow yellow petals. **FRUIT** Small, oval, black berry that resembles a grape; contains 6–12 seeds.

FLOWER

trailing petals

LEAF

pointed leaf tip

FOLIAGE AND FLOWERS

Indian Willow

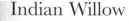

HEIGHT up to 50 ft (15 m)
TYPE Evergreen
OCCURRENCE India

The Indian willow, also known as the weeping ashoka, is often confused with the sacred ashoka tree (*Sarca indica*). The Indian willow is a common roadside tree in India and is widely used as an ornamental for its weeping branching habit. It can be seen lining the avenue leading to the Taj Mahal. A popular variety is *Polyalthia longifolia* 'Pendula', which has a very narrow, columnar shape. The parts of this tree are valued for their antimicrobial properties. **BARK** Brownish, smooth. **LEAF** Alternate, lanceolate, up to 8 in (20 cm) long, glossy green, with wavy margins. **FLOWER** Star-shaped, pale green. **FRUIT** Round black berry, 1 in (2.5 cm) wide.

wavy margins

slender, glossy leaves

FOLIAGE

UNRIPE FRUIT

berries in clusters

immature berries

KEEPING THE AIR CLEAN

Indian cities have become increasingly choked with traffic in recent years. This has greatly increased air pollution, especially the concentration of lead, which is highly toxic, in the air. The Indian willow is especially useful because it readily absorbs lead from the air, thereby reducing lead pollution. This makes it a useful bioindicator, as analysis of the leaves can indicate the levels of atmospheric lead.

Greenheart

HEIGHT up to 130 ft (40 m)
TYPE Evergreen
OCCURRENCE Guyana, French Guiana, Suriname, Brazil, introduced in Vietnam

This very large and dense forest tree is the most important timber species in Guyana and has a high commercial value. Its wood is durable when in contact with seawater and is used for building ships, docks, piers, and wharves. Since the mid-20th century, the number of trees has declined due to overexploitation of natural reserves and limited success in establishing plantations, since the tree fruits only once every 15 years. **BARK** Ash gray, smooth, dense. **LEAF** Smooth, leathery, 4–6 in (10–15 cm) long. **FLOWER** Small, whitish. **FRUIT** Nut with a large, hard, and brittle pericarp, containing a single large, fleshy seed.

Cinnamomum verum

Cinnamon

HEIGHT up to 60 ft (18 m)
TYPE Evergreen
OCCURRENCE Asia

Cinnamon is cultivated in southern India for its inner bark, which is used as a spice. Once more valuable than gold, this pale brown, aromatic spice was the most profitable spice in the Dutch East India Company trade. **BARK** Pale, pinkish brown. **LEAF** Opposite, linear-oval, waxy, 4–6 in (10–15 cm) long, and 1½–3¼ in (4–8 cm) wide, with three parallel veins. **FLOWER** Yellow-green, in axillary clusters. **FRUIT** Oval drupe, ³/₈ in (1 cm) long.

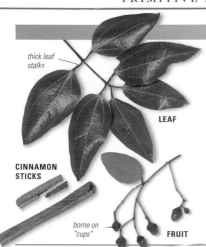

thick leaf stalks

LEAF

CINNAMON STICKS

borne on "cups"

FRUIT

Cinnamomum aromaticum

Cassia

HEIGHT up to 50 ft (15 m)
TYPE Evergreen
OCCURRENCE S. China

Cassia, a spice derived from the bark of this tree, is used as a flavoring agent, similar to cinnamon, though less prized. It is also used to repel vermin. The oil, which is distilled from the leaves, has a strong, penetrating smell and was valued

BARK

nearly parallel veins

to ½ in (1.5 cm) thick

LEAF

in biblical times.
BARK Gray, smooth. **LEAF** Long, lanceolate, leathery, reddish when young. **FLOWER** White, borne in loose umbels. **FRUIT** Elliptic, aromatic black drupe.

Cinnamomum camphora

Camphor Tree

HEIGHT up to 100 ft (30 m)
TYPE Evergreen
OCCURRENCE China, Japan

Widely planted as an ornamental, this
sturdy tree is resistant to fire and air
pollution and also acts as an effective
windbreak. It is easily distinguished
by its leaves that smell of camphor when
crushed. The leaves, twigs, and wood are
a source of camphor, which has been used
to treat ailments ranging from parasitic
infections to
toothaches. The wood
is also prized for
its red and
yellow stripes.
BARK Bright green,
tinged with red,
smooth, maturing to dark
gray-brown, with an uneven surface.
LEAF Alternate, oval, up to 5 in (12.5 cm)
long, leathery, dark green and glossy
above, green and whitish beneath,
with three distinct veins, aromatic.
FLOWER Creamy yellow
and tiny, in panicles that
are smaller than the leaves.
FRUIT Numerous, round black
berries, less than $^3/_8$ in (1 cm)
long, attached to panicles by
cuplike green cones.

wavy margins   **LEAVES**

shallow fissures /   **BARK**

green tinged with red

YOUNG SHOOT

glossy green leaves

FOLIAGE

Endiandra palmerstonii

Queensland Walnut

HEIGHT up to 115 ft (35 m)
TYPE Evergreen
OCCURRENCE Australia (N. Queensland)

Also called the black walnut, this large
tree has a spreading canopy and grows
in the lowland and upland rainforests of
northern Queensland. Its timber is used
to make furniture and veneers. The seed
of the fruit, although poisonous, is an
important traditional food for Aboriginal
peoples. After processing and cooking, it
is said to taste like bread. **BARK** Silver-
gray, smooth. **LEAF** Shiny green, ovate.

FLOWER Creamy
yellow and small,
with six segments,
hairy, scented.
FRUIT Green to
red, ribbed drupe
that is about $2^1/_4$ in
(6 cm) wide,
containing
a single large,
round seed.

buttressed base

TRUNK

Laurus nobilis

Bay Laurel

HEIGHT up to 60 ft (18 m)
TYPE Evergreen
OCCURRENCE N. Asia, Mediterranean

The bay laurel is the true laurel of Greek and Roman mythology. Considered sacred to the god Apollo, it symbolized victory and merit. It was an honor to be crowned with a garland of fruiting laurel leaves, and even today, a baccalaureate (*baca lauri*, Latin for "laurel berry") signifies achievement. The tree is now grown commercially for its aromatic leaves, which are used in cooking.
BARK Shiny gray, smooth.
LEAF Alternate, shiny dark green, leathery, 3–4 in (7.5–10 cm) long, with wavy margins, pointed tips, tapered base; red leaf stalks.

FLOWER Males and females on separate trees, in clusters on leaf axils; small, yellow, with six petals, males with numerous stamens.
FRUIT Black to purple, rounded, fleshy berry, up to 1/2 in (1.3 cm) long, on female plants.

yellow stamens

MALE FLOWERS

elliptic leaves

broadly conical habit

berries ripen from green to black

BRANCH WITH RIPE FRUIT

Persea americana

Avocado

HEIGHT up to 60 ft (18 m)
TYPE Semi-evergreen
OCCURRENCE S. Mexico

A fast-growing tree, the avocado was first cultivated in Central America, but it is now grown throughout the tropics. Its egg-shaped or pear-shaped fruits have yellowish flesh, with a buttery texture, which is exceptionally rich in proteins and oils. In its native habitat, the tree sheds its leaves briefly during the dry season, when it flowers. **BARK** Dark gray-brown, smooth.
LEAF Alternate, glossy dark green above, whitish below, variable in shape. **RIPE FRUIT**
FLOWER Pale green to yellow-green, three petal-like lobes, with nine stamens; in racemes. **FRUIT** Yellow to black drupe, speckled with yellow dots or raised spots.

round to oval seed

dense foliage

pear-shaped drupe

FRUIT-BEARING BRANCHES

Sassafras albidum

Sassafras

HEIGHT up to 65 ft (20 m)
TYPE Deciduous
OCCURRENCE E. United States

This broadly spreading tree has aromatic leaves. The bark, twigs, and leaves provide food for wildlife, particularly deer, and can be used to restore depleted soil. The orange timber is used for making barrels, buckets, and other items. Tea is brewed from its roots and the leaves are used for thickening soups. Its oil is used for making perfume.

BARK Dark gray-brown, thick.
LEAF Gray-green above, whitish beneath; juveniles with toothed margins, adults mitten-shaped or three-lobed.
FLOWER Green-yellow, petalless, borne in drooping, few-flowered, axillary racemes; males and females on separate trees.
FRUIT Dark blue, single-seeded drupe with pulpy flesh; thick red stalk.

three-lobed
adult leaf

yellow
anthers

unlobed
juvenile leaf

LEAVES

BARK

deeply
furrowed

downy young
shoots

**MALE
FLOWERS**

Umbellularia californica

lanceolate
leaf

BUDS

unopened flower
buds

California Laurel

HEIGHT up to 100 ft (30 m)
TYPE Evergreen
OCCURRENCE US (California, Oregon)

Often multi-stemmed, the California laurel has a broadly spreading habit and is found in forests and scrub in canyons and valleys. It is valuable for its pale brown timber. It has an attractive finish and is used as a veneer in furniture, paneling, and cabinetwork. **BARK** Gray-brown, thin, smooth, becoming reddish brown, scaly with age. **LEAF** Alternate, dark green, leathery, glossy above, peppery aroma when crushed.
FLOWER Yellow-green, 6–10 on each flowering stem, in leaf axils.
FRUIT Drupe, green at first, ripening to bluish black, up to 3/4 in (2 cm) wide, on yellow stalk.

FLOWERS AND FOLIAGE

MONOCOTYLEDONS

About a quarter of all flowering plants.

Monocotyledons are so called because their seeds only have one cotyledon (seed leaf), which emerges from the soil during germination. The flower parts (sepals and petals) are in multiples of three and the major leaf veins are parallel to each other and the leaf edge. The vascular bundles are scattered throughout the stem and the roots are adventitious (arising from the stem). They do not produce true wood, but have successfully evolved treelike forms. Overlapping leaf bases, thickened and enlarged cells, and prop roots are some of the strategies they use to support massive frames. Some species of *Yucca*, *Dracaena*, and *Aloe* have a thick central trunk, which may bear leafy branches. Other species, such as palms, have leaves attached at their base.

PALM TREE
Palms have a trunk that supports the leaves directly, without branches. Some species of palm can reach great heights.

MONOCOT SEEDLING
When a monocotyledon seed germinates, it sends out a root and a single seed leaf. The young plant is nourished by the food reserves (endosperm) within the seed.

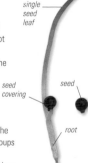

single seed leaf

seed

seed covering

root

GROUPS OF THREE
The petals of the flowers of the yucca tree are arranged in groups of three, one of the defining characters of the monocotyledons.

Pandanus tectorius

Screwpine

HEIGHT up to 30 ft (9 m)
TYPE Evergreen
OCCURRENCE Tropical Pacific

This tree has stout "root props" that grow from the bottom of the trunk and firmly anchor the tree in loose soil. They are salt-tolerant and ideal for binding sand and preventing erosion on seaward dunes. The fruit and root tips are a major food source, eaten either raw or cooked. The leaves are used for thatching and woven into mats and baskets. Regarded as the Nature Spirit (Kupua) in ancient Hawaii, this tree has been revered for centuries by Pacific people. **BARK** Prickly, with leaf scars, bearing aerial support roots. **LEAF** In spirals, pale green, usually 3–5 ft (0.9–1.5 m) long and 2–2³/4 in (5–7 cm) wide, with small upturned spines along the edges. **FLOWER** Borne on separate

woody segments   **FRUIT**

TRUNK WITH ROOT PROPS

trees; males: in clusters, 12 in (30 cm) long, of tiny, fragrant flowers, surrounded by white or cream bracts; females: in flower heads that develop into fruit.
FRUIT Resembles a pineapple, consisting of many woody segments fused together; can remain on the tree for up to 12 months.

Kingia australis

Black Gin

HEIGHT up to 25 ft (8 m)
TYPE Evergreen
OCCURRENCE S.W. Australia

A treelike perennial, which grows from a thick rhizome or underground stem, this tree is now listed as a threatened species. Fire plays an important role in its regeneration and stimulates flowering; as many as 100 flowers may bloom after the tree is exposed to fire. It is common for them to have fire-blackened trunks, which is why they are often called "blackboys." The trunk is valued for the resins it yields. Fibers from its stem pith were used to make cricket balls. **BARK** Grayish or blackish (from fire) and covered with persistent leaf bases. **LEAF** Alternate, long, linear, grasslike, near the top of the "trunk"; bunched together, appearing rather like a skirt; blue to blue-green with a silky, silvery sheen. **FLOWER** Yellowish, round, papery inflorescences, at the tip of a stout stalk that resembles a drumstick. **FRUIT** One-seeded capsule.

Xanthorrhoea australis

Grass-Tree

HEIGHT up to 6 ft (2 m)
TYPE Evergreen
OCCURRENCE Australia (New South Wales, Victoria, Tasmania)

Grass-trees are unique to the Australian bush. They are very slow-growing and can survive for many hundreds of years. Some plants may branch and have two or more heads, unlike the black gin, which has only one. The tree flowers in spring, blooming prolifically after a bush-fire. Grass-trees were a staple plant for the Aboriginals, providing food, drink, fiber, and materials for making implements and weapons. They are now valued as garden specimens. **BARK** Thick, corky, covered with leaf bases. **LEAF** Long, narrow, green, crowded at the top of the trunk.

spearlike flower spikes

spike 9¾ ft (3 m) tall

"skirt" of leaves

ABORIGINAL GLUE

A hard, waterproof resin, extracted from the leaves of the grass-tree, was used by Aboriginals in Australia as an adhesive. It was used to glue shafts and tips to spears, which had butt ends made out of the straight flower stalk.

CRAFTING SPEARS

FLOWER Very small, clustered together, in tall, straight, cylindrical spikes that arise from the leaves, with six white or cream petals, and white stamens; they contain copious amounts of nectar.
FRUIT Capsule, with hard, black seeds.

Aloe dichotoma

Quiver Tree

HEIGHT up to 25 ft (8 m)
TYPE Evergreen
OCCURRENCE S. Namibia, N.W. South Africa

The branches of this desert species repeatedly divide into two, which explains its name "dichotoma" (forked). The name "quiver tree" comes from the lightweight branches, which can be easily hollowed out and were once used by the hunters of the San tribe in southern Africa as quivers. The tree has a rounded crown topped with rosettes of leaves. The bark and fleshy leaves can store water. **BARK** Pale brown, corky and smooth, with large plates that peel off. **LEAF** Gray-green, narrow, pointed, with triangular-toothed margins. **FLOWER** Bright yellow, nectar-filled, up to 1¼ in (3 cm) long, on branched spikes. **FRUIT** Smooth, shiny capsule with narrow seeds.

Aloe barbesii

Tree Aloe

HEIGHT up to 60 ft (18 m)
TYPE Evergreen
OCCURRENCE Southern Africa

This multi-branched tree is well adapted to its dry habitat. Its prickly leaves protect it from grazing animals, and their waxy coating reduces water loss. **BARK** Pale gray, smooth. **LEAF** Succulent, long, narrow, deeply grooved. **FLOWER** Rose-pink or apricot-orange, three-branched inflorescences. **FRUIT** Spherical capsule.

cylindrical racemes

YOUNG PLANT

leaves in dense rosette

Cordyline fruticosa

Ti Plant

HEIGHT up to 10 ft (3 m)
TYPE Evergreen
OCCURRENCE S.E. Australia, tropical Pacific Islands

A popular container plant, ti is believed to have originated from Papua New Guinea. In Hawaii, its leaves are used to make hula skirts. **BARK** Gray, shiny, with horizontal leaf scars. **LEAF** Spirally arranged in tufts, at the ends of branches. **FLOWER** Yellow or red, sweetly scented; in large pendent panicles up to 12 in (30 cm) long. **FRUIT** Small red berries.

up to 30 in (75 cm) long

LEAF

glossy green

Cordyline australis

Cabbage Tree

HEIGHT up to 65 ft (20 m)
TYPE Evergreen
OCCURRENCE New Zealand

Also known as the palm lily, this popular ornamental has sweetly scented flowers. It can withstand drought and can grow in coastal habitats.
BARK Shallowly fissured. **LEAF** Long, strap-shaped, green, in tufts at the ends of branches.
FLOWER White, small, in pendent panicles 12 in (30 cm) long.
FRUIT Small pale lilac to green berries.

pale gray bark

Dracaena cinnabari

Socotra Dragon Tree

HEIGHT up to 50 ft (15 m)
TYPE Evergreen
OCCURRENCE Island of Socotra (Indian Ocean)

This tree, with its stout trunk and dense crown, has been popular since antiquity for medicinal purposes. It gets its name from its red resin, once believed to be dragon's blood. The resin is used as a varnish for violins. **BARK** Silvery, rough. **LEAF** Stiff, broad-based spiky leaves, in tufts at the end of branches. **FLOWER** Pale yellow, in clusters. **FRUIT** Yellow berry, to $3/4$ in (2 cm) wide, blackening with age.

Yucca brevifolia

Joshua Tree

HEIGHT up to 50 ft (15 m)
TYPE Evergreen
OCCURRENCE United States (California, Arizona, Nevada, Utah), Mexico

A characteristic plant of the Mojave Desert, this tree favors high desert plains. It relies on the yucca moth for pollination, but can sprout from its roots and stumps to form new plants. **BARK** Pale brown, covered with dead leaves, becoming irregularly ridged and furrowed with age. **LEAF** Strap-shaped, stiff, 6–12 in (15–30 cm) long, with sharp-pointed tips and fine-toothed edges, blue-green. **FLOWER** Bell-shaped, cream, yellow, or green, about 1½ in (4 cm) long, in upright clusters at ends of branches. **FRUIT** Fleshy capsule, pale to red-brown, 2¼–4¾ in (6–12 cm) long, 2 in (5 cm) wide, with six segments.

Areca catechu

Betel Palm

HEIGHT up to 50 ft (15 m)
TYPE Evergreen
OCCURRENCE S.E. Asia

The betel palm has a narrow, upright habit and is popular in many tropical countries for its chewable seeds, called nuts. These contain an alkaloid that acts as a stimulant. It is said to aid digestion and combat intestinal parasites and infections. **BARK** Dark green, ringed. **LEAF** Pinnate, 5–9 leaves, 30–50 dark green leaflets. **FLOWER** In horizontal stalks; males at the end and females at base of stalk. **FRUIT** Red or orange, egg-shaped berry, to 2 in (5 cm) long.

Arenga pinnata

Sugar Palm

HEIGHT up to 60 ft (18 m)
TYPE Evergreen
OCCURRENCE India, S.E. Asia

Sap from this single-stemmed tree is used to make sugar, vinegar, wine, and alcohol. **BARK** Black, fibrous, spiny. **LEAF** 20–25, pinnate, with many upright leaflets, very dark green above, silvery green beneath. **FLOWER** Yellow and showy, on long stalks. **FRUIT** Round to oval purple berry, with three seeds.

leaf to 40 ft (12 m) long

egg-shaped berry

UNRIPE FRUIT

DRAGON TREE
Found only in the Socotran Archipelago, the dragon tree (*Dracaena cinnabari*) is one of many plant and animal species unique to these islands, located off the coast of Somalia. Its characteristic canopy is thought to be typical of early trees.

Borassus flabellifer

Palmyra Palm

HEIGHT up to 65 ft (20 m)
TYPE Evergreen
OCCURRENCE India, Sri Lanka, S.E. Asia, New Guinea

The Palmyra palm is cultivated for its edible fruit and for its sap. Palms provide an important income for farmers during the dry season, when there are no crops in the field. **BARK** Dark gray-brown, with the remains of the bases of leaves, especially near the bottom; in older trees the upper trunk is grayer and smoother. **LEAF** Pointed, palmately lobed, stiff and green with a sheath and a spiny leaf stalk. **FLOWER** Males and females separate, bunched at base of oldest leaves; small, 1/8 in (3 mm) long, 3/16 in (5 mm) wide, with three sepals and three petals and either three stamens or three stigmas. **FRUIT** Rounded, smooth, reddish black when ripe, contains hard-shelled seeds within soft, fibrous, yellow pulp.

leaf 3¼–4¼ ft
(1–1.3 m) long

LEAVES

4–4¾ in
(10–12 cm)
wide

FRUIT

SUGARY SAP

Also known as the toddy or wine palm, the Palmyra palm is tapped for its sap, which has a sugar content of 14 percent. This can be boiled and made into syrup. The syrup is then left to cool and harden into lumps of sugar. It is also fermented into palm wine (toddy) or vinegar. **COLLECTING SAP**

Caryota urens

Jaggery Palm

HEIGHT up to 100 ft (30 m)
TYPE Evergreen
OCCURRENCE India, Myanmar, Sri Lanka

This tree is a source of fibers known as kitul. Its sap contains a significant percentage of sugar and is used to make an alcoholic drink. The seeds contain oxalic acid and are toxic if eaten. The fruit also needs to be handled with care since the juice can burn the skin. **BARK** Gray, covered with regularly spaced leaf scars. **LEAF** Bipinnate, 9¾–20 ft (3–6 m) long, with wedge-shaped, dark green leaflets, resemble the lower fin of a fish.

FLOWER Cream-colored, on inflorescences up to 20 ft (6 m) long, produced at the end of the tree's life and appearing first at the highest leaf level, then lower down. **FRUIT** Red drupe that is ¾ in (2 cm) wide, containing one or two dull gray seeds.

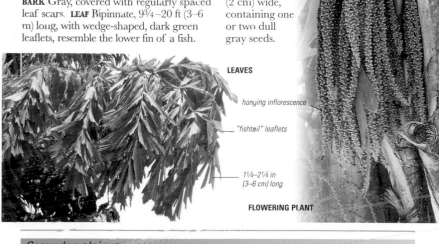

LEAVES

hanging inflorescence

"fishtail" leaflets

1¼–2¼ in (3–6 cm) long

FLOWERING PLANT

Ceroxylon alpinum

Wax Palm

HEIGHT up to 65 ft (20 m)
TYPE Evergreen
OCCURRENCE South America (Colombia, Venezuela)

A tall palm with a narrow trunk, the wax palm grows in the cloud forests of the Andes mountains at altitudes of 5,000–6,500 ft (1,500–2,000 m). The tree is endangered in Colombia because its habitat is prime coffee-growing country. **BARK** Gray and smooth, with fine horizontal leaf scars and a thin coating of wax. **LEAF** Pinnate, long, dark green above and powdery white beneath. **FLOWER** Males and females on separate trees, in loose panicles; small and greenish. **FRUIT** Bright, orange-red drupes, clustered together so that they look like a large bunch of grapes; each contains a hard, dark brown seed.

Cocos nucifera

Coconut

HEIGHT up to 100 ft (30 m)
TYPE Evergreen
OCCURRENCE S. and S.E. Asia, Central and South America, tropical Africa

Widely distributed in the tropics, this tree provides many natural products. The leaves are used for thatching, the trunk for building supports, the sugary sap makes an alcoholic drink, and its white flesh is edible. **BARK** Gray, marked by leaf scars. **LEAF** Pinnate, with stiff, strap-shaped leaflets. **FLOWER** In shoots at leaf axils; males at tip, females at base; both with six stamens and yellow-orange, lance-shaped petals. **FRUIT** Drupe composed of green outer layer (exocarp) that ripens to gray-brown, fibrous middle layer (mesocarp), hard inner layer (endocarp), surrounding a seed composed of white flesh (copra), coconut milk (endosperm), and an embryo.

ridged leaf scars

TRUNK

MATURE SEED

*mesocarp
1½–3¼ in
(4–8 cm) long*

FRUIT

COIR FROM THE SEED

Mature coconuts weigh 2¼–6½ lb (1–3 kg). Each one has a fibrous outer layer, up to 3¼ in (8 cm) thick, which helps the seed float and protects it from damage. When coconuts are harvested, the fiber, known as coir, is separated from the nut, before being cleaned and packed into bales. Coir is used to make mats and ropes.

SPINNING COIR

Copernicia prunifera

Carnauba Wax Palm

HEIGHT up to 30 ft (9 m)
TYPE Evergreen
OCCURRENCE Brazil

The heat-resistant wax harvested from the leaves gives this tree its name, and is a vital Brazilian export. Each of its approximately two dozen leaves provides about 15 lb (7 kg) of wax. **BARK** Gray, leaf bases in a spiral pattern. **LEAF** Fan-shaped, waxy, blue to green, divided into 30–60 segments. **FLOWER** Brown, on stalk. **FRUIT** Round brownish drupe, ¾–2 in (2–5 cm) wide.

LEAVES

deeply divided leaf

Corypha umbraculifera

large, fan-shaped leaves

Talipot Palm

HEIGHT up to 80 ft (24 m)
TYPE Evergreen
OCCURRENCE S. India, Sri Lanka

The largest of the fan palms, the talipot has a dramatic life history. It blooms only once in its lifetime of 30–80 years, raining down millions of flowers and fruits, but dies soon afterward.
BARK Gray. **LEAF** Palmate, up to 15 ft (4.5 m) wide, 30–40 in number; the rachis extends halfway up the leaf, bearing 110–130 spiny leaflets with split, blunt ends. **FLOWER** Cream, on tall, branched flower stalk.
FRUIT Olive green, waxy drupe, with a round seed.

divided base

LEAF STALKS

COCONUT PALM
The slender and delicate-looking *Cocos nucifera* is
deceptively robust, surviving for up to 100 years. It
is able to withstand high winds in the stormy coastal
areas in which it grows because of its strong
network of roots that anchor it to the soil.

Elaeis guineensis

Oil Palm

HEIGHT up to 65 ft (20 m)
TYPE Evergreen
OCCURRENCE W. Africa, introduced in S.E. Asia

Found in tropical rainforests, the oil palm produces the highest oil yield of any oilseed crop. **BARK** Gray, ringed with leaf scars. **LEAF** Pinnate, green leaf stalks with saw-toothed edges, with 100–150 pairs of green leaflets that are 2–4 ft (0.6–1.2 m) long and 1½–2 in (3.5–5 cm) wide. **FLOWER** Inflorescences, 4–12 in (10–30 cm) long; males: borne on short, furry branches; females: borne close to the trunk on short, heavy stalks. **FRUIT** Plumlike drupes, in large bunches, ripening to black; fleshy white mesocarp surrounds seeds that are enclosed in fibrous husk.

fruit to 1½ in (3.5 cm) long

UNRIPE FRUIT

11–17 ft (3.5–5 m) long

prominent midrib

PALM FROND

HARVESTING PALM OIL

Two kinds of oil are extracted from the palm nuts. Palm oil, which has a high unsaturated fat content, is taken from the fleshy, ivory white mesocarp while the seeds yield palm kernel oil. Both are used as cooking oils.

Hyphaene thebaica
Doum Palm

HEIGHT up to 30 ft (9 m)
TYPE Evergreen
OCCURRENCE Coastal N. and E. Africa

Unusually for a palm, this grassland and desert species has a branching trunk. **BARK** Gray, smooth lower down, leaf scars higher up. **LEAF** Pinnate, stiff, blue-green. **FLOWER** Long-branched, purple and yellow inflorescences. **FRUIT** Oval drupe, yellow-orange fibrous layer surrounding a hard seed that is 1½ in (4 cm) wide.

26–30 in (65–75 cm) long

FAN-SHAPED FRONDS

Jubaea chilensis
Chilean Wine Palm

HEIGHT up to 80 ft (25 m)
TYPE Evergreen
OCCURRENCE C. Chile (coastal areas)

Found in dry gullies and ridges with scrub, this tree has the largest trunk of all the palms. **BARK** Gray, marked with leaf scars. **LEAF** Pinnate, feathery, dull green above, gray below. **FLOWER** Purple, small, and numerous, in groups of two males to every female. **FRUIT** Round, yellow drupe, 2 in (5 cm) wide; seed, called "coquito," is like a tiny coconut.

Metroxylon sagu
Sago Palm

HEIGHT up to 50 ft (15 m)
TYPE Evergreen
OCCURRENCE S.E. Asia (probably originated in Papua New Guinea)

The starch from the sago trunk is a staple food. Trees are harvested after 12 years. **BARK** Chestnut brown, patterned with leaf bases. **LEAF** About 24, pinnate, feathery 17–26 ft (5–8 m) long; 100–190 leaflets. **FLOWER** Terminal, branched inflorescence, 10 ft (3 m) tall. **FRUIT** Straw-colored drupe.

Lodoicea maldivica
Double Coconut

HEIGHT up to 110 ft (34 m)
TYPE Evergreen
OCCURRENCE Seychelles

The seeds of this palm, the largest in the world, are very rich in fats, oils, and protein. **BARK** Gray-brown, prominent leaf scars. **LEAF** Fan-shaped, palmate veins, fringed edges, 15 ft (4.5 m) wide. **FLOWER** Male catkins at 3¼ ft (1 m) long are the longest known. **FRUIT** Large, two-lobed drupe, weighing 45 lb (20 kg).

Date Palm

Phoenix dactylifera

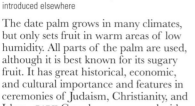

HEIGHT up to 100 ft (30 m)
TYPE Evergreen
OCCURRENCE Native to N. Africa, but introduced elsewhere

The date palm grows in many climates, but only sets fruit in warm areas of low humidity. All parts of the palm are used, although it is best known for its sugary fruit. It has great historical, economic, and cultural importance and features in ceremonies of Judaism, Christianity, and Islam. **BARK** Gray-brown, covered with remains of leaf bases in a spiral pattern. **LEAF** 20–30, pinnate, up to 20 ft (6 m) long, ascending upper leaves, downward-curving lower leaves; sharply pointed leaflets. **FLOWER** Males and females on separate trees in axillary, pendent clusters up to 4 ft (1.2 m) long; small, whitish, fragrant. **FRUIT** Oblong drupe, up to 1½ in (4 cm) long, dark orange when ripe, containing one woody seed.

DATES IN MILLIONS

Evidence suggests that the date palm was cultivated in 4000 BCE. According to the World Food and Agricultural Organization, of the 90 million trees in the world, 64 million are in Arab countries. Iraq is the top producer and exporter of dates, followed by Saudi Arabia, Egypt, and Algeria.

PACKAGED FOR EXPORT

ascending upper leaves

pendulous clusters

FRUIT

rigid, linear leaflets

FROND

Phoenix canariensis

Canary Palm

HEIGHT up to 65 ft (20 m)
TYPE Evergreen
OCCURRENCE Canary Islands

One of the most grown ornamentals of the world, this tree has a rounded crown. **BARK** Brown, thick, with prominent leaf scars. **LEAF** Pinnate, up to 18 ft (5.5 m) long, deep green, shading to yellow at stalk. **FLOWER** Males and females on separate trees; small, off-white, on stalks up to 6½ ft (2 m) long. **FRUIT** Orange drupe.

LEAVES AND FRUIT

Raphia farinifera

Raffia Palm

HEIGHT up to 33 ft (10 m)
TYPE Evergreen
OCCURRENCE Madagascar, E. Africa

This imposing African palm has the largest leaves of any tree. They are the source of raffia, a natural fiber. Its flowers are borne in clusters of thousands, on a drooping shoot that looks like a large rope. **BARK** Pale gray or brown, with leaf scars. **LEAF** Pinnate, to 65 ft (20 m) long. **FLOWER** Borne on the same inflorescence; males: on top, large, tubular; females: at bottom, small. **FRUIT** Oval, scaly brown drupe.

Roystonea regia

Royal Palm

HEIGHT up to 65 ft (20 m)
TYPE Evergreen
OCCURRENCE Native to Cuba and Honduras, but introduced in Florida

This graceful palm is notable for its salt-resistance and rapid growth. **BARK** Pale gray, smooth. **LEAF** 15–20, pinnate, bright green, with linear leaflets. **FLOWER** Males and females on same flowering shoots, both small, white. **FRUIT** Round drupe, green ripening to purple-black, with small seed.

Trachycarpus fortunei

Chusan Palm

HEIGHT up to 33 ft (10 m)
TYPE Evergreen
OCCURRENCE China

The hardiest palm, this ornamental tree occurs in mountainous regions that are often covered with snow in winter, and can survive without its leaves. Its trunk tends to be narrower at the base. **BARK** Gray or brown, coarse, becoming smooth with age. **LEAF** Unevenly divided, split halfway to leaf stalk, dark green above, silvery below, 4 ft (1.2 m) wide. **FLOWER** Males and females in branched clusters on separate trees. **FRUIT** Round to oblong, blue-black berry.

FLOWERS AND FRUIT

fruit ⅜ in (1.3 cm) wide

bright yellow flowers

prominent leaf scars

BARK

fan-shaped

FROND

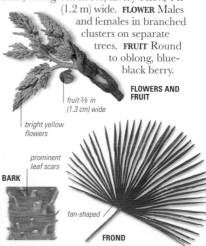

Washingtonia filifera

California Fan Palm

HEIGHT up to 60 ft (18 m)
TYPE Evergreen
OCCURRENCE US (S.E. California, W. Arizona), Mexico (Baja California)

A native of deserts and semi-arid areas, this tree is also known as the petticoat palm because its old leaves hang around the trunk like a petticoat. **BARK** Pale red-brown, smooth. **LEAF** Palmate, gray-green, with cottonlike threads; dark brown, shiny leaf base.
FLOWER White or yellow, on stalks that emerge between the leaves. **FRUIT** Black, spherical, fleshy berry up to 5 in (12.5 cm) wide, containing small, glossy red seeds.

dead leaves

BARK

FOLIAGE   *fan-shaped leaves*

Ravenala madagascariensis

Traveler's Palm

HEIGHT up to 40 ft (12 m)
TYPE Evergreen
OCCURRENCE Madagascar, widely planted in tropical areas

Traveler's palm is not a true palm and has been described as being part banana and part palm. In young plants, the trunk is underground. In mature plants, it emerges above the ground, elevating the crown. It gets its common name from the fact that when it rains, water collects in the flower bracts and leaf folds, providing a drink for travelers. **BARK** Green, with distinctive leaf scar rings. **LEAF** Up to 13 ft (4 m) long and 10–20 in (25–50 cm) wide, long stalks, arranged symmetrically on the trunk, like a giant fan. **FLOWER** Small, numerous, creamy white, held in bracts and borne in clusters 12 in (30 cm) long. **FRUIT** Brown berry, containing blue seeds.

DICOTYLEDONS
Most flowering plants, including trees.

Dicotyledons are so called because the embryo within the seed has two cotyledons (seed leaves). The leaves of dicotyledons have a complicated branching network of leaf veins. This is called reticulated or net venation. The dicotyledons have a vast range of flower forms, but the parts of the flower (petals and sepals) are mostly arranged in fives. Flowers with parts arranged in fours are less frequent, but an example is beech (*Fagus sylvatica*). In dicotyledons, the vascular bundles that contain xylem (water-conducting tissue) and phloem (sugar-transporting tissue) are arranged in a ring. Hardwood trees in this

FLOWERING IN FIVES
Almond (*Prunus dulcis*) flowers have five petals. Most dicotyledons have their flower parts arranged in fives.

stamens

petals in fives

group have xylem that contains cells called tracheids and wood vessels, plus tightly packed, thick-walled fiber cells. This makes the wood hard. An example is ebony (*Diospyros ebenum*), which has wood so dense that it sinks in water.

seed leaf

DICOTYLEDON SEEDLING
When seeds germinate, the embryonic root emerges from the seed first. The paired seed leaves emerge later.

seed covering

annual ring

ANNUAL RINGS
The vascular bundles formed in spring are much larger than those formed in summer. This difference produces "annual rings" seen in a cross-section of the trunk.

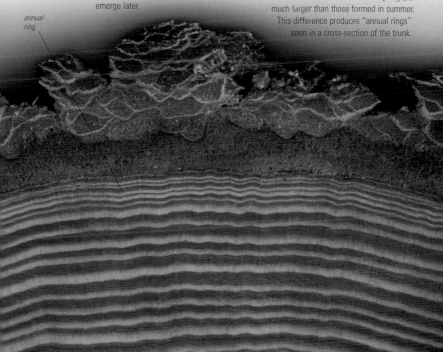

Grevillea robusta

Silk Oak

HEIGHT up to 100 ft (30 m)
TYPE Evergreen
OCCURRENCE E. Australia

Mostly planted in Australia as a shade tree for coffee and tea plantations at high altitudes, this tree is valued for its timber. It is cultivated as an ornamental for its spectacular flowers and feathery foliage. **BARK** Pale gray. **LEAF** Alternate, fernlike, 6–12 in (15–30 cm) long, gray-green above, silvery beneath. **FLOWER** Bright yellow-orange, stalked; on terminal bottlebrush-like flowering shoots that are 3¼–6 in (8–15 cm) long. **FRUIT** Brown-black, leathery seed capsules, with one or two flat, winged seeds.

flower ¾–1¼ in (2–3 cm) long

long, protruding stigma

FLOWER WITH LEAF

capsule to ¾ in (2 cm) long

IMMATURE FRUIT

PATTERNED TIMBER

The timber of the silk oak is immensely valued for its decorative, lacelike pattern. Once marketed as "lacewood," it was a leading face veneer. The heartwood is pale pink, darkening to red when dry. The timber is of medium strength and easily worked. It is used for furniture, packing cases, flooring, and paneling.

CABINET

Macadamia integrifolia

Macadamia

HEIGHT up to 65 ft (20 m)
TYPE Evergreen
OCCURRENCE New South Wales, Queensland, E. Australia

Cultivated for its nuts, the macadamia is the only Australian native plant to be grown as a major food crop. It grows in coastal rainforests and is very productive, flowering and fruiting for 3–12 months of the year. Its timber is also useful, and it is also cultivated as an ornamental. The macadamia nut can be used to make a bland salad oil, but it is usually too valuable as a dessert nut to be used in this way. **BARK** Brown, rough, but unfurrowed. **LEAF** Whorls of three, pale green or bronze when young, later green and oblong, 4 in (10 cm) wide, on leaf stalks about 1/2 in (1.5 cm) long, margins may be waxy, with a few spines. **FLOWER** Small, creamy white, petalless, borne in groups of three to four in a long axis, in racemes. **FRUIT** Round nut, hard green outer layer, and hard inner shell that protects the white kernel.

LEAVES, FLOWERS, AND FRUIT

mature leaf 4–12 in (10–30 cm) long

glossy green leaf

spreading crown

raceme

nut to 1 in (2.5 cm) wide

whorls of leaves

THE MACADAMIA NUT

Considered one of the best-tasting nuts in the world, the macadamia nut has a rich oil content of 75–80 percent. The nuts mature six to seven months after flowering and fall to the ground when ripe. After harvesting, they are dehusked, washed, and dried. The shells are cracked for processing; the shelled kernels are then vacuum-packed and shipped for sale.

PACKAGED NUTS

Mauna Loa
BITTER CANDY GLAZED
MACADAMIA
NUTS

FRESH NUTS

Platanus x *hispanica*

London Planetree

HEIGHT up to 150 ft (45 m)
TYPE Deciduous
OCCURRENCE S. Europe

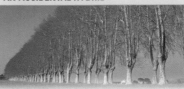

AN ACCIDENTAL HYBRID

The London planetree is a cross between *P. orientalis* (Asian planetree) and *P. occidentalis* (sycamore). According to one story, the hybrid arose in the garden of the British botanist John Tradescant. It is more likely, however, that it originated by accident in Spain or France in the mid-17th century.

A handsome ornamental with a spreading to broadly columnar crown, this tree is planted in many cities. It is suited to urban environments because its bark has the ability to renew itself by peeling off in plates to prevent its pores from getting clogged by pollution.
BARK Smooth and gray, peeling to reveal yellow or green inner bark.
LEAF Alternate, toothed, three, five, or seven pointed lobes cut about halfway to the base; shiny green above, pale matt green with downy hairs beneath.
FLOWER Petalless; males and females in separate clusters on the same tree; males yellow, females reddish. **FRUIT** Burlike, pendent achenes, covered with brown bristles, green ripening to brown.

6 in (15 cm) wide

PALMATE LEAF

up to four achenes on single stalk

peels in puzzle-like pieces

FRUIT

BARK

Platanus occidentalis

Sycamore

HEIGHT up to 100 ft (30 m)
TYPE Deciduous
OCCURRENCE E. North America

Also known as the American planetree, this massive tree has a heavy, spreading crown and zigzag branches. Its spherical fruits are used to make Christmas tree ornaments. **BARK** Thin, mottled brown, green, and white; older stems are gray-brown and scaly. **LEAF** Alternate, palmately veined, oval, with 3–5 lobes, toothed; veins below may be hairy. **FLOWER** Deep red; males and females in separate dense, spherical heads, about ³/₈ in (1 cm) wide. **FRUIT** Achene on 3–6 in (7.5–15 cm) long stalk, with a winged seed.

FOLIAGE | 4–8 in (10–20 cm) wide

Buxus sempervirens

Boxwood

HEIGHT up to 30 ft (9 m)
TYPE Evergreen
OCCURRENCE S. Europe, N. Africa, W. Asia

Well known as a garden hedge and shrub, this tree prefers lime-rich soil. **BARK** Pale brown, later cracks into small, gray, corky squares. **LEAF** Opposite, borne on squarish stems, elliptic to oblong, notched at tip, dark green above, paler or yellow-green beneath, with creamy yellow midveins.

FLOWER In small clusters of 5–6 stalkless males surrounding one short-stalked female; pale yellow, petalless, fragrant. **FRUIT** Capsule with three split horns; green becoming brown and papery, releasing glossy black seeds.

leaves 4³/₄–10 in (12–25 cm) long

urn-shaped capsule

FRUIT AND LEAVES

TOPIARY FAVORITE

Widely used in topiary, the art of clipping trees into ornamental shapes, boxwood makes a beautiful clipped hedge. Its foliage can be easily trimmed to form pyramids, cones, spirals, or rounded shapes.

POTTED ORNAMENTALS

LONDON PLANETREE
Platanus x hispanica is the archetypal city tree; it provides a pleasing dappled shade and is tolerant of both pollution and vigorous pruning. In a less restricted environment, a mature tree can reach a great size, with widely spreading branches.

Triplaris weigeltiana

Long Jack

HEIGHT up to 16 ft (5 m)
TYPE Evergreen
OCCURRENCE South America

This tree dominates forests in Surinam and old plantations in east Guyana. It is fairly invasive. **BARK** Pale gray. **LEAF** Dark green and glossy, 4–9 in (10–22 cm) long, 1½–2¼ in (4–6 cm) wide, pointed at the tip, with a prominent midvein, many pairs of side veins, and untoothed margin. **FLOWER** Males and females borne on separate spikes, each 2¼–4 in (6–10 cm) long.

cream flowers
in spikes

MALE FLOWERS

Males: tiny, cream; females: with three enlarged red-purple sepals that are about 1¼ in (3 cm) long and ³⁄₁₆ in (5 mm) wide. **FRUIT** Dry nut, ³⁄₈ in (1 cm) long.

FLOWERING BRANCHES

Charpentiera densiflora

Papala

HEIGHT up to 40 ft (12 m)
TYPE Evergreen
OCCURRENCE Hawaii (Kauri)

Moist forests located in valleys and gulches are the native habitat of this tree. It is an endangered species; fewer than 400 mature trees exist. **BARK** Smooth, grayish brown. **LEAF** Elliptic to oval, leathery, 5–16 in (13–40 cm) long. **FLOWER** Numerous, borne in panicles 9–19 in (22–48 cm) long. **FRUIT** Not described.

minute flowers

INFLORESCENCE

leaf 5–16 in
(13–40 cm) long

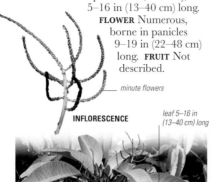

Haloxylon persicum

Saxaul

HEIGHT up to 22 ft (7 m)
TYPE Evergreen
OCCURRENCE W. Asia (Russia to Iran to China)

Found in the desert, the saxaul has a large root system that helps to stabilize sand. Its heavy, durable wood is used in carpentry and is highly valued as fuel. **BARK** Gray-white. **LEAF** Triangular, scale-like, pressed to stem, with straw-colored cusp at tip. **FLOWER** Pale yellow, solitary, ⁵⁄₃₂–⁷⁄₃₂ in (4–7 mm) long; males and females on the same plant, in scalelike bracts on dwarf side spurs of previous year's branches. **FRUIT** Round, winged nut, ⅛ in (2.5 mm) wide.

grasslike foliage

Carnegiea gigantea

Saguaro

HEIGHT up to 50 ft (15 m)
TYPE Evergreen
OCCURRENCE S.W. US (Sonora desert), Mexico

The saguaro is the world's largest cactus, and the state flower of Arizona. It grows very slowly, just over 1 in (2 cm) per year, and its massive columnar stems have a huge capacity for water storage. The oldest plants are estimated to be 200 years old. **BARK** Smooth, waxy, green.

NECTAR-FILLED CACTUS

The saguaro flowers every year even if there is no rainfall. The creamy-white petals surround a tube. Yellow stamens form a circle at the top of the tube. At the bottom of the tube is nectar. This, and the color of the flowers, attract birds, bats, and insects that pollinate the flowers.

dense group of stamens

OPEN FLOWERS

creamy white petals

FLOWERING STEM   *downward-pointing spines*

LEAF Stout spines, 2 in (5 cm) long, in clusters on the stem's vertical ribs.
FLOWER Bell-shaped, waxy, fragrant, about 4–4¾ in (10–12 cm) long and 3½–4¾ in (9–12 cm) wide, in clusters at the ends of stems and branches; numerous stamens surround a tube; only a few open at a time, and each one lasts only one night. **FRUIT** Greenish to reddish, oval, edible berry; contains red pulp and small, black seeds.

SAGUARO
Saguaro (*Carnegiea gigantea*) is supremely equipped
for survival in the scorching deserts of the American
West. In particular, its "pleated" trunk and branches
expand to allow maximum uptake of water during
rare periods of rainfall.

Phytolacca dioica

Bella Umbra

HEIGHT up to 60 ft (18 m)
TYPE Evergreen
OCCURRENCE Argentina, Brazil, Uruguay

Also known as ombu or belhambra, this fast-growing, herbaceous tree has a broad trunk with high water content. The only tree to live on the Pampas grasslands in South America, it is well adapted to grassland fires and scarcity of water due to a fire-resistant trunk that can store water. Its poisonous sap keeps browsing animals away. This tree is also valued for the shade it provides. **BARK** Pale brown, very spongy. **LEAF** Dark, glossy green, ovate or elliptic. **FLOWER** Small, greenish white, in clusters. **FRUIT** In clusters on stalks like a mass of curled up caterpillars, green turning crimson when ripe, up to 3/8 in (1 cm) wide.

ovate leaf

LEAVES AND FLOWERS

flowers in long racemes

Nuytsia floribunda

Fire Tree

HEIGHT up to 33 ft (10 m)
TYPE Evergreen
OCCURRENCE Western Australia

Also known as the Western Australian Christmas Tree, this evergreen shrub or small tree is semi-parasitic, getting water and nutrients from the roots of grasses and other plants up to 500 ft (150 m) away. Its spectacular flowers bloom for several months around Christmas. Its thin, long leaves give the tree an untidy appearance. **BARK** Rough, gray-brown. **LEAF** Linear, dark green. **FLOWER** In clusters on branched inflorescences. **FRUIT** Dry nut with three broad, leathery wings.

FLOWERS

yellow-orange flowers

Santalum album

dark green, glossy leaves

brownish red flowers

LEAVES AND FLOWERS

BARK

Sandalwood

HEIGHT up to 30 ft (9 m)
TYPE Evergreen
OCCURRENCE China, India, Indonesia, Philippines

This tree is renowned for its oil and wood, which is used for making perfumes, herbal medicines, and fine furniture. It is a semi-parasitic tree, requiring roots of other plants to grow successfully. **BARK** Reddish brown. **LEAF** Elliptic-lanceolate, up to 1¼ in (3 cm) long, on thin stalks. **FLOWER** Small, in branched cymes. **FRUIT** Small, dark red, one-seeded drupe.

Cercidiphyllum japonicum

Katsura Tree

HEIGHT up to 60 ft (18 m)
TYPE Deciduous
OCCURRENCE China, Japan

The katsura tree is valued as a shade or specimen tree. In fall, its leaves have a fragrance of burned sugar or strawberries. **BARK** Initially smooth with many pores, becoming darker and splitting into thin, curling strips with age. **LEAF** Heart-shaped with bluntly-toothed margins, 2–3¼ in (5–8 cm) long, purple when emerging, turning scarlet to yellow in fall. **FLOWER** Male and female flowers on separate trees, inconspicuous in

LEAVES | fall coloration

reddish bracts, appearing before the leaves. **FRUIT** Small (to ¾ in/2 cm long) curved seed pods in small clusters, initially red.

LEAVES

conical to rounded habit

opposite arrangement

Liquidambar orientalis

Asian Sweetgum

HEIGHT up to 40 ft (12 m)
TYPE Deciduous
OCCURRENCE Turkey

This tree's resin has been used medicinally for over 700 years. **BARK** Purple-gray, corky. **LEAF** Alternate, palmate, cut into five three-lobed sections. **FLOWER** White, arranged in small, round solitary heads. **FRUIT** Spiny, globe-shaped capsule.

FALL LEAVES   orange, scarlet, or purple coloration

Liquidambar styraciflua

Sweetgum

HEIGHT up to 75 ft (23 m)
TYPE Deciduous
OCCURRENCE E. and S. United States

This tree has a pyramidal shape when young, becoming rounded with age. **BARK** Pale gray, later deeply fissured. **LEAF** Alternate, leathery, glossy green. **FLOWER** Solitary, yellow-green, rounded heads. **FRUIT** Spiny, spherical, brown.

LEAVES AND YOUNG FRUIT

fruit 1–1¼ in
(2.3–3 cm) wide   palmate leaf

LABEL TO COME

Parrotia persica

Ironwood

HEIGHT up to 40 ft (12 m)
TYPE Deciduous
OCCURRENCE Iran

This is an ideal specimen tree with its pest-free nature, noninvasive roots, and superb fall colors. **BARK** Silver, green, white, and brown when peeling. **LEAF** Alternate, oblong to oval, wavy to toothed margins, hairy, glossy green in summer, young leaves red-purple. **FLOWER** Petalless, many deep crimson stamens, emerge before leaves. **FRUIT** Dry, pale brown capsule ⅜ in (1 cm) wide, contains seeds.

wavy margin

leaf ¾–5 in
(2–12.5 cm)
long   **LEAVES**

Staphylea pinnata

European Bladdernut

HEIGHT up to 15 ft (4.5 m)
TYPE Deciduous
OCCURRENCE S.E. Europe, W. Asia

This tree is very popular as an ornamental. **BARK** Grayish brown, smooth. **LEAF** Opposite; 3–7 leaflets, oblong to oval, toothed, dull green above, pale below. **FLOWER** White, stalked, about ⅜ in (1 cm) long, in drooping panicles. **FRUIT** Inflated, papery capsule, with edible seeds.

LEAVES, FLOWERS, AND FRUIT   leaf 2–4¾ in (5–12 cm) long

Terminalia catappa

Indian Almond

HEIGHT up to 60 ft (18 m)
TYPE Deciduous
OCCURRENCE S. and S.E. Asia

The spreading, horizontal branches of this species make it an ideal shade tree, although it is invasive. Its fruit has many medicinal uses. **BARK** Smooth and gray. **LEAF** In clusters, oblong to oval, 12 in (30 cm) long, 6 in (15 cm) wide, shiny green.

FLOWER In long terminal clusters, 6 in (15 cm) long, males and females on same tree; females greenish white. **FRUIT** Oval drupe, with corky fiber covering a green to yellow husk that turns reddish when ripe; thin, green inner flesh encloses nut that tastes of almonds.

FRUIT | drupe 2–3 in (5–7.5 cm) long

Lawsonia inermis

Henna

HEIGHT up to 20 ft (6 m)
TYPE Evergreen
OCCURRENCE N. Africa, S.W. Asia

The red-orange dye extracted from the leaves of the henna tree is used for body art and as a hair colorant. **BARK** Grayish brown. **LEAF** Opposite pairs, 3/8–1 1/4 in (1–3 cm) wide. **FLOWER** Four-petaled, red, white, pink, or yellow, fragrant, in terminal clusters. **FRUIT** Berry, containing 40–45 small seeds.

leaf 3/8–2 in (1.2–5 cm) long

greenish brown fruit

LEAVES

FRUIT

Corymbia ficifolia

Red Flowering Gum

HEIGHT up to 40 ft (12 m)
TYPE Evergreen
OCCURRENCE S.W. Australia

This tree is widely planted as an ornamental. **BARK** Fibrous, dark gray to brown. **LEAF** Oval, dull green. **FLOWER** Bright red stamens around yellow centers. **FRUIT** Urn-shaped capsule.

FLOWERS

flowers in clusters

leaf 3–9 in (7.5–22.5 cm) long

Eucalyptus brassiana

Cape York Redgum

HEIGHT up to 100 ft (30 m)
TYPE Evergreen
OCCURRENCE Australia (Queensland), Papua New Guinea

Native to the Cape York peninsula, this is a popular shade tree. Its flowers are an important food source for bees. **BARK** Gray-white, smooth, peeling in narrow strips. **LEAF** Stalked, gray-green, yellowish or red midvein. **FLOWER** Umbels with 3–7 stalked, white flowers. **FRUIT** Semi-spherical, dry capsule, 1/4–4 in (6–10 mm) long.

Eucalyptus delegatensis

Alpine Ash

HEIGHT up to 260 ft (80 m)
TYPE Evergreen
OCCURRENCE S.E. Australia, Tasmania

The alpine ash is a high-altitude, sub-alpine tree that can tolerate extreme environmental conditions. It is a fast-growing timber tree and produces high-quality wood. **BARK** Rough, fibrous below, main branches smooth and stringy. **LEAF** Alternate; adults narrowly lanceolate, stalked, curved with uneven base, dull green with reddish tint; juveniles gray-green and broader. **FLOWER** Creamy white, in numerous axillary umbels of 7–11. **FRUIT** Goblet-shaped dry capsule, 3/8 in (1 cm) long, usually with four valves.

Eucalyptus camaldulensis

River Redgum

HEIGHT up to 130 ft (40 m)
TYPE Evergreen
OCCURRENCE Australia

This tree, with its broadly columnar or spreading crown, is widespread in its native range. Its timber is hard, durable, and termite-resistant. Its pollen and nectar make high-quality honey. **BARK** Smooth, mottled white, gray, brown, or red. **LEAF** Alternate, gray-green, quite thick, turning oval to lanceolate with age. **FLOWER** In axillary clusters of 7–11 creamy white flowers. **FRUIT** Semi-spherical capsule, 7/32–5/16 in (7–8 mm) long, 3/16–1/4 in (5–6 mm) wide, yellow seeds.

long white stamens

leaves to 8 in (20 cm) long

LEAF AND FLOWER

Eucalyptus deglupta

Kamarere

HEIGHT up to 225 ft (67 m)
TYPE Evergreen
OCCURRENCE Papua New Guinea

Also known as the rainbow gum, the kamarere tree is notable for its beautiful multicolored bark. Its timber is used for pulp. **BARK** Shades of green, brown, and gray, prickly, peeling. **LEAF** Lanceolate, untoothed, darker green above, paler green beneath. **FLOWER** Creamy white, in numerous axillary umbels of 7–11. **FRUIT** Round, dry capsule.

BARK peeling in vertical strips

faint lateral veins

LEAF

Eucalyptus diversicolor

Karri

HEIGHT up to 260 ft (80 m)
TYPE Evergreen
OCCURRENCE Western Australia

An extremely tall tree, karri is a rich source of timber and provides shade. **BARK** Smooth, variously colored, shedding in flakes. **LEAF** Opposite, broadly lanceolate, thick. **FLOWER** Creamy white, in axillary clusters. **FRUIT** Dry round to oval capsule, with a stalk.

BARK

dense crown

Eucalyptus gunnii

Cider Gum

HEIGHT up to 120 ft (36 m)
TYPE Evergreen
OCCURRENCE Tasmania

This tree is one of the hardiest species of *Eucalyptus*. **BARK** Reddish brown, gray, rough at base. **LEAF** Adults alternate, gray-green, sickle-shaped, aromatic; juveniles opposite, rounded, silvery blue. **FLOWER** Creamy white, with numerous stamens. **FRUIT** Dry, gray capsule.

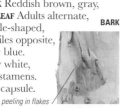

BARK

peeling in flakes

LEAVES

Eucalyptus globulus

Bluegum

HEIGHT up to 230 ft (70 m)
TYPE Evergreen
OCCURRENCE Australia

Found in Tasmania, southern Victoria, and New South Wales, this vigorous, large tree forms dense thickets. It is the Tasmanian floral emblem. Its four subspecies differ mainly in the flower arrangement and the shedding of bark. It has strong, durable wood, which is used as fuel, and its oil is used in perfumes and soap-making. The bluegum tree is also a rich source of pollen and nectar for honey. **BARK** Rough, grayish blue, usually peeling in long ribbons on upper trunk and branches. **LEAF** Adults alternate, dark green, 4–12 in (10–30 cm) long, 1–2 in (2.5–5 cm) wide; juveniles silvery, blue-gray, broad, to 6 in (15 cm) long. **FLOWER** White, 2 in (5 cm) wide, with numerous long white stamens; borne singly, in pairs, or in threes in leaf axils. **FRUIT** Grayish, woody, prominently ridged capsule, 1 in (2.5 cm) wide.

LEAVES

sickle-shaped leaf

RIVER REDGUM
The most widely distributed of all *Eucalyptus* species, river redgum (*Eucalyptus camaldulensis*) is tolerant of a wide variety of conditions. It is typically found along watercourses, as here in a flooded area close to the Murribidgee River, South Australia.

Eucalyptus marginata

Jarrah

HEIGHT up to 165 ft (50 m)
TYPE Evergreen
OCCURRENCE Western Australia

This tree is well adapted to its dry habitat, which is prone to fire. It has long roots and develops large underground swellings called lignotubers that store carbohydrates, allowing young trees to grow back after a fire. One of Australia's most important hardwood trees, it is extensively harvested for its durable, dark red timber. As a result, untouched jarrah forest has undergone a sharp decline. **BARK** Rough, grayish brown bark, shedding in long strips. **LEAF** Adults: alternate, shiny dark green above and paler beneath, lanceolate, with a narrow, flattened or channeled stalk; juveniles: dull gray-green without stalks. **FLOWER** White, very fragrant, appearing at the top of the tree in umbels of 7–11. **FRUIT** Round capsules, that are ⅓–½ in (1–1.5 cm) long, with a flat central disk.

FEAST FOR ALL

The jarrah tree is a rich source of nectar and pollen for bees. Its scented flowers bloom once in two years, attracting bees to pollinate them, and the resulting dark-colored honey is nutritious and full of flavor. Research has also shown that jarrah forest honey has anti-bacterial properties and can be used to heal wounds. Nectar from the tree is a food source for insects, birds, and marsupials as well.

HONEY

TRUNKS   *vertical fissures*

Eucalyptus microtheca

Coolibah

HEIGHT up to 65 ft (20 m)
TYPE Evergreen
OCCURRENCE Australia (except Victoria and Tasmania)

A fast-growing, single- or multi-trunked tree, the coolibah grows well in arid and semi-arid areas and can be used to control erosion. Its timber is one of the strongest in the world. **BARK** Gray brownish, thick, fibrous, rough, does not peel off. **LEAF** Adults: narrowly lanceolate, 2¼–8 in (6–20 cm) long, dull green above and paler beneath, slightly thick and leathery; juveniles: broader, brighter green. **FLOWER** White, very small, short-stalked, in branched or compound umbels of 3–7. **FRUIT** Short-stalked capsule, 1¼–2 in (3–5 cm) long, with black seeds.

Eucalyptus microcorys

Tallowwood

HEIGHT up to 180 ft (55 m)
TYPE Evergreen
OCCURRENCE Australia (New South Wales, Queensland)

The tallowwood's low-branching habit and dense, spreading crown make it an effective windbreak. It is found in wet forests or rainforest margins, usually on slopes. This tall tree has strong, durable timber that takes a good polish. It is also used as an ornamental, for hedging, and as a shade tree. Koalas depend on it for food and shelter. **BARK** Soft, flaky, fibrous, brown to yellow-brown, with surface pores. **LEAF** Alternate, lanceolate, glossy dark green, stalked. **FLOWER** Small, creamy white, arranged in umbels in groups of five; hermaphroditic (has both male and female organs), pollinated by bees. **FRUIT** Narrow, funnel-shaped capsule.

Eucalyptus pilularis

Blackbutt

HEIGHT up to 230 ft (70 m)
TYPE Evergreen
OCCURRENCE New South Wales and Queensland (coastal plains)

This important commercial tree grows well in coppices, provides good fuel, and is also a source of food for the koala, insects, and other animals. **BARK** Rough, fibrous, shedding in strips. **LEAF** Dark green, narrowly lanceolate, curved. **FLOWER** White, small, in axillary clusters of 7–15. **FRUIT** Woody capsule.

Eucalyptus pauciflora

Snowgum

HEIGHT up to 100 ft (30 m)
TYPE Evergreen
OCCURRENCE S.E. Australia

Long-lived and slow-growing, this tree has a crooked trunk and twisted branches. **BARK** Smooth, green, gray, or cream, sheds in ribbons. **LEAF** Adults: thick, glossy and waxy, linear-lanceolate; juveniles: more oval, dull gray-green. **FLOWER** White, scented, borne in clusters of 11 or more in leaf axils. **FRUIT** Semi-spherical or conical capsule.

adult leaf

flower clusters

LEAVES AND FLOWERS

SNOW GUM
Eucalyptus pauciflora is a highly adaptable tree
that thrives in many different situations, including
exposed ridge tops and snowy and wet conditions.
It is found primarily in the Snowy Mountains of
southeastern Australia.

Mountain Ash

Eucalyptus regnans

HEIGHT up to 300 ft (90 m)
TYPE Evergreen
OCCURRENCE Australia

This is the tallest hardwood tree in the world. **BARK** White or gray, smooth, rough base. **LEAF** Alternate, stalked, lanceolate. **FLOWER** White, small, in axillary clusters. **FRUIT** Pear-shaped, three-valved capsule.

TRUNK   *bark peels in strips*

Surinam Cherry

Eugenia uniflora

HEIGHT up to 25 ft (8 m)
TYPE Evergreen
OCCURRENCE South America

The Amazon rainforest is this tree's native habitat. **BARK** Pale brown, thin, and peeling. **LEAF** Opposite, oval to lanceolate. **FLOWER** White, with four curved petals. **FRUIT** Round berry, with orange-red pulp.

FRUIT-BEARING BRANCH   *dark red drupe*

glossy deep green foliage

Paperbark Tree

Melaleuca quinquenervia

HEIGHT up to 100 ft (30 m)
TYPE Evergreen
OCCURRENCE E. Australia, introduced in US (Florida)

In Australia, this tree grows on the eastern coast and is planted in parks. However, in Florida, it can grow into immense forests and virtually eliminate all other vegetation. **BARK** Whitish, spongy. **LEAF** Alternate, short-stalked, narrowly elliptic, flat, leathery, with five parallel veins. **FLOWER** Small, white, with united stamens, borne at branch tips in brushlike spikes. **FRUIT** Cylindrical or squarish woody capsule with several seeds.

peeling in many layers

BARK

Christmas Tree

Metrosideros excelsa

HEIGHT up to 80 ft (25 m)
TYPE Evergreen
OCCURRENCE New Zealand

Known as the Christmas tree because it flowers at Christmas, this coastal tree has long, hanging roots that enable it to cling to rocky cliffs. **BARK** Pale gray brown, plated. **LEAF** Leathery, hairy below, to 4 in (10 cm) long. **FLOWER** At branch tips in racemes, with small petals and several long stamens. **FRUIT** Papery capsule.

FLOWERS   *bright red stamens*

Psidium guajava

Guava

HEIGHT up to 25 ft (8 m)
TYPE Evergreen
OCCURRENCE American tropics,
cultivated in warm regions worldwide

Probably originating in southern Mexico, this tree can be invasive and forms dense thickets. In some countries, the fruit forms the basis of an important industry. The wood is used for carpentry, fuel wood, and charcoal. The bark and leaves contain tannin, and are also used in traditional medicine. **BARK** Pale reddish brown,

smooth, peeling in large flakes, green-gray inner bark. **LEAF** Opposite, brittle, oval to oblong-elliptic, hairy beneath. **FLOWER** White, 1 in (2.5 cm) wide, with 4–5 petals, many white stamens; in groups of 1–4 in leaf axils. **FRUIT** White-yellow or faintly pink berry, up to 4 in (10 cm) long; granular, sweet-sour, juicy pulp.

PRESERVING PULP

The guava fruit is high in vitamin C. Uncooked guavas are used in salads or desserts. The fruit is commonly cooked to eliminate its strong odor. The fruit can be stewed, canned, jellied, or made into paste and "cheese." Guava juice and guava nectar are popular drinks, while guava syrup can also be used to flavor desserts.

GUAVA CHEESE

UNRIPE FRUIT

HALVED RIPE FRUIT

yellow seeds

LEAVES

10–20 pairs of prominent veins

Syzygium aromaticum

Clove

HEIGHT up to 40 ft (12 m)
TYPE Evergreen
OCCURRENCE Indonesia (Molucca Islands), Philippines

The flower buds of the clove tree have been used as a spice for thousands of years. One of the earliest references to cloves says that people who visited the Chinese emperor had to place a few in their mouths to sweeten their breath. The tree has been

DENSE FOLIAGE

pyramidal habit

introduced throughout the tropics. Today, the main producers of cloves and clove oil are the islands of Zanzibar and Pemba, off the coast of East Africa. The tree once played an important part in world history. Wars were fought in Europe and with the native Moluccan islanders to secure rights to the lucrative clove trade. In 1816, the Dutch destroyed the trees in order to raise prices. This led to a bloody native insurrection, which proved to be a disaster for the Dutch. **BARK** Grayish and smooth. **LEAF** Oblong, up to 6 in (15 cm) long, fragrant. **FLOWER** Red and white, bell-shaped, in terminal clusters. **FRUIT** One-seeded berry.

glossy surface

LEAVES

yellow calyx

FLOWER BUDS

CLOVES AND CLOVE OIL

Cloves, the flower buds of the tree, are harvested and dried before they open, and are widely used as a spice. The oil extracted from cloves is used in cosmetics, confectionery, and herbal medicine. It also has a mild anesthetic effect and is used externally to treat toothaches.

CLOVES   **CLOVE OIL**

Syzygium cumini

Jambolan

HEIGHT up to 100 ft (30 m)
TYPE Evergreen
OCCURRENCE Indonesia, India

The jambolan is a tropical and sub-tropical tree. Juice is extracted from its fruit, which is eaten both raw and cooked. In the Philippines and Suriname, it is used to make vinegar and liquor. All parts of the tree are used in traditional medicine. **BARK** Gray, smooth; the base is rough and flaking. **LEAF** Opposite, oblong; pink when young, dark green when mature. **FLOWER** Rose pink to white, in branched, fragrant clusters at stem tips; 4–5 fused petals, many stamens. **FRUIT** Purple-black, oval berry, up to 2 in (5 cm) long, whitish, juicy pulp with one seed.

Syzygium malaccense

Malaysian Apple

HEIGHT up to 60 ft (18 m)
TYPE Evergreen
OCCURRENCE S.E. Asia, Pacific Islands

This tropical tree is grown for its edible fruit, yielding more than 200 lb (100 kg) per tree. **BARK** Gray, smooth, and mottled. **LEAF** Opposite, leathery, dark green, soft. **FLOWER** Fragrant, in clusters of 2–8, with a funnel-like base, topped by five thick green sepals and four (usually pink to dark-red) petals; many stamens. **FRUIT** Pear-shaped, deep red, white, or pink berry.

TREE IN FLOWER

Tibouchina urvilleana

Princess Flower

HEIGHT up to 16 ft (5 m)
TYPE Evergreen
OCCURRENCE Brazil

Widely cultivated in warm regions for its showy flowers that bloom for most of the year and its velvety foliage, this tree is a popular ornamental. **BARK** Pale brown, thin. **LEAF** Opposite, lanceolate-ovate, dark green, often with red edges, and 3–5 prominent veins. **FLOWER** Purple blossoms, 5 in (12.5 cm) wide, with hooked stamens, held in terminal panicles above foliage. **FRUIT** Dry, hard brown capsule.

FLOWERS IN FULL BLOOM

Chrysobalanus icaco

Coco Plum

HEIGHT up to 20 ft (6 m)
TYPE Evergreen
OCCURRENCE US (S. Florida) to N. South America, Africa

Usually shrubby, the coco plum grows in tropical coastal areas and is useful for stabilizing dunes and soil. **BARK** Gray-brown, with lenticels. **LEAF** Alternate, leathery, shiny dark green above, paler beneath, short-stalked. **FLOWER** Several, in cymes at ends of branches, with 4–5 white petals. **FRUIT** White to purple, plumlike drupe, with spongy, whitish, edible flesh.

rounded or elliptic leaves

fruit up to 1¼ in (3 cm) wide

LEAVES AND FRUIT

Parinari curatellifolia

Mobola

HEIGHT 26–40 ft (8–12 m)
TYPE Evergreen
OCCURRENCE Tropical Africa

The mobola tree is a prized fruit tree in tropical Africa. **BARK** Rough, with deep fissures; emits a hissing sound when cut. **LEAF** Alternate, oblong to elliptic, with a rounded or tapering base. **FLOWER** Yellow-green, in drooping panicles, fragrant. **FRUIT** Plum-shaped, olive-green drupe.

Populus alba

White Poplar

HEIGHT up to 100 ft (30 m)
TYPE Deciduous
OCCURRENCE Europe, C. and W. Asia, N. Africa

This tree is useful for land stabilization, particularly in coastal areas, and makes an excellent park ornamental. **BARK** Whitish gray, smooth; base develops deep fissures with age. **LEAF** Alternate, 3–5 lobes, wavy margins, white when young, turning shiny dark green above and white beneath with age. **FLOWER** Males and females borne on separate trees, petalless, in catkins; males: gray, with crimson red anthers; females: greenish yellow. **FRUIT** Green capsule with fluffy seeds.

ADULT LEAVES

spreading habit

Pangium edule

Kepayang

HEIGHT up to 130 ft (40 m)
TYPE Evergreen
OCCURRENCE Malaysia, Indonesia, Philippines, Papua New Guinea

The kepayang tree's parts are highly toxic, but the seed is edible when thoroughly washed. **BARK** Reddish to dark brown, smooth or fissured. **LEAF** Alternate, spiral, ovate to cordate, dark green above. **FLOWER** Bright pale green, axillary; male in clusters; female solitary. **FRUIT** Brown, berrylike, soft when ripe.

oblong-ovoid fruit

FRUIT

LEAF

fissured bark

TRUNK

Populus grandidentata

Bigtooth Aspen

HEIGHT up to 65 ft (20 m)
TYPE Deciduous
OCCURRENCE N.E. and N.C. United States, S.E. Canada.

coarsely toothed margins

ovate to rounded leaves

This tree is a major source of wood pulp for paper and hardboard. It is also used as supplementary food for cattle. **BARK** Thin, pale grayish green, base irregularly fissured when old. **LEAF** Alternate, dark green above, hairy beneath, turning smooth with age. **FLOWER** Males and females on separate trees in cylindrical catkins; males with pale red anthers; females green. **FRUIT** Pear-shaped capsule, hairy seeds.

Populus x canadensis

Carolina Poplar

HEIGHT 50–65 ft (15–20 m)
TYPE Deciduous
OCCURRENCE Garden origin

This tree is a hybrid between the eastern cottonwood (*P. deltoides*) and the Lombardy poplar (*P. nigra*). **BARK** Pale gray-brown, deeply fissured. **LEAF** Alternate, dark green, broadly triangular, finely toothed margins. **FLOWER** Males and females separate, in drooping, cylindrical catkins; males with pale red anthers; females green. **FRUIT** Small capsule, with hairy seeds.

broadly columnar habit

Populus balsamifera

Balsam Poplar

HEIGHT up to 100 ft (30 m)
TYPE Deciduous
OCCURRENCE North America

This tree was used by American Indians for its medicinal properties and to make glue and soap. Today, its soft wood is used for pulp and rough timber. **BARK** Pale gray to brown, smooth; grows darker and furrowed with age. **LEAF** Alternate, ovate, shiny dark green above, pale green below; resinous smell. **FLOWER** Green, small, petalless; males and females on separate trees, in cylindrical, pendent catkins. **FRUIT** Small, green capsule; seeds with fluffy hairs.

pointed tip

finely toothed margins

conspicuous veins

LEAF

Populus deltoides

Eastern Cottonwood

HEIGHT up to 100 ft (30 m)
TYPE Deciduous
OCCURRENCE E. United States

This tree is valued for pulp and paper production. **BARK** Greenish yellow; dark gray, furrowed with age. **LEAF** Alternate. **FLOWER** Catkins; males with pale red anthers; females green. **FRUIT** Capsule.

Populus maximowiczii

Doronoki

HEIGHT up to 100 ft (30 m)
TYPE Deciduous
OCCURRENCE N.E. Asia, Japan

Doronoki wood was used for making matchsticks, boxes, and pulp. Today, in Japan, it is used for stabilizing stream banks and sand. **BARK** Greenish white, turning gray, deeply fissured with age. **LEAF** Alternate, leathery, elliptic-ovate, toothed margins. **FLOWER** Males and females on separate trees; green, petalless, in hanging, cylindrical catkins. **FRUIT** Capsule, with fluffy seeds.

rounded crown

FRUIT WITH SEEDS

fluffy hairs

WHITE POPLAR
Populus alba, with its distinctive white trunk and
dark markings, is an extremely vigorous tree that
often outcompetes other species. This tendency can,
however, be useful for pioneer planting in areas
where other trees are less easily established.

Populus nigra

Lombardy Poplar

HEIGHT up to 100 ft (30 m)
TYPE Deciduous
OCCURRENCE Europe, W. Asia

The "Mappa burl" veneer is made from the bossed trunk of this tree. **BARK** Dark gray-brown, deeply furrowed. **LEAF** Alternate, triangular to ovate, with finely toothed margins, shiny dark green above, pale green beneath. **FLOWER** In long catkins, males with red anthers; females green. **FRUIT** Small capsule, fluffy-haired seeds.

translucent margins

LEAVES

small, green capsules

Populus tremula

European Aspen

HEIGHT up to 100 ft (30 m)
TYPE Deciduous
OCCURRENCE Europe, N. Africa, W. Asia

The flattened leaf stalks of this tree make the leaves quiver with a distinctive sound. **BARK** Smooth, pale gray, diamond-shaped lenticels, becoming darker, rough and ridged. **LEAF** Alternate, round, toothed, shiny dark green above, pale green below. **FLOWER** In long catkins, males with red anthers; females green. **FRUIT** Small capsule, with fluffy-haired seeds.

broadly ovate to rounded

LEAF

catkins bearing fluffy-haired seeds

Populus tremuloides

Quaking Aspen

HEIGHT up to 100 ft (30 m)
TYPE Deciduous
OCCURRENCE C. North America, W. North America (from Mexico to Alaska)

This aspen reproduces by means of vegetative suckers and forms stands of clones, the largest being a male clone in Utah that occupies 17.2 acres and has more than 47,000 stems. **BARK** Thin, smooth, whitish to pale yellow-brown. **LEAF** Alternate, broadly ovate, 1–3 in (2–7 cm) long. **FLOWER** Cylindrical catkins; males with pinkish red anthers; females green. **FRUIT** Small capsule.

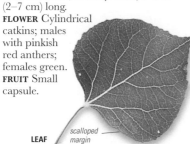

LEAF scalloped margin

Populus trichocarpa

Black Cottonwood

HEIGHT up to 200 ft (60 m)
TYPE Deciduous
OCCURRENCE W. North America

Like most poplars, the wood of this tree is light. It is used as pulp for high-grade book and magazine paper. It peels easily and is used in plywood and crate manufacture. **BARK** Ashy gray, deeply divided into broad, rounded ridges, breaks up in flakes. **LEAF** Alternate, ovate-lanceolate to triangular, shiny dark green above, whitish to rusty beneath. **FLOWER** Catkins, long, cylindrical; males with light purple anthers; females green. **FRUIT** Small capsule.

Salix alba

White Willow

HEIGHT up to 80 ft (25 m)
TYPE Deciduous
OCCURRENCE Europe, W. Asia, N. Africa

The bark of the willow tree has valuable medicinal properties. It is a natural source of salicin, which is the active ingredient of the analgesic drug aspirin. **BARK** Gray-brown, deeply fissured. **LEAF** Alternate, bluish green below with silky hairs. **FLOWER** In cylindrical catkins, petalless; males yellow; females green. **FRUIT** Small green capsule.

lanceolate leaf

LEAVES

Salix babylonica

Weeping Willow

HEIGHT up to 33 ft (10 m)
TYPE Deciduous
OCCURRENCE China

This willow was previously cultivated as a waterside tree. **BARK** Gray-brown, with irregular fissures. **LEAF** Alternate, lanceolate, toothed, grayish green beneath. **FLOWER** Cylindrical catkins; males yellow; females green. **FRUIT** Green capsule.

Salix purpurea

Purple Osier

HEIGHT up to 17 ft (5 m)
TYPE Deciduous
OCCURRENCE Europe, N Asia

There are several commercial cultivars of this small, shrubby tree. **BARK** Olive-gray. **LEAF** Alternate or sub-opposite, oblanceolate, finely toothed near tip, green to bluish white below, sparsely hairy. **FLOWER** Cylindrical catkins, petalless; males yellow; females green. **FRUIT** Small green capsule.

ASPEN
Pictured here in the Targhee National Forest, Idaho, the golden autumn foliage of the aspen (*Populus tremula*) is one of the hallmark sights of the North American fall. However, this species also grows widely in Europe and Asia.

Salix × sepulcralis

Golden Weeping Willow

HEIGHT 30–65 ft (9–20 m)
TYPE Deciduous
OCCURRENCE Garden origin

A hybrid between *S. alba* and *S. babylonica*, this tree has a rounded, spreading crown and drooping shoots. The largest "weeping" willow is 'Chrysocoma'.
BARK Pale gray-brown. **LEAF** Alternate, margins finely toothed, smooth below or covered with silky hairs, ending in long tapered points. **FLOWER** Catkins; borne on separate trees, cylindrical, individual flowers small, petalless; males yellow; females green. **FRUIT** Small green capsule, with fluffy white seeds.

SACRED WAY, BEIJING

Weeping willows are used as ornamentals worldwide and are associated with death in many cultures. A symbol of sorrow and mourning, these trees are often planted near graveyards and tombs, as on this road leading to the Ming Tombs in Beijing. *S. babylonica* is also known as the tree of inspiration and enchantment.

shallow fissures

BARK

LEAVES

lanceolate leaf

Aleurites moluccana

Candlenut

HEIGHT up to 80 ft (25 m)
TYPE Evergreen
OCCURRENCE Thailand, Malaysia to
W. Polynesia and E. Australia

Also known as the kukui nut or kemiri, this tree has an irregular and whitish crown. **BARK** Rough, with lenticels. **LEAF** Alternate and spiral, ovate, dark green. **FLOWER** Greenish white, males and females on same plant in terminal panicles. **FRUIT** Bunches of 3–6 nuts, olive to yellowish green.

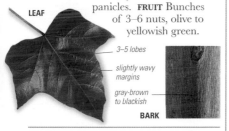

LEAF

3–5 lobes

slightly wavy margins

gray-brown to blackish

BARK

Euphorbia ingens

Tree Euphorbia

HEIGHT up to 33 ft (10 m)
TYPE Deciduous
OCCURRENCE Mozambique, Zimbabwe, South Africa

The latex of this densely branched tree is extremely toxic. **BARK** Gray, roughly fissured. **LEAF** Oblanceolate on seedlings and young plants, triangular on old growth. **FLOWER** Reddish. **FRUIT** Semi-spherical capsule, with 2–3 cavities.

fleshy terminal branches

Baccaurea ramiflora

Rambai

HEIGHT up to 50–80 ft (15–25 m)
TYPE Evergreen
OCCURRENCE India to S. China, Thailand, Malay Peninsula, Andaman Islands

The crown of this tree is irregular and dense; the branches are pagoda-like. **BARK** Grayish brown, smooth or slightly flaky. **LEAF** Alternate, ovate to ovate-lanceolate, smooth to sparsely hairy below. **FLOWER** Yellowish green; males and females borne on separate plants in inflorescences on branches and trunk. **FRUIT** Drooping clusters of spherical nuts, red to orange-pink, turning purple when ripe; edible, sweet-sour taste.

Euphorbia candelabrum

Candelabra Tree

HEIGHT up to 40 ft (12 m)
TYPE Deciduous
OCCURRENCE E. Africa

The fleshy terminal branches of this succulent tree form a round crown. **BARK** Gray with rough fissures. **LEAF** Oblanceolate on seedlings and young plants, triangular on old growth. **FLOWER** Greenish yellow, on the topmost segment of every branch. **FRUIT** Semi-spherical capsule, with 2–3 cavities.

green stems

Hevea bracillensis

Rubber Tree

HEIGHT up to 100 ft (30 m)
TYPE Semi-deciduous
OCCURRENCE Tropical South America, introduced to S.E. Asia

Rubber trees were widely cultivated in Southeast Asian plantations for the abundance of white latex in their trunks, which was extracted and processed to make natural rubber. However, erratic supplies during World War II led to the development of synthetic rubber and a decline in the importance of natural rubber. **BARK** Grayish to pale brown, smooth, with rings. **LEAF** Alternate, trifoliate, with smooth, elliptic leaflets. **FLOWER** Greenish yellow, petalless, borne in axillary panicles; males and females on the same branch. **FRUIT** Oval capsule, with three lobes and furrowed seeds.

NATURAL RUBBER

The invention of the pneumatic tire gave an impetus to the development of rubber. It was also used for waterproofing fabrics. At first, rubber was exported from Brazil, but the seeds of the tree were smuggled to Britain and promoted across its colonies. Today, Thailand is one of the largest producers.

RUBBER TAPPING

untoothed margin

LEAFLETS

Mallotus philippensis

Kamala Tree

HEIGHT up to 80 ft (25 m)
TYPE Evergreen
OCCURRENCE Tropical Asia, Australia

The kamala tree has a short, often fluted trunk, and a dense crown. The red powder that covers the fruit was formerly collected and used as a natural dye, producing brilliant yellows and oranges. It is still used in small quantities by craft dyers. In India, the fruit is used in Ayurvedic medicine. **BARK** Gray-brown and smooth. **LEAF** Alternate, ovate to lanceolate, on reddish brown branchlets. **FLOWER** Greenish, small; males and females on separate trees; males solitary or in spikes; females in terminal and axillary spikes or racemes. **FRUIT** Three-lobed capsule that is covered with orange to reddish granules and contains black seeds.

RIPE FRUIT ON BRANCHES

Vernicia fordii

Tung

HEIGHT up to 65 ft (20 m)
TYPE Deciduous
OCCURRENCE S. China, Myanmar, N. Vietnam

This tree is cultivated for the oil in its seeds. Tung oil is used in paints, polishes, varnishes, and brake linings, and is the main ingredient in "teak oil." **BARK** Smooth. **LEAF** Alternate, ovate, with a heart-shaped base. **FLOWER** Pink, large; males and females on the same plant. **FRUIT** Oval to pear-shaped, green to purple capsule with 4–5 seeds.

shallow lobes

two red glands

LEAVES

LEAF BASE

Caryocar nuciferum

Souari Nut

HEIGHT up to 130 ft (40 m)
TYPE Evergreen
OCCURRENCE South America

This tree usually flowers at night and is pollinated by bats. The fruit is coated by a fibrous husk and the fat from the kernels provides oil. Brazilians use the fruit to make liquor. The timber is very durable and is used to build boats. **BARK** Dull gray, develops deep, vertical cracks. **LEAF** Opposite, trifoliate, elliptic to elliptic-lanceolate leaflets, sometimes slightly toothed. **FLOWER** Large, powderpuff-like, 2–8, with blood-red petals, several stamens, in racemes. **FRUIT** Soft, woody, kidney-shaped nuts with edible yellow pulp.

Calophyllum inophyllum

Alexandrian Laurel

HEIGHT up to 65 ft (20 m)
TYPE Evergreen
OCCURRENCE India, Indonesia, Philippines, Papua New Guinea, Malaysia, Pacific Islands

Found on sandy and rocky seashores, this tree is also known as the kamani. It has a broad crown, often with gnarled, horizontal branches, and is sometimes planted as a street tree in coastal areas.

BARK Gray-brown to blackish, deeply fissured, with yellow sap. **LEAF** Opposite, elliptic to obovate-elliptic. **FLOWER** Borne in axillary racemes, 4–8 white petals, with numerous yellow stamens. **FRUIT** Yellowish green, globose drupe.

untoothed margins

spherical fruit   **LEAVES WITH FRUIT**

Garcinia mangostana

Mangosteen

HEIGHT 20–80 ft (6–25 m)
TYPE Evergreen
OCCURRENCE Known only in cultivation

The mangosteen is probably the most highly praised tropical fruit and is usually eaten fresh. Cultivated trees of this species are always female, and they reproduce asexually, producing offspring that are identical to themselves. Together, they are thought to form a clone that has descended from a single parent plant. **BARK** Dark brown to black, flaking. **LEAF** Opposite, oblong to elliptic, smooth surface and margins. **FLOWER** Solitary or paired at the tips of the branchlets; large, fleshy petals, yellow-green with reddish edges. **FRUIT** Dark purple and globose berry, with the seed enveloped in an edible white structure (arillode).

RIPE FRUIT

edible layer

LEAVES WITH FRUIT   unripe fruit   glossy, deep green leaf

Rhizophora mangle

Red Mangrove

HEIGHT up to 80 ft (25 m)
TYPE Evergreen
OCCURRENCE US (S. Florida), West Indies, coasts of tropical America, W. Africa

This species dominates mangrove swamps in the Western Hemisphere. Its bark has been a source of tannin, dyes, and medicines. **BARK** Gray to gray-brown, developing scaly ridges. **LEAF** Opposite, leathery, elliptic to obovate-elliptic. **FLOWER** Pale yellowish green; four sepals and four petals. **FRUIT** Leathery, initially conical berry, germinating on parent tree.

LEAVES WITH FRUIT

untoothed leaf margin

embryonic root

Erythroxylum coca

Coca

HEIGHT 12–20 ft (3–6 m)
TYPE Evergreen
OCCURRENCE South America

an addictive drug. **BARK** Grayish white, **LEAF** Alternate, oval to elliptical, 1½–9¾ in (4–7 cm) long. **FLOWER** Solitary or in clusters in the leaf axils, small, yellowish green. **FRUIT** Red drupe.

The shrublike coca plant has many small branchlets, bearing leaves containing the alkaloid cocaine. It is one of the oldest domesticated shrubs, its cultivation dating as far back as 2,000–3,000 years. In the past, cocaine was used in tonics and patent medicines. It is now recognized as

COCA LEAVES

The tradition of chewing of coca leaves is deeply entrenched among the Andean Indians, who use it to increase physical energy and to reduce the perception of pain, hunger, and thirst. The coca leaf has great mythical and mystical significance in their culture and religion and is a symbol of Andean Indian identity.

RED MANGROVE
The red mangrove (*Rhizophora mangle*) is well adapted to aquatic conditions, such as those seen here on the coast of Boipeba Island, Brazil. Stilt roots support the plant above the water, while aerial roots extend to the surface to aid aeration.

Bilimbi

Averrhoa bilimbi

HEIGHT up to 50 ft (15 m)
TYPE Evergreen
OCCURRENCE India, S.E. Asia

Also called the cucumber tree, this tree has a short trunk and erect branches. The fruit is sour and usually not eaten raw. **BARK** Pinkish brown, smooth, sometimes slightly flaky. **LEAF** Alternate, pinnate, crowded at ends of branches, with a terminal leaflet; leaflets are ovate, in 7–19 pairs, sometimes hairy. **FLOWER** In small panicles, five petals, yellowish green or purplish, marked with dark purple, fragrant. **FRUIT** Oval to egg-shaped or nearly cylindrical berry, faintly five-sided, yellowish green to whitish.

Starfruit Tree

Averrhoa carambola

HEIGHT up to 50 ft (15 m)
TYPE Evergreen
OCCURRENCE S.E. Asia, Florida

This many-branched, bushy tree has a broad crown, with drooping branches. **BARK** Pale brown, smooth. **LEAF** Alternate, pinnate, with a terminal leaflet, sometimes hairy. **FLOWER** In axillary panicles, pale red with a purple heart. **FRUIT** Egg-shaped berry, orange-yellow when ripe.

5 prominent ribs

3–6 pairs of leaflets

FRUIT　　**FLOWERS AND LEAVES**

Soapbark Tree

Quillaja saponaria

HEIGHT up to 65 ft (20 m)
TYPE Evergreen
OCCURRENCE Chile, Peru

First used by the Mapuche people of Chile, the bark extract of this tree is utilized as a foaming agent in beverages and a wetting agent in photography. **BARK** Gray-brown, finely pustular, turning darker and tough. **LEAF** Alternate, elliptic to ovate, margins smooth to toothed. **FLOWER** White, in terminal flat-topped clusters. **FRUIT** Follicle with winged seeds.

LEAVES　simple, leathery leaves

Davidson Plum

Davidsonia pruriens

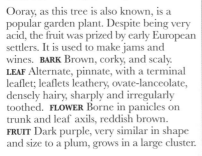

HEIGHT up to 33 ft (10 m)
TYPE Evergreen
OCCURRENCE Australia (Queensland)

Ooray, as this tree is also known, is a popular garden plant. Despite being very acid, the fruit was prized by early European settlers. It is used to make jams and wines. **BARK** Brown, corky, and scaly. **LEAF** Alternate, pinnate, with a terminal leaflet; leaflets leathery, ovate-lanceolate, densely hairy, sharply and irregularly toothed. **FLOWER** Borne in panicles on trunk and leaf axils, reddish brown. **FRUIT** Dark purple, very similar in shape and size to a plum, grows in a large cluster.

Acacia aneura

Mulga

HEIGHT 16–33 ft (5–10 m)
TYPE Evergreen
OCCURRENCE Australia

This erect, spreading tree or shrub in rare cases reaches 56 ft (18 m) in height and is an exceedingly variable species with about ten varieties. It is long-lived and is such a prominent part of the Australian scrubland that areas in which it grows are referred to as "mulga country" or "mulga lands." The tree is of economic importance as fodder for grazing animals. **BARK** Dark gray, fissured. **LEAF** Straight or slightly curved, highly variable in shape, narrow, blue-green to gray-green, smooth or finely hairy. **FLOWER** Golden yellow, in stalked axillary, cylindrical spikes. **FRUIT** Flat, broad pod that is narrowly winged, ripening to brown.

Acacia dealbata

Silver Wattle

HEIGHT up to 65 ft (20 m)
TYPE Evergreen
OCCURRENCE S.E. Australia, Tasmania

TREE IN FLOWER

A broadly conical to spreading tree, the silver wattle is widely cultivated in the Mediterranean region. **BARK** Smooth, green or blue-green, turning almost black with age. **LEAF** Alternate, bipinnate, 4³/₄ in (12 cm) long, divided into numerous leaflets, about ³/₁₆ in (5 mm) long each, untoothed, blue-green, and finely hairy. **FLOWER** In panicles of small, rounded clusters; individual flowers are small, bright yellow, and have numerous stamens. **FRUIT** Flattened pod, ripening from green to blue-green to brown.

Acacia farnesiana

Sweet Acacia

HEIGHT 5–26 ft (1.5–8 m)
TYPE Evergreen
OCCURRENCE Tropical America, parts of Africa, Australia

This small tree or thorny shrub is also called golden mimosa. Its flowers are used to produce "Cassie" perfume, which is an ingredient of many cosmetics and fine perfumes. **BARK** Dark brown, smooth. **LEAF** Alternate, bipinnate with linear to oblong leaflets in 10–25 pairs. **FLOWER** Mostly bisexual, in axillary, rounded flower heads, with numerous stamens; sweetly scented. **FRUIT** Sausage-like, brownish black pod.

bright golden yellow
flower head

LEAVES AND FLOWER

Acacia longifolia

Sydney Golden Wattle

HEIGHT up to 33 ft (10 m)
TYPE Evergreen
OCCURRENCE E. Australia

One of the hardiest acacias, this invasive tree was introduced into cultivation in 1792. It is fast-growing and excellent for screening purposes, but is short-lived. **BARK** Gray, fissured. **LEAF** Straight, linear to elliptic, with 2–4 prominent primary veins. **FLOWER** Golden to lemon yellow, arranged in cylindrical heads. **FRUIT** Rough brown pod.

leaf 2–6 in (5–15 cm) long

yellow flower spikes

FLOWERING BRANCHLET

Acacia mearnsii

Black Wattle

HEIGHT 16–100 ft (5–30 m)
TYPE Evergreen
OCCURRENCE S.E. Australia

Although this upright tree grows wild in woodland, it is also grown commercially for tannin from its bark. **BARK** Gray-brown, smooth. **LEAF** Alternate, bipinnate, with linear to oblong leaflets. **FLOWER** In panicles, creamy white to pale yellow, fragrant. **FRUIT** Gray, hairy or smooth pod with black seeds.

LEAVES AND FLOWERS

rounded flower heads

16–70 pairs of leaflets

Acacia mangium

Mangium

HEIGHT 33–100 ft (10–30 m)
TYPE Evergreen
OCCURRENCE E. Australia, Aroe Islands, S. Moluccas, S.E. Asia

Planted as an exotic, this tree grows well on poor soil. It is grown for pulp and paper production. **BARK** Gray to dark brown, corrugated or cracked. **LEAF** Elliptic. **FLOWER** Greenish white to cream, in loose spikes. **FRUIT** Pod with black seeds.

Acacia melanoxylon

Blackwood

HEIGHT up to 80 ft (25 m)
TYPE Evergreen
OCCURRENCE E. and S. Australia

This erect or spreading tree is found in wet forests. Its wood is used for paneling. **BARK** Dark gray-black, deeply fissured, somewhat scaly. **LEAF** Alternate, narrowly elliptic to oblanceolate. **FLOWER** Cream, spherical flower heads in short racemes. **FRUIT** Elongated, twisted pod with black seeds.

bipinnate juvenile leaves

undivided adult leaves

LEAVES

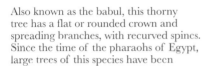
Acacia nilotica

Prickly Acacia

HEIGHT up to 65 ft (20 m)
TYPE Deciduous
OCCURRENCE Introduced in Arabia and India

Also known as the babul, this thorny tree has a flat or rounded crown and spreading branches, with recurved spines. Since the time of the pharaohs of Egypt, large trees of this species have been exploited for their dark brown wood, which is strong and durable, and nearly twice as hard as teak. It makes an excellent fuel wood and good-quality charcoal. Being termite-resistant, the timber is especially suitable for railroad ties. **BARK** Dark red-brown, thin, rough and fissured. **LEAF** Alternate, bipinnate, often with glands on leaf stalk. **FLOWER** Globose, scented, in axillary flower heads. **FRUIT** Dark brown pod that splits open when ripe, compressed over the seeds.

BRANCHES

long, light gray spines

7–25 pairs of leaflets

bright yellow flower heads

LEAVES AND FLOWER HEADS

GUM ARABIC

Babul trees are a source of gum arabic. A piece of bark is removed and incisions are made in the surrounding bark with a mallet or hammer. The reddish gum is then extracted and is formed into rounded or oval "tears." Almost completely soluble and tasteless, it is resistant to insects and water because of its resins. Although inferior to other forms of gum arabic, it is used commercially in the manufacture of candles, inks, matches, and paints. The uses of gum arabic date back about 5,000 years to the ancient Egyptians.

GUM ARABIC "TEARS"

Acacia pycnantha

Golden Wattle

HEIGHT up to 25 ft (8 m)
TYPE Evergreen
OCCURRENCE S.E. Australia

The golden wattle is the official floral emblem of Australia, and its bark is one of the richest sources of tannin in the world, although nowadays it is rarely used commercially. **BARK** Dark grayish brown, smooth or finely fissured. **LEAF** Sickle-shaped to oblanceolate, smooth, with prominent midrib. **FLOWER** In racemes, about five flower heads. **FRUIT** Flat, linear pod.

golden yellow flowers

FLOWERS

deep green foliage

TREE IN FLOWER

Acacia seyal

Shittim

HEIGHT 20–50 ft (6–15 m)
TYPE Evergreen
OCCURRENCE N. Tropical Africa (Sahel zone)

This tree has an umbrella-shaped crown. Gum talha obtained from this species, similar to gum arabic from *A. senegal*, is used as a thickener and emulsifier. **BARK** Rust-red or pale green, smooth, peeling, with a rusty, powdery coating. **LEAF** Alternate, bipinnate; 10–22 pairs of linear leaflets. **FLOWER** Bright yellow, in axillary, spherical flower heads. **FRUIT** Slightly curved, pendent pod.

Acacia xanthophloea

Fever Tree

HEIGHT 50–80 ft (15–25 m)
TYPE Semideciduous
OCCURRENCE East Africa

With its spreading branches and open crown, this acacia grows mainly in depressions and shallow pans where underground water is present or surface water collects. Early European settlers mistakenly associated it with fever since people living near its swampy habitat contracted malarial fever. The young branches are covered with paired thorns. **BARK** Lime green to greenish yellow, luminous, slightly flaking, and coated with a yellow powdery substance. **LEAF** Alternate, bipinnate. **FLOWER** Borne in ball-like clusters on shortened side shoots at the nodes and toward the ends of branches, bright golden yellow, sweetly scented. **FRUIT** Yellow-brown pod.

Albizia julibrissin

Silk Tree

HEIGHT 20–40 ft (4–12 m)
TYPE Semideciduous
OCCURRENCE Asia, Mediterranean region, introduced in United States

FLOWERS

fluffy, pinkish flowers

A popular ornamental in warm climates, this short-lived tree has an umbrella-shaped crown. **BARK** Pale brown, smooth. **LEAF** Alternate, bipinnate. **FLOWER** In axillary clusters of about 20. **FRUIT** Flat, gray-brown pod.

40–60 leaflets

Amherstia nobilis

Pride of Burma

HEIGHT up to 40 ft (12 m)
TYPE Evergreen
OCCURRENCE Known only in cultivation

Widely cultivated in the tropics, this tree was found in the wild only once, in 1865. All the trees now in existence are progeny of a cultivated temple plant collected by the botanist Nathaniel Wallich in 1829. **BARK** Dark ash gray. **LEAF** Alternate, pinnate, with 6–8 pairs of leaflets, red to pink. **FLOWER** Five petaled, bright red with yellow spots, in pendent racemes. **FRUIT** Flattened pod.

petal-like bracts   *oblong leaves*   **LEAVES AND FLOWERS**

Bauhinia variegata

Orchid Tree

HEIGHT up to 50 ft (15 m)
TYPE Semideciduous
OCCURRENCE E. Asia (India to China)

leaf 4–6 in (10–15 cm) wide

heart-shaped leaf base

flower 3–5 in (7.5–12.5 cm) wide

FLOWER AND LEAVES

Widely planted as an ornamental tree in warmer regions of the world, this tree is also called the camel's-foot tree. It blooms for several months. The bark has been used as a tannin, a dye, and an astringent. The flowers can be eaten as a vegetable. **BARK** Gray-brown, smooth. **LEAF** Alternate, cleft in two lobes, up to one-third of surface, butterfly-shaped. **FLOWER** In a few clusters at the tips of branches, appearing when the tree is leafless; five petals, clawed, broad, in shades of lavender to purple or white, with a dark purple central petal. **FRUIT** Flat, oblong pod.

FEVER TREE
The species name of the graceful fever tree (*Acacia xanthophloea*) is derived from the Greek for "yellow" (*xanthos*) and "bark" (*phloios*). Its open crown is popular with nesting birds, and its leaves, flowers, and pods are a useful food source for animals.

Butea monosperma

Flame of the Forest

HEIGHT 33–50 ft (10–15 m)
TYPE Deciduous
OCCURRENCE India, S.E. Asia

The flowers of this tree yield a bright orange dye known as "butein." **BARK** Pale brown to grayish. **LEAF** Alternate, trifoliate, with ovate leaflets. **FLOWER** In racemes, bright orange-red, densely hairy. **FRUIT** Pod with single seed near tip.

Cassia fistula

Golden Shower

HEIGHT 23–65 ft (7–20 m)
TYPE Deciduous
OCCURRENCE Mainland S.E. Asia, Sri Lanka

Widely cultivated in the tropics, this tree has a narrow crown and slender, drooping branches. **BARK** Pale brown, slightly cracked. **LEAF** Pinnate, alternate. **FLOWER** Large, in pendulous racemes. **FRUIT** Long, cylindrical pod.

flowers with yellow petals

ovate shape

LEAFLET

Cassia javanica

Rainbow Shower

HEIGHT up to 65 ft (20 m)
TYPE Deciduous
OCCURRENCE S.E. Asia

The pink shower, as this tree is also known, has a spreading crown. It is cultivated as an ornamental. **BARK** Gray-brown with black pustules. **LEAF** Pinnate, alternate, 10–20 pairs of broadly elliptic to ovate-oblong leaflets, shiny above, hairy beneath. **FLOWER** Pink, dark red, or pink and white, in racemes from short, leafless shoots. **FRUIT** Cylindrical black pod.

Castanospermum australe

Black Bean Tree

HEIGHT up to 130 ft (40 m)
TYPE Evergreen
OCCURRENCE E. Australia, Fiji, New Caledonia

Commonly cultivated as an ornamental, this tree is valued for its wood, which is one of Australia's most prized cabinet timbers. **BARK** Gray to brown, rough with small pustules. **LEAF** Pinnate, with terminal leaflet, and alternate, 9–17 oblong-elliptic leaflets, glossy green above, paler beneath. **FLOWER** Orange-red and yellow, in axillary racemes. **FRUIT** Woody, spongy pod, with 3–5 beanlike brown seeds.

cylindrical pod

FRUIT

Ceratonia siliqua

Carob

HEIGHT up to 33 ft (10 m)
TYPE Evergreen
OCCURRENCE Uncertain, probably Arabian Peninsula

Unknown in the wild, this tree has been cultivated since ancient times, originally propagated by the Greeks. Its alternative names, locust tree and St. John's bread, were derived from the Bible. St. John the Baptist is said to have sustained himself on the sweet, pulpy pods of this tree when wandering in the wilderness. The pods are used as fodder for livestock and also as a substitute for cocoa.

CARATS FROM CAROB

The Greek name of the carob tree is "keration" from which the word "carat" is derived. Carob pod seeds have a uniform and consistent weight. In the ancient world, jewelers, seeking a standard weight measurement for gems, began to use the seeds to assess the value of individual stones.

CAROB PODS

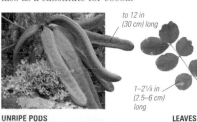

to 12 in (30 cm) long

1–2¼ in (2.5–6 cm) long

UNRIPE PODS

LEAVES

BARK Brown, rough. **LEAF** Alternate, pinnate; 2–5 pairs of oval leaflets with rounded tips, shiny dark green above, paler beneath. **FLOWER** Green, tinted red, axillary or borne on the branches and trunk, in small clusters. **FRUIT** Oblong, leathery pod, containing soft, pale brown pulp and 5–15 flattened, hard seeds.

Cercis canadensis

Eastern Redbud

HEIGHT 40–50 ft (12–15 m)
TYPE Deciduous
OCCURRENCE N.E. and C. North America

This popular, small ornamental tree has several cultivars with white flowers, pendulous forms, and one with purple leaves called 'Forest Pansy'. American Indians used extracts from the bark and roots as medicine. **BARK** Brown-gray, fissured and scaly plates, sometimes flaking in strips; cinnamon-orange inner bark revealed with age.
LEAF Alternate, broadly ovate to rounded, with a heart-shaped base, palmately veined, smooth.
FLOWER Pink, borne in clusters on old wood.
FRUIT Pinkish-red pod that ripens to brown.

pointed tip

untoothed margin

LEAF

Cercis siliquastrum

Judas Tree

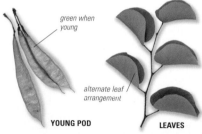

HEIGHT up to 33 ft (10 m)
TYPE Deciduous
OCCURRENCE S.E. Europe, W. Asia

According to legend, this is the tree on which Judas Iscariot hanged himself. The unopened buds are pickled or used as a caper substitute. **BARK** Gray-brown, finely fissured, cracking into small rectangular plates. **LEAF** Rounded, with a heart-shaped base, smooth on both sides, palmately veined. **FLOWER** In clusters on the branches and trunk, appearing before the leaves. **FRUIT** Flat pod, ripening to brown.

rose-purple flowers

irregular crown

green when young

alternate leaf arrangement

YOUNG POD

LEAVES

Colophospermum mopane

Mopane

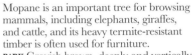

HEIGHT up to 100 ft (30 m)
TYPE Deciduous
OCCURRENCE Southern Africa

Mopane is an important tree for browsing mammals, including elephants, giraffes, and cattle, and its heavy termite-resistant timber is often used for furniture. **BARK** Grayish brown, deeply and vertically fissured. **LEAF** Alternate, deeply two-lobed, butterfly-like. **FLOWER** In small, green sprays. **FRUIT** Flat, crescent-shaped pod.

Colvillea racemosa

Colville's Glory Tree

HEIGHT 25–65 ft (8–20 m)
TYPE Deciduous
OCCURRENCE Madagascar

This plant is cultivated in the tropics as an ornamental. **BARK** Copper brown, with small, corky lenticels. **LEAF** Alternate, bipinnate, with 15–30 leaflets. **FLOWER** In grapelike cylindrical to conical clusters. **FRUIT** Two-valved, straight pod.

red and orange
flowers

gray-green
leaves

Cynometra caulitlora

Nam-Nam

HEIGHT up to 50 ft (15 m)
TYPE Evergreen
OCCURRENCE Known only in cultivation

Small and many-branched, this tree has a knotty trunk. The tree is known for its edible fruit, which grows directly from the trunk, mostly at the base, instead of from the branches. The nam-nam fruit has a pleasantly sweet-sour taste when ripe. In its unripe state it can be pickled or stewed with sugar. **BARK** Grayish brown, dappled, scaly. **LEAF** Alternate, pinnate, with 1–2 pairs of ovate to ovate-lanceolate, smooth leaflets, rarely covered with hairs. **FLOWER** Cauliflorous (growing directly from knots on the trunk), in compact clusters, with white petals, and pinkish white sepals curved back like petals. **FRUIT** Ovoid to kidney-shaped pod that is hard, rough, and knobby, greenish yellow to brown.

Brazilian Tulipwood

HEIGHT 25–40 ft (8–12 m)
TYPE Deciduous
OCCURRENCE Brazil (Bahia)

The Brazilian tulipwood usually has multiple trunks and grows taller in the forest than in open areas. Its wood is greatly sought-after for its color and flowerlike fragrance, and has been exported from Brazil for many decades.

The identity of the wood remained a mystery for years, and its scientific description was available only in 1966, after a living tree was tracked down in Bahia. **BARK** Red-brown, peeling in narrow strips. **LEAF** Alternate, pinnate, with a terminal leaflet; 5–9 oblong-elliptic leaflets, with pointed tips, sometimes densely hairy beneath. **FLOWER** Terminal and lateral, white, pealike, in corymblike inflorescence. **FRUIT** Elliptical pod.

African Blackwood

HEIGHT up to 30 ft (9 m)
TYPE Semi-deciduous
OCCURRENCE E. Africa

Found in deciduous woodlands and dry savannas, the African blackwood usually has many branches, which bear thick spines at the nodes. Its wood produces

a beautiful musical tone and is used for making complex musical instruments, especially woodwinds. It is also used to make chess pieces and ornamental boxes. **BARK** Pale gray, smooth and papery, sometimes peeling off in strips. **LEAF** Alternate, pinnate with a terminal leaflet; 7–13 leaflets. **FLOWER** White to pale pink, fragrant, pealike, in axillary or terminal panicles. **FRUIT** Thin, narrow, papery pod.

BLACKWOOD MUSIC

Clarinets made of African blackwood are known for their rich, mellow tone. The fine-grained, dense wood lends itself to the intricate machining needed for the manufacture of complex woodwind instruments. It can also withstand extreme temperatures.

CLARINET

Dalbergia nigra

Brazilian Rosewood

HEIGHT 50–65 ft (15–20 m)
TYPE Deciduous
OCCURRENCE Brazil (Bahia to São Paulo)

This tree yields a heavy, hard, dark-colored wood that is streaked with black. It is highly prized as a cabinet timber and is used in the manufacture of guitars and pianos. The tree has been overexploited to the verge of extinction and it is now illegal to trade in the species. However, some types of guitars are still made from the wood, and people can log old stumps left in the forest. The strong odor of the heartwood is due to the presence of "nerolidol," an essential oil.

FINE FURNITURE

Prized for its exotic and beautifully figured appearance, Brazilian rosewood was a favorite among cabinet-makers of the 18th and 19th centuries. Today, these pieces are highly sought-after by collectors.

REGENCY BRAZILIAN ROSEWOOD CABINET

BARK Red-brown, thin, peeling in longitudinal plates. **LEAF** Alternate, pinnate with a terminal leaflet; 11–17 oblong leaflets that are softly hairy when young and become smooth with age. **FLOWER** Violet, fragrant and pealike, borne in lateral flowering shoots. **FRUIT** Winged pod.

peeling plates

BARK

Delonix regia

Royal Poinciana

HEIGHT up to 50 ft (15 m)
TYPE Deciduous
OCCURRENCE Madagascar,
widely planted

Considered one of the most colorful trees in the world for its scarlet-red blossoms,

this fast-growing tree was introduced worldwide by Wenzel Bojer in 1828 from an isolated specimen in northeast Madagascar. The tree is found in conspicuous, spreading groups in forests, on karst limestone and escarpments. **BARK** Pale gray, smooth but crumbling surface. **LEAF** Alternate, pinnate or bipinnate; 10–25 pairs of primary leaflets, each with 15–30 pairs of secondary leaflets; elliptic to oblong, smooth or covered with short hairs. **FLOWER** In racemes, four spoon-shaped, spreading petals, fifth petal larger with yellowish white and scarlet markings, the rest scarlet-red. **FRUIT** Linear, leathery dark brown pod, to 23½ in (60 cm) long.

large, showy flowers

petals to 3 in (7.5 cm)

FLOWERS

blue-gray seeds

POD AND SEEDS

AN ENDANGERED SPECIES

Although widely cultivated as a street tree the world over for its spreading branches, dense foliage, and striking flowers, this tree is endangered in the wild. The IUCN Red List classifies the native Madagascan population of the tree as globally vulnerable. It is threatened because it occurs in a charcoal production area.

URBAN PLANTING

Dipteryx odorata

Tonka Bean

HEIGHT 80–130 ft (25–40 m)
TYPE Evergreen
OCCURRENCE Orinoco region of Guyana and Venezuela, introduced in West Indies

This tree is tall, with a compact crown. Tonka bean seeds yield coumarin, used to give fragrance to pipe tobacco and soaps. Its bark is used in shipbuilding. **BARK** Gray, smooth and flaky, becoming furrowed and corky with age. **LEAF** Alternate, pinnate; leaflet oblong. **FLOWER** White, in axillary spikes. **FRUIT** Small, one-seeded pod.

oval fruit

black, wrinkled beans

SEEDS

FRUITING TREE

Erythrina caffra

Coast Coral Tree

HEIGHT 30–40 ft (9–12 m)
TYPE Deciduous
OCCURRENCE E. Africa, South Africa

Found in coastal forests, this tree has large flowers that produce vast amounts of nectar. Its coral-red seeds are used to make necklaces. **BARK** Gray-brown, sometimes with prickles. **LEAF** Alternate with three broadly ovate sharp-tipped leaflets up to 7 in (18 cm) long. **FLOWER** In clusters, pealike. **FRUIT** Narrow pod; poisonous seeds.

scarlet-orange petals

FLOWER

spreading crown

Erythrina crista-galli

Crybaby Tree

HEIGHT up to 25 ft (8 m)
TYPE Deciduous
OCCURRENCE South America

The crimson flowers of this short-trunked tree are pollinated by carpenter bees and hummingbirds. The tree contains alkaloids and has been used for medicinal purposes. **BARK** Gray, smooth, sometimes with thorns. **LEAF** Alternate, with three leaflets, whitish beneath, often with spines. **FLOWER** Groups of 1–3 at ends of twigs, with five petals. **FRUIT** Large, long, thin brown pods.

FLOWERS AND LEAVES

pealike crimson flowers

elliptic to ovate leaflets

Falcataria moluccana

Sau

HEIGHT up to 130 ft (40 m)
TYPE Deciduous
OCCURRENCE E. Malaysia, Indonesia (Molucca Islands), Papua New Guinea to Solomon Islands

This tree has been introduced into several Southeast Asian countries and other tropical regions. It has a flat, spreading, very wide crown and grows extremely rapidly, even on nutrient-poor soil. A one-year old tree may reach a height of more than 20 ft (6 m), while a ten-year old tree can reach a height of

FLOWERS

blackish seeds

POD

yellowish brown mature pod

nearly 100 ft (30 m). The sau is often planted as an ornamental and for reforestation. It is also used in coffee-growing areas as a shade tree. **BARK** Greenish white to gray, smooth, sometimes slightly warty. **LEAF** Alternate, bipinnate, with 15–25 pairs of elliptic, sickle-shaped, smooth leaflets. **FLOWER** Cream to greenish white, stalkless, numerous, borne in lateral panicles. **FRUIT** Flat, narrow, thin-walled pod.

TRUNK

LIGHT WOOD

The soft, light wood of the Sau tree is used to make matchsticks and to manufacture pulp and low-density particleboard. It is a high quality core material for plywood, pallets and crating, and chopsticks. The wood is also used for lightweight construction, paneling, furniture components, toys, wooden shoes, and musical instruments.

MATCHSTICKS

Gleditsia triacanthos

Honey Locust

HEIGHT 75–150 ft (22–45 m)
TYPE Deciduous
OCCURRENCE N.E. and C. US

The trunk of this tree has large, branched spines. The wood was formerly prized for bows, timber, and fenceposts. Its pods are filled with a sticky pulp that is sweet and flavorful, but irritating to the throat. American Indians used the pulp as a

bright green turns to yellow

FALL LEAVES

sweetener and thickening agent, and as a medicine. **BARK** Dark gray-brown, deeply fissured. **LEAF** Alternate, first leaves from the spurs on the old wood pinnate, later leaves on the new shoots bipinnate; 18–28 elliptic to ovate, minutely toothed leaflets. **FLOWER** Pale yellow-green, in narrow racemes. **FRUIT** Dark reddish brown pod with seeds embedded in a succulent pulp.

leaflet to 1½ in (4 cm) long

BRANCHLET

twisted pod

FRUIT

Gymnocladus dioica

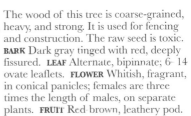

pointed tips

LEAFLETS

Kentucky Coffee Tree

HEIGHT 72–105 ft (22–32 m)
TYPE Deciduous
OCCURRENCE C. and E. United States

The wood of this tree is coarse-grained, heavy, and strong. It is used for fencing and construction. The raw seed is toxic. **BARK** Dark gray tinged with red, deeply fissured. **LEAF** Alternate, bipinnate; 6–14 ovate leaflets. **FLOWER** Whitish, fragrant, in conical panicles; females are three times the length of males, on separate plants. **FRUIT** Red-brown, leathery pod.

Koompassia excelsa

Tualang

HEIGHT up to 260 ft (80 m)
TYPE Evergreen
OCCURRENCE Malay Peninsula, Sumatra, Borneo

This massive tree mostly grows in river valleys and on hill slopes. It is rarely felled, since its timber is hard, and is more valued for the honeycombs in its branches.
BARK Gray with a greenish tinge, smooth.
LEAF Alternate, pinnate, elliptic, slightly hairy beneath. **FLOWER** In many-flowered panicles at the ends of shoots; fragrant, creamy white petals. **FRUIT** Winged pod.

7–12 leaflets

LEAVES

Koompassia malaccensis

Kempas

HEIGHT up to 150 ft (45 m)
TYPE Evergreen
OCCURRENCE Malay Peninsula, Sumatra, Borneo

The kempas tree usually has steep buttresses up to 10 ft (3 m) long. Its wood makes an excellent heavy timber and is now increasingly used for parquet flooring. **BARK** Gray-brown, narrow, fine fissures, somewhat flaky. **LEAF** Alternate, pinnate; 5–9 ovate-elliptic to oblong leaflets with one terminal leaflet; slightly hairy beneath. **FLOWER** Small, faintly scented, borne in terminal panicles; round-tipped white petals greenish at the base. **FRUIT** Pod.

spreading crown

Laburnum anagyroides

Golden Chain

HEIGHT up to 23 ft (7 m)
TYPE Deciduous
OCCURRENCE C. and S. Europe

Also known as laburnum, this tree has a narrow, irregular crown. It is rarely planted in public places because it is very poisonous. **BARK** Greenish brown, smooth, becoming shallowly fissured with age. **LEAF** Alternate, with three leaflets, dull green above, gray-green beneath, silky. **FLOWER** In terminal drooping racemes, pealike. **FRUIT** Linear brown pod.

elliptic leaflets

golden yellow flowers

TREE IN FLOWER

LEAVES AND FLOWERS

Leucaena leucocephala

Lead Tree

HEIGHT up to 30 ft (9 m)
TYPE Evergreen
OCCURRENCE S. Mexico,
N. Central America

Introduced throughout the tropics and naturalized in many places, this tree is used in reforestation, erosion control, and soil improvement projects. It is a prolific seed producer, and can regenerate and spread rapidly. It has a wispy crown. The green parts are used as a fodder and green manure. The wood is used to make pulp or small poles. **BARK** Gray-brown, with small, pale brown spots, smooth. **LEAF** Alternate, bipinnate, with

LEAVES AND FLOWERS

RIPE PODS

10 20 pairs of linear to oblong, dull green leaflets that are smooth above, hairy beneath, and fold up at night. **FLOWER** Borne in solitary or paired, spherical heads. **FRUIT** Strap-shaped pod.

yellowish white head

FLOWERS

Parkia biglobosa

Locust

HEIGHT up to 70 ft (21 m)
TYPE Semi-evergreen
OCCURRENCE W. Africa

The locust tree has a wide crown and a short, crooked trunk. Its seeds are used to produce fermented thickening flour. **BARK** Gray, rough, with longitudinal fissures. **LEAF** Alternate, bipinnate; lanceolate leaflets. **FLOWER** Bright red, spherical, drooping heads of about 2,000 tightly-packed individual flowers; opens at night. **FRUIT** Long, pale brown pod, with black seeds in a sweet pulp.

FOLIAGE

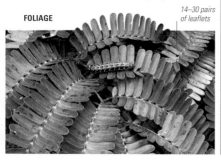

14–30 pairs of leaflets

Parkia speciosa

Petai

HEIGHT up to 150 ft (45 m)
TYPE Evergreen
OCCURRENCE S.E. Asia

This steeply buttressed tree has an umbrella-shaped crown. **BARK** Reddish brown, becoming flaky. **LEAF** Alternate, bipinnate, glandular at base; 20–35 pairs of leaflets. **FLOWER** Creamy white, long-stalked. **FRUIT** Large green pod.

pendulous pods

FRUIT

Peltophorum pterocarpum

Yellow Flamboyant

HEIGHT 30–50 ft (9–15 m)
TYPE Deciduous
OCCURRENCE Tropical Asia, E. Australia

This tree bears flowers for a large part of the year and has a low, forked trunk. Usually found along the coast, it has been planted as a shade and street tree in areas with a monsoon climate. **BARK** Dark brown, vertically furrowed, red inner bark. **LEAF** Alternate, bipinnate; 8–20 pairs of elliptic-oblong leaflets. **FLOWER** Bright yellow, axillary racemes or terminal panicles; petals are wrinkled, with a reddish mark at the center. **FRUIT** Flattened, oblong to elliptic pod.

yellow flowers

spreading crown

Pericopsis elata

Afromosia

HEIGHT up to 115 ft (36 m)
TYPE Semi-deciduous
OCCURRENCE W. and C. Africa

The afromosia tree has a flat-topped crown, with spreading branches. Its trunk is fluted and its buttressed base is bare of branches for up to 80–100 ft (25–30 m). It is found in drier areas of semi-deciduous forests. An important timber tree, the afromosia yields a hard, heavy, and dark-colored wood that is streaked with black. The timber is considered an alternative to teak and is often used for boat-building, joinery, flooring, and decorative veneers. However, the species is now endangered in most of its range because of over-exploitation of its timber and minimal regeneration. **BARK** Creamy gray, smooth, peeling off in patches to expose the soft orange inner bark.
LEAF Alternate, pinnate with a terminal leaflet, usually with nine elliptic to ovate, smooth leaflets.
FLOWER Cream to greenish white, pealike, in slender terminal panicles.
FRUIT Long, flat, winged pod.

orange underbark

buttresses up to 9¾ ft (3 m) from base

Prosopis chilensis

rounded crown

Algarroba

HEIGHT 10–33 ft (3–10 m)
TYPE Deciduous
OCCURRENCE Bolivia, Peru, Argentina, Chile

The algarroba is an important tree in its native semi-desert habitat. It is valued for the shade, fuel, and concentrated forage it provides. The tree is a staple food for cattle in arid regions. The unripe green pods are bitter and of little value, but the ripe pods, which contain sugar, make excellent fodder. **BARK** Gray-brown, sometimes fissured. **LEAF** Alternate, bipinnate, with 10–30 linear leaflets. **FLOWER** Greenish white to yellow, up to ³⁄₁₆ in (5 mm) long, arranged in axillary, cylindrical spikes or racemes that are 2–4 in (5–10 cm) long. **FRUIT** Broad, straight pod, 4–8 in (10–20 cm) long, flat and yellow when ripe, borne in drooping clusters; contains pale brown seeds, enclosed in a scaly seed coat.

Prosopis glandulosa

Honey Mesquite

HEIGHT up to 50 ft (15 m)
TYPE Deciduous
OCCURRENCE S. United States, Mexico, introduced in Australia, India, Saudi Arabia, S.W. Africa

The Aztec name for tree, "mesquite," gives this tree its common name. A small tree or shrub with zigzag branches and thorn-like spines, mesquite often forms thickets in sandy, alluvial flats. Like other semidesert species of the genus *Prosopis*, the mesquite is used for shade, fuel, and concentrated forage. In addition, it was the most important gum-yielding species of North America in the past. The seeds of the pod were ground into flour and processed to make bread, which was a staple food for native peoples of the deserts of the southwestern United States. **BARK** Reddish brown, fissured. **LEAF** Alternate, bipinnate with 6–17 linear to oblong, smooth leaflets. **FLOWER** In axillary spikes, small, greenish yellow, with inconspicuous, short-lobed petals. **FRUIT** Long, flat pod, with oblong seeds.

USES OF MESQUITE

The dense hardwood of this tree is excellent for woodworking and is used for fencing. The bark has been used medicinally for the treatment of eye problems, skin ulcers, and sore throats, as well as a digestive aid. The clear sap is used to make candy and a black dye is extracted from the darker sap.

MESQUITE WOOD

pod 4–12 in (10–30 cm) long

FRUIT

flower spike

greenish yellow flowers

FLOWERS

Pterocarpus indicus

Angsana

HEIGHT 33–165 ft (10–50 m)
TYPE Deciduous
OCCURRENCE S.E. Asia, E. Asia, Pacific Islands

Also called rosewood, this is the national tree of the Philippines. Its trunk is often twisted and gnarled, usually buttressed. **BARK** Yellowish to greenish brown, flaking in thin plates; inner bark yields red sap. **LEAF** Alternate, pinnate with 5–11 leaflets. **FLOWER** Borne in axillary racemes, yellow to orange-yellow, fragrant. **FRUIT** Circular pod.

smooth leaf surface

seed

ovate to oblong leaflets with wavy margins

LEAVES AND FRUIT

LEAVES

Pterocarpus santalinus

Red Sandalwood

HEIGHT up to 25 ft (8 m)
TYPE Deciduous
OCCURRENCE Asia, S. India

This tree is found in dry, tropical forests, often on dry, rocky soils. The timber, much sought-after for furniture-making, is also used for producing dyes. In India, the felling of these trees is strictly monitored, and export is forbidden. **BARK** Blackish brown, flaking deeply. **LEAF** Alternate, trifoliate or rarely with five leaflets. **FLOWER** Few, in terminal racemes. **FRUIT** Spherical pod with thickened seed-bearing portion and wavy wings.

rectangular flakes

broadly elliptic leaflet

BARK

LEAF

Robinia pseudoacacia

Black Locust

HEIGHT up to 80 ft (25 m)
TYPE Deciduous
OCCURRENCE United States, Europe

Also known as false acacia, this tree has a narrow crown and spiny branches. **BARK** Gray-brown, furrowed. **LEAF** Alternate, pinnate with elliptic to ovate leaflets. **FLOWER** White and pealike, in pendent racemes. **FRUIT** Drooping pod with red-brown valve.

7–21 leaflets

reddish brown calyx

LEAVES AND FLOWERS

Samanea saman

Rain Tree

HEIGHT up to 65 ft (20 m)
TYPE Evergreen
OCCURRENCE Mexico, Guatemala,
South America (Peru, Bolivia, Brazil)

Introduced into many tropical regions, such as the West Indies, Sri Lanka, India, and, in 1876, Singapore, this tree is widely cultivated. Its large, domed canopy provides plenty of shade, making it an important roadside and park tree. **BARK** Dark gray, rough, and deeply furrowed into thin plates or corky ridges. **LEAF** Alternate, bipinnate, with 6–16 squarish to elliptic leaflets, increasing in size from bottom to top of the tree; shiny above, with fine hairs below. **FLOWER** Spherical pink flower heads in stalked clusters. **FRUIT** Straight or curved pod, with a sweet pulp; pods smell of honey when broken.

CICADA "RAIN"

The common name of this species, "rain tree," refers to the falling of "honeydew," a watery waste excreted by cicadas after they suck sap from the tree. While feeding, the cicadas squirt out this liquid. When large numbers of cicadas feed on the canopy, moisture drips from the tree, creating the effect of a rain shower.

CICADA

FLOWER HEADS

ring of pink petals

broad crown

Sophora japonica

Pagoda Tree

HEIGHT up to 80 ft (25 m)
TYPE Deciduous
OCCURRENCE China, Korea

As the name suggests, the pagoda tree was frequently planted in temple gardens. It is of historical significance as an agroforestry tree recorded as far back as the 6th century. It was introduced into western horticulture in 1753 and is now planted on streets and in parks. **BARK** Gray-brown, prominently ridged and fissured. **LEAF** Alternate, pinnate, with a terminal leaflet, dark green above, blue-green beneath, softly hairy. **FLOWER** White, pealike, fragrant, in loose, hanging panicles at ends of shoots. **FRUIT** Pod, highly constricted between the seeds and resembling a string of beads.

spreading habit

round crown

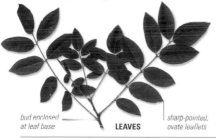

bud enclosed at leaf base **LEAVES** sharp-pointed, ovate leaflets

---

Tamarindus indica

Tamarind

HEIGHT up to 80 ft (25 m)
TYPE Evergreen
OCCURRENCE E. Africa, India, widely cultivated in other tropical countries

This tree has a short trunk, drooping branches, and a rounded crown. The edible sweet and sour pulp in its pods is an important ingredient in many chutneys and sauces. **BARK** White-gray, rough, with irregular scales. **LEAF** Alternate, pinnate, without a terminal leaflet; 10–20 pairs of elliptic-oblong, usually smooth leaflets. **FLOWER** Red in bud opening yellow to cream, in racemes at the sides and ends of shoots. **FRUIT** Pod, with a dry outer shell, pulpy inside.

5 unequal lobes

FLOWER
flower up to 1 in (2.5 cm) long

Crataegus monogyna

Singleseed Hawthorn

HEIGHT up to 33 ft (10 m)
TYPE Deciduous
OCCURRENCE Europe, N. Africa, W. Asia

This small tree has spiny branches; old trees often have fluted trunks. An herbal medicine for circulatory problems is extracted from its fruit and leaves.
BARK Dark orange-brown or pink-brown; cracking into rectangles. **LEAF** Alternate, smooth, deeply cut into 3–7 lobes, glossy dark green above, paler beneath.
FLOWER White, fragrant, in dense clusters on shoots.
FRUIT Oval red pome, with one seed.

pink anthers
FLOWERS

leaves 2 in (5 cm) long

fruit ½ in (1.2 cm) wide

FRUIT

Cydonia oblonga

Quince

HEIGHT up to 25 ft (8 m)
TYPE Deciduous
OCCURRENCE Caucasus, N. Iran, South America, Mediterranean region

The fruit of this small tree is an important crop in South America and the Mediterranean. **BARK** Purplish gray-brown, flaking to orange-brown.
LEAF Alternate, ovate to oblong, with untoothed margins. **FLOWER** Terminal, solitary, large with five whitish to pink petals.
FRUIT Large, fragrant, pear-shaped pome, downy when young, yellow when ripe.

FRUIT

fruit 4 in (10 cm) long

LEAVES AND FLOWERS

flower 2 in (5 cm) wide

Eriobotrya japonica

Loquat

HEIGHT up to 20 ft (6 m)
TYPE Evergreen
OCCURRENCE China, Japan, India, Australia, South America, California, Mediterranean, South Africa

In the unusual flowering cycle of this tree, the flowers bloom with the onset of winter and the edible fruit ripens by spring. It has a dense, rounded, glossy dark green canopy.
BARK Dark gray, smooth, and flaking.
LEAF Alternate, smooth above, hairy beneath, toothed margins.
FLOWER Large, white, fragrant, in terminal racemes. **FRUIT** Pear-shaped to oval pome.

oblong to obovate leaves

yellow fruit

FRUITING TREE

RIPE FRUIT

Malus trilobata

Turkish Crab Apple

HEIGHT up to 50 ft (15 m)
TYPE Deciduous
OCCURRENCE S.W. Asia, N.E. Greece

This narrowly conical tree grows in evergreen thickets in Asia and Greece. The flowers bloom in early summer. **BARK** Gray-brown, cracking into numerous small, square plates. **LEAF** Alternate, long-stalked, deeply cut into three lobes, smooth above, hairy beneath; glossy dark green turning yellow, red, and purple in fall. **FLOWER** White, cup-shaped, with five petals and yellow anthers, appearing from woolly buds, borne in small clusters at the end of shoots. **FRUIT** Small, hard, green or red-green pome, up to 1¼ in (3 cm) wide.

flowers up to 1½ in (4 cm) wide

leaves up to 3½ in (9 cm) long

LEAVES AND FLOWERS

FRUIT

¾–1¼ in (2–3 cm) across

Malus sylvestris

Wild Apple

HEIGHT 25–40 ft (8–12 m)
TYPE Deciduous
OCCURRENCE Caucasus, N. Iran

This tree is an ancestor of most cultivated apples and is used as graft stock for many commercial varieties. It is found in hedgerows and at woodland edges. **BARK** Gray-brown to purple-brown, peeling in rectangular flakes. **LEAF** Alternate, elliptic to obovate, with toothed margins and a rounded leaf base. **FLOWER** Large, in clusters on short shoots. **FRUIT** Spherical, green to yellowish red pome.

pink to white flowers

FLOWERS

Prunus africana

Red Stinkwood

HEIGHT 10–130 ft (3–40 m)
TYPE Evergreen
OCCURRENCE Africa, Madagascar

In Africa the bark of this tree is used as a traditional medicine for chest pain, malaria, and fevers. An extract from the pulverized bark is also an ingredient of medications used in the treatment of prostate gland enlargement, but methods of extraction, which involve excessive debarking and felling of trees, are threatening the species. **BARK** Dark brown to blackish, tough, resinous, peeling. **LEAF** Alternate, glossy dark green, elliptic to oblong, smooth surface, finely toothed margin. **FLOWER** Small, white to yellowish, in racemes on special shoots. **FRUIT** Oval drupe, red to black when ripe.

Prunus armeniaca

Apricot

HEIGHT up to 33 ft (10 m)
TYPE Deciduous
OCCURRENCE C. and W. Asia, N. China

The apricot tree, with its rounded crown and open canopy, was originally cultivated in northeastern China over 3,000 years ago. The species is now widely cultivated for its sweet edible fruit. Historically, apricots were grown from seedlings, and a few improved cultivars exist. **BARK** Red-brown, smooth,

LEAVES AND FRUIT

and glossy. **LEAF** Alternate, glossy dark green, broadly ovate to rounded with abruptly tapered tip, usually rounded base and finely toothed margin. **FLOWER** Large with five white to pink petals, borne singly on old wood in spring before the leaves emerge. **FRUIT** Spherical, fleshy drupe, yellow-flushed orange-red, with a hard, smooth stone enclosing an edible white seed.

leaf to 4 in (10 cm) long

orange-red flesh

single stone

FRUIT

APRICOT PRODUCTS

Jam and preserves are made from the sweet cooked pulp of the apricot fruit. The Romans introduced apricots to Europe in 70–60 BCE, and European settlers brought the tree to North America. Turkey is the world's largest producer of apricots. **JAM**

Prunus avium

Sweet Cherry

HEIGHT up to 80 ft (25 m)
TYPE Deciduous
OCCURRENCE Europe, W. Asia, North America

Also known as wild cherry, sweet cherry wood has been used for veneer, and also for furniture-making, particularly in France. The roots of this tree can cause problems for nearby buildings. The double-flowered cultivar 'Plena' is a popular ornamental tree. **BARK** Red-brown, peeling in horizontal bands. **LEAF** Alternate, elliptic to oblong or obovate, dull green above, covered with soft hairs below. **FLOWER** Large, white, borne in clusters on short shoots before the leaves emerge. **FRUIT** Spherical, bitter or sweet, edible red drupe.

FLOWERS

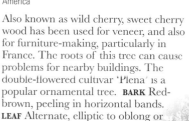

leaf to 6 in (15 cm) long

red berry

LEAVES AND FRUIT

Prunus cerasifera

Cherry Plum

HEIGHT up to 33 ft (10 m)
TYPE Deciduous
OCCURRENCE Known only in cultivation

Also called Myrobalan plum, this tree has a rounded crown. It is commonly used as a rootstock for grafting domestic plums and is often planted as an ornamental. 'Pissardii', its best-known cultivar, has

FLOWERS

pink flowers and purple leaves; 'Nigra' is the selection from this cultivar that is usually grown today. **BARK** Purple-brown, thinly scaly, with horizontal orange-brown lenticels, becoming fissured with age. **LEAF** Alternate, ovate to elliptic or obovate with toothed margins, smooth above, covered with soft hairs below. **FLOWER** White, rarely pink, borne singly or in clusters, before the leaves. **FRUIT** Spherical, red or yellow, plumlike drupe.

APRICOT FLOWER
Stamens of the apricot (*Prunus armeniaca*) flower
as revealed by a scanning electron micrograph. Each
stamen is made up of a green filament with a red
anther at its tip, which releases pollen. The pollen is
carried by insects to the female parts of the flower.

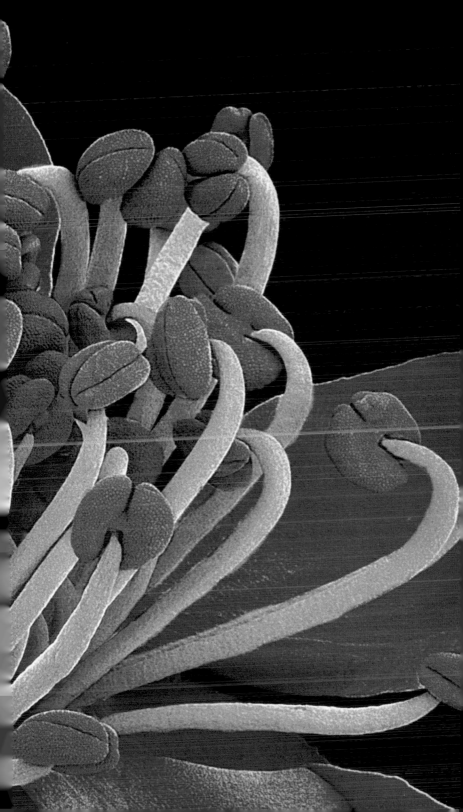

Prunus cerasus

Sour Cherry

HEIGHT up to 33 ft (10 m)
TYPE Deciduous
OCCURRENCE Garden origin

This tree was cultivated from wild populations growing around the Caspian and Black seas. It has a broadly rounded crown. **BARK** Purple-brown, rough, scaly. **LEAF** Alternate, elliptic to ovate, with toothed margins. **FLOWER** In clusters of 3–5. **FRUIT** Spherical, sour-tasting drupe.

large white flowers

leaves 2–5 in (5–12 cm) long

red to black drupe

BRANCH WITH FLOWERS

FRUIT

Prunus laurocerasus

Cherry Laurel

HEIGHT up to 33 ft (10 m)
TYPE Evergreen
OCCURRENCE E. Europe, S.W. Asia

This large, common shrub is found in parks and woodland. **BARK** Dark gray-brown, smooth. **LEAF** Alternate, obovate. **FLOWER** Small, white and fragrant, borne in racemes. **FRUIT** Purple-black conical drupe.

dark green leaf

berrylike fruit

wide, spreading habit

LEAVES AND FRUIT

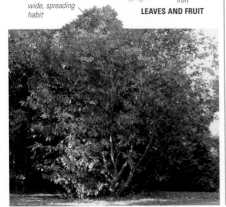

Prunus x domestica

Plum

HEIGHT up to 33 ft (10 m)
TYPE Deciduous
OCCURRENCE Garden origin

Many cultivars of this tree are grown for its culinary plum. Its crown is broad and spreading. **BARK** Gray-brown, fissured with age. **LEAF** Alternate, elliptic to obovate, toothed margins. **FLOWER** In clusters on short shoots, five white petals. **FRUIT** Ovoid drupe, yellow, red, or purple, sweet or sharp taste.

dull green surface

3 in (7.5 cm) long

LEAVES

FRUIT

Prunus mume

Japanese Apricot

HEIGHT 20–33 ft (6–10 m)
TYPE Deciduous
OCCURRENCE China, Japan

Cultivated for over 1,500 years for its variously colored blossoms, this Japanese apricot has more than 300 cultivars. It has a rounded crown. **BARK** Gray to greenish. **LEAF** Alternate, ovate, hairy, sharply toothed margins. **FLOWER** Large, white to pink to red, and fragrant; borne singly or in pairs on old wood. **FRUIT** Spherical to ovoid drupe, fleshy, yellow, barely edible.

Prunus dulcis

Sweet Almond

HEIGHT up to 25 ft (8 m)
TYPE Deciduous
OCCURRENCE C. and W. Asia, North Africa

Widely cultivated since ancient times for its green, edible fruit and as an ornamental, the almond thrives in the United States, which today is by far the largest producer of almonds in the world, producing 75 percent of the world's crop. The tree has a spreading crown and smooth green or red-flushed shoots.
BARK Dark gray, cracking into small pieces.
LEAF Alternate, ovate-

FLOWERS

flower to 2 in (5 cm) wide

HISTORY OF THE ALMOND

Explorers ate almonds while traveling on the "Silk Road" between Asia and the Mediterranean. Before long, almond trees flourished in the Mediterranean, especially in Spain and Italy. The almond tree was brought to California from Spain in the mid-1700s by Franciscan priests.

ALMONDS

lanceolate to narrowly elliptic, smooth, finely toothed margin, dark green.
FLOWER Borne on lateral spurs before the leaves, solitary or in pairs, large, pink to whitish. **FRUIT** Oval, compressed drupe, velvety outside, dry and leathery flesh enclosing a smooth, pitted stone with an edible kernel.

leaf to 4¾ in (12 cm) long

LEAVES AND FRUIT

flesh splits open as fruit ripens

Prunus padus

European Bird Cherry

HEIGHT up to 50 ft (15 m)
TYPE Deciduous
OCCURRENCE Europe, N. Asia to Japan

The conical crown of this tree becomes rounded with age. **BARK** Gray-brown, smooth. **LEAF** Elliptic to obovate, finely toothed. **FLOWER** White, fragrant. **FRUIT** Spherical black drupe.

alternate leaves
drooping racemes

Prunus serrulata

Flowering Cherry

HEIGHT up to 65 ft (20 m)
TYPE Deciduous
OCCURRENCE China, Japan, Korea

This Asian cherry has several cultivars. In spring, many of them produce dazzling semi-double flowers. **BARK** Purple-brown or grayish. **LEAF** Alternate, ovate-oblong to obovate. **FLOWER** Pink to white, in clusters of 2–5. **FRUIT** Fleshy, purple-red to black drupe.

notched petals

FLOWERS

Prunus spinosa

Blackthorn

HEIGHT up to 16 ft (5 m)
TYPE Deciduous
OCCURRENCE Europe, N. Africa, N. Asia

Also known as sloe, this many-branched and thicket-forming tree has spiny branches. **BARK** Dark blackish brown. **LEAF** Alternate, elliptic-ovate to obovate, toothed. **FLOWER** Single or in pairs, white, small. **FRUIT** Spherical, smooth drupe.

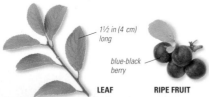

1½ in (4 cm) long

blue-black berry

LEAF   **RIPE FRUIT**

Prunus subhirtella

Winter-Flowering Cherry

HEIGHT up to 33 ft (10 m)
TYPE Deciduous
OCCURRENCE Japan

sharply toothed margin

bronze-green young leaf

deep green mature leaf

LEAVES

This tree has a rounded crown and upright branches. One popular cultivar, 'Autumnalis', flowers throughout mild winters, when its branches are bare of leaves. **BARK** Gray-brown, smooth, with horizontal lenticels. **LEAF** Alternate, elliptic to ovate. **FLOWER** Pale pink to white, notched petals, in clusters of 2–4 on short shoots. **FRUIT** Spherical, fleshy black drupe.

Prunus persica

Peach

HEIGHT up to 25 ft (8 m)
TYPE Deciduous
OCCURRENCE China

Cultivated since ancient times, this tree has many different varieties, with differing shapes, flowers, and fruit. The tree's shape can be bushy or weeping, and its flowers single- or double-petaled. Peaches typically have downy-skinned fruit, with yellow or white flesh. However, in nectarines, the fruit's skin is smooth—a difference controlled by a single gene. **BARK** Dark gray, becoming fissured with age. **LEAF** Alternate, narrowly elliptic to lanceolate, with finely toothed margins. **FLOWER** Borne singly or in pairs, pink, sometimes white. **FRUIT** Large, spherical drupe, with velvety or smooth skin; sweet, fleshy, white or orange-yellow pulp, with a deeply pitted stone and a white seed.

1½ in (4 cm) wide

pitted stone

FRUIT AND SEED

FLOWERS

ORIGINS OF THE PEACH

Peaches were probably the first fruit crop domesticated in China about 4,000 years ago. The tree was introduced to Persia (Iran) by way of the ancient silk trading routes. Greeks and Romans spread the peach throughout Europe and England in 300–400 BCE. Peaches then came to North America with the explorers of the 16th and 17th centuries.

PEACH TREE IN BLOOM

red-flushed skin

3¼ in (8 cm) wide

FLOWERING CHERRY
In Japan, which is famous for its flowering cherry trees (*Prunus serrulata*), the brief blossom season in March–April is a time of celebration, marked by parties, or "hanami," held in the shade of the trees. This tree is popular worldwide as an ornamental.

Prunus x yedoensis

Yoshino Cherry

HEIGHT up to 50 ft (16 m)
TYPE Deciduous
OCCURRENCE Japan, of garden origin

Also known as the flowering cherry, this fast-growing Japanese hybrid is one of the favorite cultivated cherry trees of Japan. With its broadly spreading crown, arching branches, and spectacular display of early spring flowers, it is now a very popular ornamental tree throughout the world, especially as an avenue tree. It was planted on United States soil for the first time in 1912, when the people of Japan presented the tree as a gift of friendship. **BARK** Purple-gray, with thick bands of corky lenticels. **LEAF** Alternate, elliptic to obovate, 2½ in (6 cm) wide, with tapered tips and sharply toothed margins; they are pale green and downy when young, particularly on the underside,

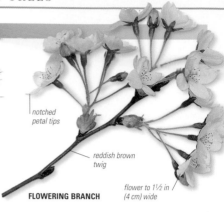

notched petal tips

reddish brown twig

flower to 1½ in (4 cm) wide

FLOWERING BRANCH

the surface becoming smooth and glossy with age. **FLOWER** Pale pink, fading to nearly white, with five large petals, numerous, borne in small clusters on side spurs in early spring, before the young leaves emerge. **FRUIT** Fleshy, spherical drupe, red at first, ripening to black.

leaf to 14½ in (1 cm) long

**LEAVES AND
UNRIPE FRUIT**

fruit to ½ in (1.2 cm) wide

CHERRY PLANTING

Mass planting (originally of *P. serrula*) on riversides was popularized by the Shogun rulers of Japan. Initiated by Yoshimune Tokugawa (1716–45), the planting of cherry trees was backed by the slogan that cherries can purify river water.

JAPANESE PAINTING

Pyrus communis

Pear

HEIGHT up to 65 ft (20 m)
TYPE Deciduous
OCCURRENCE Known only in cultivation (grown in gardens and orchards); occasionally naturalized in Europe

A broadly conical to columnar tree, the pear is a hybrid of several European species. Along with its cultivars, it is widely grown for its edible fruit. In its wild form, it has a spiny habit when young. It is usually found in woodlands and scrub. **BARK** Dark gray, cracking into rectangular plates. **LEAF** Alternate, ovate to elliptic, glossy deep green. **FLOWER** Five white petals with deep pink anthers, in clusters on short shoots. **FRUIT** Fleshy, yellowish green pome.

toothed margins

LEAVES

FRUIT-BEARING BRANCHES

to 4 in (10 cm) long

RIPE FRUIT

CULTIVATED PEARS

The original pear fruit were small, hard, gritty, sour, and astringent, and may have resembled the stewing pears that survive today. There are over 5,000 cultivated varieties of pears, of which 10–25 are commercially grown. In the US, 75 percent of the pears cultivated are "Bartletts," which is the same as the British "Williams" pear, and of which there are greenish yellow and red varieties.

RED PEAR

WILLIAMS PEAR

Pyrus pyrifolia

Chinese Pear

HEIGHT up to 40 ft (12 m)
TYPE Deciduous
OCCURRENCE C. and W. China

This tree was brought into cultivation in China 3,000 years ago. **BARK** Dark gray to purplish brown. **LEAF** Alternate, ovate to ovate-oblong, bristle-toothed margins. **FLOWER** White, borne in clusters of 6–9. **FRUIT** Brown to yellow, rounded pome.

FLOWERS AND LEAVES

five petals

reddish new leaves

Pyrus salicifolia

Willow Pear

HEIGHT up to 33 ft (10 m)
TYPE Deciduous
OCCURRENCE W. Asia

This spreading tree has slender, pendent shoots and willow-like leaves. It is considered one of the best cultivated ornamental pears. **BARK** Pale gray-brown. **LEAF** Alternate, lanceolate. **FLOWER** Large, white, on short shoots. **FRUIT** Yellow-brown pome, hairy; later smooth.

tapering tips

UNRIPE FRUIT

in clusters

FLOWERS   LEAVES

Sorbus aria

Whitebeam

HEIGHT up to 80 ft (25 m)
TYPE Deciduous
OCCURRENCE Europe

This tree is found on well-drained chalk and limestone. **BARK** Gray, cracking with age. **LEAF** Alternate, ovate to elliptic-oblong, covered with hairs when young, pale green above, whitish hairs beneath. **FLOWER** In flattened terminal clusters, with five white petals. **FRUIT** Red-orange, spherical to egg-shaped pome.

Sorbus aucuparia

European Mountain Ash

HEIGHT up to 50 ft (15 m)
TYPE Deciduous
OCCURRENCE N. Africa, W. Asia

The dried berries of this tree are used mainly in the food and beverage industries. **BARK** Gray, smooth. **LEAF** Alternate, pinnate, with 9–15 elliptic to lanceolate leaflets. **FLOWER** White, in flat clusters. **FRUIT** Orange-red pome.

LEAVES AND FLOWERS

pointed tips

RIPE FRUIT

Sorbus domestica

Whitty Pear

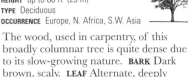

HEIGHT up to 65 ft (20 m)
TYPE Deciduous
OCCURRENCE S. Europe, N. Africa, S.W. Asia

This broadly columnar tree, once grown for its fruit, is now becoming rare. **BARK** Dark brown, scaly. **LEAF** Alternate, pinnate; oblong to lanceolate leaflets, smooth above, hairy beneath. **FLOWER** White, in large clusters. **FRUIT** Yellow-green pome.

pyramidal clusters

berrylike pome

FLOWERS

FRUIT WITH LEAVES

Sorbus torminalis

Wild Service Tree

HEIGHT up to 80 ft (25 m)
TYPE Deciduous
OCCURRENCE Europe, N. Africa, S.W. Asia

The wood, used in carpentry, of this broadly columnar tree is quite dense due to its slow-growing nature. **BARK** Dark brown, scaly. **LEAF** Alternate, deeply lobed at base. **FLOWER** White, in flattened clusters. **FRUIT** Small, brown, rounded pome.

open flower clusters

cracking in scaly plates

LEAVES AND FLOWERS

triangular-ovate lobes

BARK

Hovenia dulcis

Raisin Tree

HEIGHT up to 33 ft (10 m)
TYPE Deciduous
OCCURRENCE China, Japan, Korea

The fruit stalks of this tree are edible while the fruit itself is not. **BARK** Smooth, gray when young, paler and furrowing with age. **LEAF** Alternate, toothed, long-stalked. **FLOWER** Cream to greenish white, small. **FRUIT** Purple-black, fleshy drupe.

oval crown

Ziziphus jujuba

Jujube

HEIGHT up to 33 ft (10 m)
TYPE Deciduous
OCCURRENCE S. Europe, N. Africa, W. Asia, China, S. United States

This tree has been cultivated in China for more than 4,000 years. It has a broad crown and drooping branches. The sweet fruit can be dried or candied. **BARK** Gray to dull black, rough. **LEAF** Alternate, smooth or slightly hairy on the veins below. **FLOWER** Yellowish green, small, in axillary cymes. **FRUIT** Purple-red, egg-shaped, fleshy drupe.

irregularly cracked

BARK

finely toothed margins

3 main veins

LEAVES

Ziziphus lotus

Lotus

HEIGHT up to 7 ft (2 m)
TYPE Deciduous
OCCURRENCE S. Europe, N. Africa

stalkless leaves

LEAVES

A sprawling shrubby tree, the lotus has zigzag branches that are armed with spines. It is well adapted to drought and hot climates. It is thought to be the source of the famous sweet fruit from which the ancient lotus-eaters of North Africa took their name. It was believed that once the fruit was eaten or liqueur made from it was consumed, travelers gave up all desire to return to their native lands. The fruit, which is rich in vitamins and in sugar, is eaten fresh, pickled or dried, or made into confectionery. Its mealy flesh can also be made into a fermented drink. In the Arabian Peninsula, a kind of bread is made from the fruit, which is dried and then pounded in a wooden mortar to separate the stones. The meal is mixed with water and formed into cakes that resemble sweet gingerbread. The common name of this tree should not be confused with various types of water lilies. **BARK** Pale ash gray. **LEAF** Alternate, ovate to oblong, smooth, with slightly toothed margins and three lateral veins. **FLOWER** Small, with yellow petals, in axillary clusters. **FRUIT** Yellow to reddish brown, rounded drupe, with sweet, edible flesh.

Trema micrantha

Guacimilla

HEIGHT 8–33 ft (2.5–10 m)
TYPE Evergreen
OCCURRENCE US (Florida), Mexico, West Indies, Central and South America

This fast-growing species produces soft wood used to make tea chests and matchsticks. **BARK** Dark or gray-brown, shallowly furrowed. **LEAF** In flat sprays, ovate, toothed, pale green above, white-hairy beneath. **FLOWER** Petalless, greenish white calyx, in clusters. **FRUIT** Spherical orange drupe.

alternate leaves

FOLIAGE

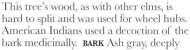

Ulmus americana

American Elm

HEIGHT 100–120 ft (30–36 m)
TYPE Deciduous
OCCURRENCE E. US, S.E. Canada

This tree's wood, as with other elms, is hard to split and was used for wheel hubs. American Indians used a decoction of the bark medicinally. **BARK** Ash gray, deeply fissured, with scaly ridges.

LEAF

doubly toothed margins

LEAF Alternate, ovate-oblong to elliptic, downy beneath. **FLOWER** Reddish, tiny, petalless, in axillary clusters on long, drooping stalks. **FRUIT** Nutlet, notched at top, with hairy margin.

slender zig-zag twigs

red anthers

FLOWERING SHOOT

Ulmus glabra

Wych Elm

HEIGHT up to 130 ft (40 m)
TYPE Deciduous
OCCURRENCE N. and C. Europe, W. Asia

The wych elm has a broad crown and short trunk. Its wood is very durable in wet conditions and was popular for troughs, cribs, and coffins. It is still used for the construction of breakwaters for coastal defenses and harbors. **BARK** Gray, smooth. **LEAF** Alternate, elliptic to oblong-obovate, coarse and uneven at bases, double-toothed margins, dark green and roughly hairy above, usually downy beneath. **FLOWER** Tiny, with reddish anthers, petalless, in dense, axillary clusters. **FRUIT** Smooth nutlet surrounded by a membranous wing.

prominent veins | **LEAF**

FLOWER CLUSTERS

Ulmus procera

English Elm

HEIGHT up to 100 ft (30 m)
TYPE Deciduous
OCCURRENCE W. Europe

Regarded by some as a variety of *Ulmus minor*—*Ulmus minor* var. *vulgaris*—the English elm was probably introduced into Britain by the Romans, who used this tree to train grapevines. It has a broad, columnar habit, strong branches, and shoots that can become corky when the tree is a few years old. This elm reproduces by means of suckers that grow extensively around its base.

DUTCH ELM DISEASE

Dutch elm disease, which was first identified in the Netherlands, is a yeastlike fungus that is spread by elm bark beetles. It was first recorded in Britain in 1927, but the devastating infection that killed 12 million English Elm trees in the 1970s was the result of an aggressive form of the disease that came from North America.

ELM BARK BEETLE

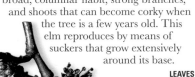

flowers open on bare shoots

FLOWER CLUSTERS

LEAVES

double-toothed margin

BARK Gray-brown, smooth when young, becoming fissured with age.
LEAF Alternate, very variable in shape, elliptic to obovate, with an unequal base; dark green and rough to the touch above, hairy beneath.
FLOWER Reddish, petalless, in dense clusters. **FRUIT** Nutlet, slightly notched, smooth, surrounded by a narrow membranous wing. Nearly all the seeds are infertile.

Ulmus pumila

Siberian Elm

HEIGHT up to 80 ft (25 m)
TYPE Deciduous
OCCURRENCE N. China, E. Siberia, Korea

Broadly columnar in shape, this fast-growing tree is sometimes planted as a windbreak in North America.
BARK Grayish brown, deeply furrowed.
LEAF Alternate, elliptic to elliptic-lanceolate.
FLOWER Red, very small, petalless, in dense clusters. **FRUIT** Winged, slightly notched nutlet.

LEAVES

sharply toothed margins

Celtis australis

Nettle Tree

HEIGHT up to 80 ft (25 m)
TYPE Deciduous
OCCURRENCE S. Europe, W. Asia, N. Africa

This tree has a broadly columnar to spreading crown. **BARK** Gray, smooth.
LEAF Alternate, narrowly oval, sharply toothed, dark green and scaly above, gray-green and softly hairy beneath.
FLOWER Greenish, tiny, petalless, long-stalked, open singly or in small clusters.
FRUIT Ovoid purple-brown to blackish drupe.

*to 6 in
(15 cm) long*

LEAVES

Zelkova serrata

Japanese Zelkova

HEIGHT up to 100 ft (30 m)
TYPE Deciduous
OCCURRENCE China, Korea, Japan

The wood of this tree is valued for making furniture, lacquer-ware, and trays. It grows on moist soil near streams.
BARK Smooth, gray, flaking with age.
LEAF Alternate, ovate to ovate-oblong or elliptic, dark green with scattered hairs above, smooth or slightly hairy below, sharply toothed.
FLOWER Green, small, petalless; males and females in separate clusters. **FRUIT** Small spherical drupe.

*to 4¾ in
(12 cm) long*

LEAVES

Celtis occidentalis

Common Hackberry

HEIGHT up to 130 ft (40 m)
TYPE Deciduous
OCCURRENCE N.E. and N.C. United States

Although the fruit of this tree is not very fleshy, it was used by American Indians to flavor food. **BARK** Smooth, dark brown, scaly with age. **LEAF** Alternate, ovate to ovate-oblong, sharply toothed near the tip.
FLOWER Greenish, small, petalless, singly or in small clusters. **FRUIT** Berrylike, orange-red to purple, edible drupe.

*broadly columnar
crown*

Artocarpus altilis

Breadfruit

HEIGHT up to 100 ft (30 m)
TYPE Evergreen/Deciduous
OCCURRENCE New Guinea, Pacific Islands

Widely cultivated for its edible fruit, the breadfruit tree has a straight trunk and a wide crown with large, spreading branches. **BARK** Gray, smooth; exudes sticky white latex. **LEAF** Alternate, large, with 5–11 lobes, pointed tips, glossy bright green above, stiff hairs beneath, with prominent yellowish nerves; stipules are large and conical, leaving scars encircling the stem at the nodes when they fall off. **FLOWER** Males and females borne on the same tree, inconspicuous, grouped in fleshy inflorescences; males: yellowish brown, densely set on a drooping, cylindrical to club-shaped spike; females: upright, in a rounded to oval prickly head which develops into a compound fruit.

warty surface

FRUIT

yellow-green fruit

FRUIT Spherical to oblong syncarp, often with a warty or spiny surface, 4–12 in (10–30 cm) wide, borne singly or in clusters of two or three at the ends of branches; white, starchy when unripe, usually fragrant when ripe, few seeds, sometimes seedless.

FOLIAGE | leaves in spirals

MALE FLOWER | cylindrical spike

STARCH STAPLE

This food pounder from Tahiti, known as a *poi*, was used to grind breadfruit pulp. Captain James Cook wrote of this process in his journal: "Of breadfruit they make two or three dishes by beating it with a stone pestle till it makes a paste, mixing water or cocoa nut liquor or both with it, adding ripe plantains..."

POUNDER

LEAVES AND FRUIT

waxy surface

unripe fruit

Artocarpus heterophyllus

Jackfruit

HEIGHT 33–65 ft (10–20 m)
TYPE Evergreen
OCCURRENCE S.E. Asia, known only in cultivation

The fruit of this tree is the largest tree-borne fruit in the world. It can be eaten fresh, dried as confectionery, or canned. The pulp is used to flavor beverages and ice cream. The seeds can be roasted and used as table nuts. **BARK** Blackish brown, thick; exudes white latex. **LEAF** Alternate, elliptic to obovate. **FLOWER** Males and females borne on the same tree; males: on new wood among the leaves, small, ellipsoidal, and covered with pollen when mature; females: larger than the males, borne on short stalks on the stem and branches. **FRUIT** Yellowish brown syncarp, up to 110 lb (50 kg) in weight, covered with conical warts, waxy, golden yellow, aromatic pulp; 30–500 oval seeds, surrounded by a thick, gelatinous jacket.

green coloration

YOUNG BARK

Antiaris toxicaria

Upas Tree

HEIGHT up to 150 ft (45 m)
TYPE Evergreen
OCCURRENCE India to S. China, Malaysia, Africa

The upas tree has a conical crown and its trunk is sometimes buttressed. The latex is toxic and contains cardiac glycosides, which can cause heart failure. It has been widely used by some tribal peoples in north India and Borneo to poison arrowheads. **BARK** Yellowish to grayish white, smooth, usually with lenticels; exudes creamy white, watery latex; it has a fibrous inner bark. **LEAF** Alternate, oblong-elliptic to obovate, hairy, sometimes toothed. **FLOWER** Males and females on the same tree; males: fleshy, green, with rounded heads; females: solitary in a pear-shaped receptacle. **FRUIT** Purple-red pear-shaped drupe, ripening to black, immersed in a fleshy receptacle.

BARK

Broussonetia papyrifera

Paper Mulberry

HEIGHT 33–65 ft (10–20 m)
TYPE Deciduous
OCCURRENCE S.E. Asia

FRUIT

red ripening
fruit

The name "paper mulberry" comes from
the fine fiber that this tree yields from its
inner bark, which is used to make paper
and Polynesian tapa cloth (used for
ceremonial purposes, clothing, and
bedding). The tree has a broadly
spreading habit and bristly shoots.
BARK Dark gray-brown, smooth; exudes
white latex. **LEAF** Alternate, ovate to
elliptic-ovate, purplish at first, turning
matt green; hairy and scaly above,
densely hairy beneath, unlobed or with
3–5 lobes on young trees, with scalloped

WASHI AND TAPA

In China, bark fibers of the paper mulberry were used to
make paper and bark cloth from 105 CE, and continues to
be used in the making of some lampshades. By the 6th
century, classic washi paper-making had reached Japan.
Early Polynesian voyagers took the tree and the skills of
making bark-cloth with them to the Pacific, and it is here
that tapa cloth-making reached its highest art.

**PAPER-
MAKING**

to toothed margins. **FLOWER** Males and
females on separate trees; males: white, in
drooping, cylindrical catkins; females:
green, in dense, spherical heads.
FRUIT Spherical syncarp in clusters, the
fleshy part turning orange-red.

**LEAVES AND
FLOWERS**

leaf to 8 in
(20 cm) long

female flowers
with purple
stigmas

LEAVES

Ficus benghalensis

Indian Banyan

HEIGHT up to 80 ft (25 m)
TYPE Evergreen
OCCURRENCE India

This spreading tree is a strangling fig, with massive pillar roots that have grown downward from another tree. In this species, the branches root themselves (a process known as layering) over a large area. It is because of this characteristic and its longevity that the banyan is a symbol of immortality and an integral part of the myths and legends of India. It is also the national tree of India. The English name comes from "banians," the Hindu merchants who often set up markets in the shade of the tree.
BARK Pale brown to gray, smooth; exudes white latex. **LEAF** Alternate, ovate, with heart-shaped base, smooth and leathery, untoothed. **FLOWER** Males and females on the same tree; tiny, enclosed in a fig receptacle.
FRUIT Figlike; small, round, rose-red.

fruit to ½ in (1.5 cm) wide

RIPE FRUIT

TRUNK

LEAVES

leaf 5–10 in (12.5–25 cm) long

THE LARGEST BANYAN TREE

Beginning life as a seedling in the crown of a date palm in 1782, this Banyan tree in the Indian Botanical Gardens at Howrah, Kolkata (Calcutta), is now reputed to be the world's largest, covering some 4 acres (1.6 hectares), appearing like a small forest in itself.

Ficus benjamina

Weeping Fig

HEIGHT up to 65 ft (20 m)
TYPE Evergreen
OCCURRENCE India to S. China,
S.E. Asia, N. Australia, Pacific Islands

A strangling fig that often grows into a large spreading tree, the weeping fig usually has many hanging aerial roots, some of which develop into independent trunks. While it remains small as a houseplant, in the wild it develops a dense, spreading crown. There are several ornamental cultivars, and it is popular for bonsai. **BARK** Pale brown to grayish white; exudes white latex. **LEAF** Alternate, ovate to elliptic, smooth and leathery. **FLOWER** Tiny, enclosed in a fig receptacle; males near the opening, females beneath. **FRUIT** Round, stalkless fig, red with white dots.

leaf to 15 in
(3 cm) long

red fruit

**LEAF AND
FRUIT**

Ficus carica

Common Fig

HEIGHT up to 33 ft (10 m)
TYPE Deciduous
OCCURRENCE W. Asia, introduced in
Mediterranean region

This tree has been cultivated for thousands of years for its edible fruit. Its remains have been found at Neolithic sites dating back to 5000 BCE. The Arab expansion in the 6th–8th centuries brought new and better cultivars to the Mediterranean region. Today, there are about 700 known cultivars. **BARK** Grayish brown, smooth and porous. **LEAF** Alternate, ovate to round with heart-

shaped base, 3–5 deep lobes, toothed or wavy margins, rough above, softly hairy beneath. **FLOWER** Tiny, fleshy, numerous, enclosed in a hollow fig receptacle; males on the inner walls near the small opening at the top, females beneath. **FRUIT** Reddish purple, pear-shaped to globose fig.

divided into
deep lobes

long stalk

LEAF

Ficus elastica

Indian Rubber Tree

HEIGHT 65–100 ft (20–30 m)
TYPE Evergreen
OCCURRENCE S. and S.E. Asia

Often grown as a houseplant, this strangling fig can attain an impressive size in the wild. It has numerous, slender aerial roots on its trunk and main branches. It is widely planted as an ornamental and street tree. There are several cultivars, including ones with variegated leaves. **BARK** Pale gray, smooth. **LEAF** Alternate, smooth and leathery, glossy dark green, with pink to purplish stipules. **FLOWER** Tiny, enclosed in a fig receptacle; males near the opening, females beneath. **FRUIT** Oblong, stalkless fig, turning yellow when ripe.

variegated leaves

HOUSEPLANT FOLIAGE

Ficus macrophylla

Moreton Bay Fig

HEIGHT 50–180 ft (15–55 m)
TYPE Evergreen
OCCURRENCE E. Australia

One of Australia's largest figs, this massive strangler has a deeply buttressed trunk. When mature, its crown can be up to 165 ft (50 m) wide, sometimes supported by prop roots. **BARK** Gray-brown, smooth; exudes white latex. **LEAF** Alternate, dark green above, golden brown beneath. **FLOWER** Tiny, enclosed in a fig receptacle; males near the opening, females beneath. **FRUIT** Globose fig, purple when ripe.

ovate to elliptic leaves

white dots on ripe fig

LEAVES AND FIGS

MORETON BAY FIG
The enormous buttress roots of this fig species (*Ficus macrophylla*) make it suitable only for parks and large open spaces. The scale of the root system is matched by the width of its spreading crown. The examples seen here are located in Hawaii.

Ficus religiosa

Bo-Tree

HEIGHT 50–115 ft (15–35 m)
TYPE Deciduous
OCCURRENCE C. and E. India

Also known as bodhi tree or pipal, this tree has a broad crown and a fluted or ribbed trunk. It is said to be the tree under which the Buddha meditated for six years and achieved enlightenment. The daughter of the Indian king Ashoka took a shoot of the Buddha's tree to Sri Lanka in the 3rd century BCE. It was planted at the Mahavihara monastery, where it still flourishes today. **BARK** Gray, smooth, or with shallow longitudinal fissures. **LEAF** Alternate, ovate, with slightly wavy

long, pointed tip

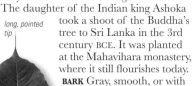

LEAVES

SACRED TREE

The bo-tree is sacred to both Hindus and Buddhists. It is widely cultivated, particularly near Buddhist temples, and worship of the tree is considered homage to the Hindu Trinity of Brahma, Vishnu, and Shiva.

BUDDHIST TEMPLE

margins. **FLOWER** Red, minute; males and females on the same tree, enclosed in a fig receptacle. **FRUIT** Fig; greenish yellow, turning red, rounded and flat-topped, stalkless, in pairs.

broad crown

Ficus sycomorus

Sycamore Fig

HEIGHT 26–100 ft (8–30 m)
TYPE Evergreen
OCCURRENCE Tropical Africa, Arabian Peninsula

In its native habitat, the sycamore fig is found primarily in savanna areas along riverbanks, where the soil remains humid even during the hot and dry summer. Cultivated today in Egypt, Israel, and Syria, it was introduced to Egypt during the First Dynasty (3000 BCE). In the absence of its pollinators, tiny insects called the chalcidoid wasps, the Egyptians worked out a way to cause the fruit to develop without fertilization. The wood of the tree was frequently used for the construction of coffins (sarcophagi). **BARK** Greenish yellow to creamy brown, smooth. **LEAF** Alternate, ovate to elliptic, rough to the touch, heart-shaped base, slightly wavy margin. **FLOWER** Males and females borne on the same tree, enclosed in a fig receptacle, minute; males near the opening of the fig, females below. **FRUIT** Green fig, turning yellowish to reddish when ripe.

spreading crown

TRUNK | short and buttressed

Ficus sumatrana

Strangler Fig

HEIGHT up to 130 ft (40 m)
TYPE Evergreen
OCCURRENCE S.E. Asia

Like its many relatives, this rainforest fig is a parasite that uses other trees for support. It begins life high in the forest canopy, as a seed dispersed by birds. Initially, the young fig takes root among mosses and dead leaves, but as it grows, it sends out long roots that snake their way to the ground. Over a period of years, these roots surround the host tree's trunk, preventing further growth. Eventually, the host tree dies and rots away, leaving the fig standing in its place. **BARK** Pale brown to grayish white. **LEAF** Alternate, elliptic to ovate-oblong. **FLOWER** Males and females in a fig receptacle; males near the opening, females beneath, **FRUIT** Yellowish to orange-red fig, with minute hairs.

aerial root

smooth texture

STRANGLER CLASPING HOST

Maclura pomifera

Osage Orange

HEIGHT up to 65 ft (20 m)
TYPE Deciduous
OCCURRENCE S. and C. United States

Often used as a hedge plant outside its native habitat, this tree was cultivated extensively by American Indians for its roots and durable wood, which was used for making weapons and a yellow dye. It has a short trunk and an irregular to rounded crown. **BARK** Orange-brown, scaly ridges with irregular furrows, with milky sap. **LEAF** Alternate, ovate to oblong-lanceolate, smooth surface, glossy dark green above, turning yellow in fall. **FLOWER** Males and females on separate trees, both small and inconspicuous; males: in short, terminal racemes; females: in flower heads. **FRUIT** Cluster of green to orange syncarps.

untoothed margins

clusters up to ⅜ in (1 cm) long

yellow-green flowers

to 14 in (10 cm) wide

pointed tip

LEAVES

FRUIT

FLOWERS

Milicia excelsa

Iroko

HEIGHT up to 165 ft (50 m)
TYPE Deciduous
OCCURRENCE Tropical Africa

Also known as the African teak, the iroko has a straight and cylindrical trunk, usually with short buttresses. It is one of the most important timber trees of Africa, often used as a teak substitute. East Africa once was a major source, but the tree has been logged out in the region. West Africa, despite overexploitation, remains an important supplier. The timber is used mainly for construction. **BARK** Gray to brown-black, rough; exudes white latex. **LEAF** Alternate, elliptic, 4–8 in (10–20 cm) long. **FLOWER** Males and females on separate trees; males: white, borne on slender, pendent, catkinlike spikes; females: greenish, in short cylindrical spikes. **FRUIT** Wrinkled, fleshy, caterpillar-like syncarp, green, 2–3 in (5–7.5 cm) long, 1 in (2.5 cm) thick.

brown to dark-brown wood

IROKO WOOD

Morus alba

White Mulberry

HEIGHT up to 45 ft (14 m)
TYPE Deciduous
OCCURRENCE Native to C. and N. China, cultivated in Asia, Europe, United States

In about 550 CE, two monks smuggled silk-worm eggs and seeds of the white mulberry, the food plant of silkworms, out of China. This led to the start of the European silk industry, breaking the monopoly of the "Silk Road" trade from Asia. Usually, the tree has a spreading round crown, but there are cultivars with pyramidal and pendulous forms, large or cut-leaved forms, and several non-fruiting varieties used for landscaping. **BARK** Pale brown to gray, smooth; later develops scaly ridges.

LEAF Alternate, toothed, ovate to rounded, smooth above, hairy below. **FLOWER** Small, green; males: in pendent, spikelike inflorescences; females: in compact clusters. **FRUIT** In clusters, stalked, fleshy, edible syncarps, purple-red when ripe.

leaf to 8 in (20 cm) long

fruit to 1 in (2.5 cm) long

LEAVES AND FRUIT

spreading crown

Morus nigra

Black Mulberry

HEIGHT up to 33 ft (10 m)
TYPE Deciduous
OCCURRENCE Native to W. Iran, cultivated in China, W. Asia, Europe

Since antiquity, this tree has been popular in southern Europe for its edible fruit. **BARK** Orange-brown, ridged, fissured. **LEAF** Alternate, broadly ovate, roughly hairy above, smooth beneath. **FLOWER** Small, green; males in pendent racemes; females in clusters. **FRUIT** Fleshy syncarps in clusters, purple-red when ripe.

toothed leaf margin

LEAVES AND FRUIT

fruit to 1 in (2.5 cm) long

Cecropia peltata

Trumpet Tree

HEIGHT up to 65 ft (20 m)
TYPE Evergreen/Deciduous
OCCURRENCE C. and N. South America, West Indies, naturalized in parts of Africa

In the rainforests, Aztec ants inhabit the hollow stems of this tree. **BARK** Gray-brown, smooth, ringed. **LEAF** Alternate, rounded, dark green, rough above, dense white hairs beneath. **FLOWER** Yellowish green, small, in drooping, catkinlike spikes. **FRUIT** Long, thin, pencil-like pod, fleshy.

lobed leaves   **BRANCHES**

Musanga cecropioides

Umbrella Tree

HEIGHT up to 65 ft (20 m)
TYPE Semi-evergreen
OCCURRENCE Africa (Guinea to Zaire, Angola, and eastward to Uganda)

Fast-growing and invasive, the umbrella tree has a straight trunk, conspicuous roots, and a spreading crown. Its light wood is used to make floats and rafts. **BARK** Gray to brownish green, smooth with large lenticels. **LEAF** Alternate, 12–15 oblanceolate leaflets radiating from stalk tip, grayish-white feltlike hair below. **FLOWER** Axillary, males in branched clusters; females in compact heads on long stalks. **FRUIT** Yellowish green, oval, succulent.

LEAVES

Dendrocnide excelsa

Gympie Stinger

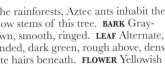

HEIGHT 33–130 ft (10–40 m)
TYPE Deciduous
OCCURRENCE E. Australia (New South Wales and Queensland)

The stinging hairs on the leaves of this tree contain a virulent poison. **BARK** Yellowish gray, ringed. **LEAF** Alternate, with toothed margins. **FLOWER** Yellowish green, small. **FRUIT** Small achene, on a fleshy stalk.

LEAVES

heart-shaped base

Dendrosicyos socotranus

Cucumber Tree

HEIGHT up to 20 ft (6 m)
TYPE Deciduous
OCCURRENCE Yemen (Socotra Island)

Sometimes cultivated as a succulent, this tree is found among coastal vegetation. **BARK** Pallid dirty white. **LEAF** Alternate, ovate to round, five-lobed, tendrils absent. **FLOWER** Yellow, borne on the same plant in axillary clusters. **FRUIT** Orange, cylindrical berry with a beaked tip.

pendulous branches

thick trunk

Nothofagus cunninghamii
Myrtle Beech

HEIGHT up to 100 ft (30 m)
TYPE Evergreen
OCCURRENCE Australia (Victoria, Tasmania)

A large rainforest tree, this species can also grow as a shrub at high altitudes. **BARK** Dark, scaly. **LEAF** Alternate, small, ovate, bluntly toothed margin, base tapered to blunt. **FLOWER** Males and females in groups of 1–4. **FRUIT** Husk (cupule), usually containing three nuts.

Nothofagus antarctica
Antarctic Beech

HEIGHT up to 115 ft (35 m)
TYPE Deciduous
OCCURRENCE South America (Chile)

The Antarctic beech was introduced into cultivation in 1830. **BARK** Gray, scaly. **LEAF** Alternate, ovate, often heart-shaped, sometimes shallowly lobed. **FLOWER** Males and females in groups of 1–4. **FRUIT** Husk (cupule) with three nuts.

fruit husk

wavy leaf margin

BRANCHLET WITH FRUIT

Nothofagus solanderi
Black Beech

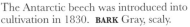

HEIGHT up to 80 ft (25 m)
TYPE Evergreen
OCCURRENCE New Zealand

The timber of this tree is used for general construction. **BARK** Black, rough, and furrowed. **LEAF** Alternate, elliptic-oblong, dark green, smooth above, grayish white hairs below **FLOWER** Males and females in groups of 1–4. **FRUIT** Husk (cupule), containing 2–3 nuts.

short point on leaf tip

FOLIAGE

Castanea dentata
American Chestnut

HEIGHT 16–33 ft (5–10 m)
TYPE Deciduous
OCCURRENCE N. United States

Decimated by chestnut blight, this species is now rare in the wild. **BARK** Dark grayish brown, scaly. **LEAF** Alternate. **FLOWER** Males in long spikes; females on spikes or at the base. **FRUIT** Spiny husk, with 2–3 nuts.

LEAVES

lanceolate-oblong

FRUIT

LEAVES

coarse, bristly teeth

Castanea sativa

European Chestnut

HEIGHT up to 100 ft (30 m)
TYPE Deciduous
OCCURRENCE S.E. Europe, naturalized elsewhere

The European chestnut has been cultivated for 3,000 years. In some parts of Europe, the fruit formed an important food source and item of exchange because it could be ground into flour. The expansion of the tanning industry, which uses its bark, coincided with the "ink disease" that infected European trees in the late 19th century. This led to a rapid reduction of the chestnut forests. Alcohol can be made from the fruit; chestnut beer is still produced in Corsica. Today, China and Korea supply 55 percent of the annual production of chestnuts. **BARK** Gray, smooth, becoming fissured and spirally twisted. **LEAF** Alternate, oblong-lanceolate, dull dark green above, paler and hairy below. **FLOWER** Small, creamy yellow, in pendulous, spikelike catkins. **FRUIT** Spiny husk, enclosing 2–3 nuts.

green husks

FRUIT

male and female flowers clustered on same spike

FLOWERS

FAVORED NUTS

Before potatoes were introduced, chestnuts were the basic food of the poor in much of southern Europe. Today, throughout most of Europe, cultivated chestnuts are a delicacy. Roasted chestnuts are a wintertime favorite on both sides of the Atlantic.

Castanea pumila

Chinkapin

HEIGHT up to 50 ft (15 m)
TYPE Deciduous
OCCURRENCE S.E. United States

The chinkapin is often shrubby and forms dense thickets. **BARK** Reddish brown, platelike scales. **LEAF** Alternate, elliptic-oblong, sharply toothed, gray hairs below. **FLOWER** Yellowish; males in erect spikes; females solitary, short-stalked. **FRUIT** Nut surrounded by a spiny husk.

FLOWERING SHOOT

yellow-green leaf

flowers in catkins

Chrysolepis chrysophylla

Giant Chinkapin

HEIGHT 50–100 ft (15–30 m)
TYPE Evergreen
OCCURRENCE S.W. United States

This broadly conical tree is often used as an ornamental. **BARK** Dark red-brown, with scales and ridges. **LEAF** Alternate, leathery, lanceolate, dark green above, golden yellow below. **FLOWER** Creamy white; male catkins on erect spikes; female stalkless. **FRUIT** Nutlets, about 1–3, surrounded by a spiny husk, which ripens in two years.

male flower

LEAVES, FLOWERS, AND FRUIT

Fagus crenata

Japanese Beech

HEIGHT up to 100 ft (30 m)
TYPE Deciduous
OCCURRENCE Japan

The Japanese beech is considered to be the finest beech species for bonsai because of its small, neat foliage and thin, delicate twigs. Like the European beech, the bark turns white with age. **BARK** Gray, smooth. **LEAF** Alternate, ovate to elliptic, with wavy margins. **FLOWER** Males in catkins; females inconspicuous in leaf axils. **FRUIT** Husk with long bristles, splitting into four to reveal the nut.

FOLIAGE

glossy green leaves

Fagus grandifolia

American Beech

HEIGHT 70–80 ft (20–24 m)
TYPE Deciduous
OCCURRENCE N.E. United States

The American beech produces abundant fruit every 3–5 years. **BARK** Blue-gray, smooth. **LEAF** Alternate, ovate-oblong, 9–14 lateral veins, dark green, with coarsely toothed margin. **FLOWER** Males in drooping clusters; tiny females in the leaf axils. **FRUIT** Nut, enclosed by husk.

FALL FOLIAGE

female flower

Fagus sylvatica

European Beech

HEIGHT up to 100 ft (30 m)
TYPE Deciduous
OCCURRENCE Europe, excluding the north

A slow-growing tree with a majestic, spreading crown, the European beech casts a deep shade when it is in full leaf. Its fine-grained timber is used for furniture and parquet floors. There are many cultivars—pendulous, columnar, and cut-leaved—which may have green, purple, or variegated leaves.
BARK Smooth, blue-gray. **LEAF** Alternate, ovate to elliptic, with silky hairs, margins with rounded teeth, 5–9 lateral veins.

glossy dark green

to 2–4 in (5–10 cm) long

FRUIT

FLOWER Yellow males in pendulous clusters; green females, inconspicuous, in leaf axils. **FRUIT** Woody husk that has long, straight bristles and splits into four to reveal one or two edible nuts.

Quercus alba

White Oak

HEIGHT 80–100 ft (25–30 m)
TYPE Deciduous
OCCURRENCE N.E. North America

The wood of the White Oak is used for furniture, flooring, and veneers. **BARK** Pale gray, divided into narrow, flat scales. **LEAF** Alternate, oblong to ovate lobes, hairy when young. **FLOWER** Yellow-green males in catkins; bright red, unstalked females. **FRUIT** Rounded acorn that matures in the first season.

untoothed lobes

scaly cup

ACORN

LEAVES

Quercus coccinea

Scarlet Oak

HEIGHT up to 80 ft (25 m)
TYPE Deciduous
OCCURRENCE E. North America

This widespread American oak gets its name from its spectacular fall colors. **BARK** Pale gray-brown with irregular ridges. **LEAF** Alternate, elliptic, dark green above, triangular-toothed lobes. **FLOWER** Males in slender catkins; females on short hairy stalks. **FRUIT** Acorn enclosed up to one-half in a glossy cup.

FALL LEAVES

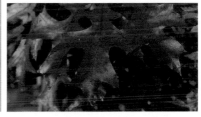

Quercus cerris

European Turkey Oak

HEIGHT up to 115 ft (35 m)
TYPE Deciduous
OCCURRENCE C. and S. Europe

Long, frilly, threadlike stipules, which surround the buds, characterize this oak. **BARK** Dark brown, furrowed. **LEAF** Alternate, oval or oblong, 4–9 pairs of lobes. **FLOWER** Males in yellow-green catkins; females unstalked. **FRUIT** Acorn.

variable leaf lobing

LEAVES

Quercus ilex

Holly Oak

HEIGHT 65–90 ft (20–27 m)
TYPE Evergreen
OCCURRENCE S. Europe

This spreading, extremely hardy tree is considered an excellent species for cultivation. **BARK** Gray to blackish, scaly, divided into small squares. **LEAF** Alternate, ovate to lanceolate, glossy dark green above, whitish down beneath that turns gray with age. **FLOWER** Males in catkins; females on short, downy stalks. **FRUIT** Acorn enclosed in a scaly cup.

rounded crown

BEECH
The graceful beech (*Fagus sylvatica*) is sometimes named "the Lady of the Woods." Beech woods are a rich habitat for many animals who feed on beech nuts, including squirrels and wild boar. This beech forest is located in Hertfordshire, England.

Quercus imbricaria

Shingle Oak

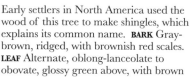

HEIGHT 65–100 ft (20–30 m)
TYPE Deciduous
OCCURRENCE W. to N.E. United States

Early settlers in North America used the wood of this tree to make shingles, which explains its common name. **BARK** Gray-brown, ridged, with brownish red scales. **LEAF** Alternate, oblong-lanceolate to obovate, glossy green above, with brown hairs beneath. **FLOWER** Males in golden yellow catkins; females on short, stout stalks. **FRUIT** Acorn, one-third to one-half covered by cup.

ACORN

overlapping red-brown scales

LEAVES

Quercus macrolepis

Valonia Oak

HEIGHT up to 50 ft (15 m)
TYPE Semi-deciduous
OCCURRENCE S. Europe to W. Asia

The acorn cups of this tree have a high content of tannin and were formerly in high demand, with Turkey being the leading exporter. **BARK** Dark, fissured. **LEAF** Alternate, elliptic to oblong, with 3–7 pairs of triangular, bristle-tipped lobes; smooth above, densely woolly beneath. **FLOWER** Males in catkins; females on short stalks. **FRUIT** Acorns, up to 2 in (5 cm) wide, with elongated scales.

Quercus pubescens

Downy Oak

HEIGHT 50–65 ft (15–20 m)
TYPE Deciduous
OCCURRENCE S. Europe, W. Asia

up to 4 in (10 cm) long

shallow lobes

LEAVES

This oak has a broadly spreading crown and hairy young shoots. **BARK** Gray-brown, deeply furrowed. **LEAF** Alternate, obovate, deeply cut into 4–8 pairs of lobes, dark gray-green above, paler gray-green, with velvety hairs beneath. **FLOWER** Males in drooping catkins; females inconspicuous, on short stalks. **FRUIT** Ovoid acorn, up to 1½ in (4 cm) long, one-third to one-half enclosed in a cup covered with dense, overlapping, downy scales; ripens in the tree's first year.

Quercus petraea

Sessile Oak

HEIGHT 80–130 ft (25–40 m)
TYPE Deciduous
OCCURRENCE Europe, W. Asia

Also called durmast oak, this tree is often found on light, poor soils. **BARK** Fissured, gray-brown. **LEAF** Alternate, obovate, smooth beneath, with an acute base, distinctly stalked. **FLOWER** Males in catkins; females on short stalks. **FRUIT** Ovoid acorns, in stalkless clusters.

rounded lobes

LEAVES

Quercus robur

English Oak

HEIGHT 80–130 ft (25–40 m)
TYPE Deciduous
OCCURRENCE Europe, W. Asia, N. Africa

Also known as pedunculate oak, this tree has a spreading habit and smooth shoots. Oak forests were once a valuable resource for industrial and naval activities. Its bark is also used in the tanning industry. A famous heritage tree in Britain is "The Major" in Sherwood Forest, which is estimated to be 800 years old; legend has it that Robin Hood hid in this tree. **BARK** Grayish brown, vertically ridged. **LEAF** Alternate, obovate, with 5–9 lobes, dark green above, blue-green beneath. **FLOWER** Males in drooping catkins; females inconspicuous, on short stalks. **FRUIT** Ovoid, long-stalked acorns, one-third to one-half enclosed in a cup, initially green, ripening to brown in first year.

lobed leaves

young acorn

UNRIPE ACORNS

fissured surface

overlapping scales on cup

BARK

MATURE ACORN

SHIPBUILDING

From Viking longboats to Lord Nelson's flagship, HMS *Victory*, oak has a long history in shipbuilding. Some 6,000 oak trees were used to build the *Victory*. Trees planted in 1802 are now being used to repair the same ship.

LONGBOAT

SESSILE OAK
Quercus petraea is the species from which French oak wine barrels are usually made. These trees can grow up to 130 ft (40 m) tall and may live for up to 1,000 years, although in a woodland setting such as this, they may not reach such great stature or age.

Quercus rubra

Red Oak

HEIGHT 60–80 ft (18–25 m)
TYPE Deciduous
OCCURRENCE E. North America

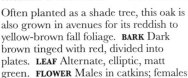

Often planted as a shade tree, this oak is also grown in avenues for its reddish to yellow-brown fall foliage. **BARK** Dark brown tinged with red, divided into plates. **LEAF** Alternate, elliptic, matt green. **FLOWER** Males in catkins; females on short stalks. **FRUIT** Large acorns.

bristle-tipped lobes

in shallow cup

LEAF　　　　　　　**ACORNS**

Quercus velutina

Black Oak

HEIGHT 70–80 ft (20–25 m)
TYPE Deciduous
OCCURRENCE C. and
N.E. North America

The black oak has a broadly spreading habit. Its bark was formerly used in the tanning industry and to prepare a yellow dye. **BARK** Dark brown to black, with a scaly surface. **LEAF** Alternate, ovate to oblong, 3–4 pairs of triangular-toothed lobes, glossy above, slightly hairy below with tufts of rusty hairs in the vein axils. **FLOWER** Males in slender catkins; females on short, hairy stalks. **FRUIT** Ovoid acorns, enclosed halfway in the cup, maturing in the second year.

large terminal tooth

ridged and furrowed

MATURE BARK

LEAVES

Quercus macrocarpa

Bur Oak

HEIGHT up to 130 ft (40 m)
TYPE Deciduous
OCCURRENCE E. North America

The acorns of this broadly spreading tree are larger than those of any other North American oak. **BARK** Gray, rough, deeply furrowed. **LEAF** Obovate, deeply cut into round-ended lobes, broader toward the base, glossy green and smooth above, paler and hairy beneath. **FLOWER** Males in yellow, drooping catkins; females inconspicuous, borne separately on the same plant. **FRUIT** Acorn, enclosed in a cup that is rimmed with a fringe of scales.

widely spaced lobes

LEAVES

Quercus suber

Cork Oak

HEIGHT up to 65 ft (20 m)
TYPE Evergreen
OCCURRENCE W. Mediterranean, especially Portugal

Cork forests form an environmentally friendly ecosystem, rich in wildlife. These broadly spreading trees grow on hills in open woodland. The cork is harvested every 9–12 years. Bottle corks account for 15 percent of production by weight but 65 percent of value of a $3 billion industry. Stripping the bark, from which cork is produced, does not damage the living tissue of the plant, which grows a new outer layer within a few years. **BARK** Thick, furrowed, and corky, with prominent ridges. **LEAF** Alternate, ovate to oblong, toothed margins, covered with minute gray felt beneath. **FLOWER** Males: borne in slender catkins; females: inconspicuous, on short downy stalks, borne separately on the same plant. **FRUIT** Acorn, enclosed halfway in the cup, covered by elongated gray-brown scales, matures in the first season.

CORKY OLD WHISTLER

The oldest cork oak is the "Whistler" (so called because of the numerous songbirds nesting in its canopy), which was planted in 1783 and last harvested in 2000. Located in the Alentejo region of Portugal, it has been producing cork every nine years since 1820. The average Cork Oak produces enough for 4,000 corks per harvest; the Whistler produces about 100,000 corks.

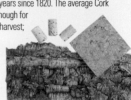

CORK

pale gray brown

BARK

2¼ in (7 cm) long

dark green above

LEAVES

Morella cerifera

Wax Myrtle

HEIGHT 20–40 ft (6–12 m)
TYPE Evergreen
OCCURRENCE S.E. United States

The leaves of this tree are aromatic when crushed. Early European settlers would boil the fruit and skim off the wax, which could then be used to make candles. **BARK** Smooth, pale gray. **LEAF** Alternate, oblanceolate, usually coarsely toothed above center; dark glands above, bright orange glands beneath. **FLOWER** Males and females on separate trees, both in short, spikelike catkins. **FRUIT** Spherical, pale green drupe.

yellow-green leaves

LEAVES

fruit coated with pale bluish wax

BRANCH WITH FRUIT

Morella faya

Fire Tree

HEIGHT up to 26 ft (8 m)
TYPE Evergreen
OCCURRENCE Azores, Canary Islands, Madeira Islands, naturalized in Hawaii

Introduced into Hawaii by Portuguese laborers who made wine from the fruit, this tree has since become a serious invasive weed, although it is not invasive in its native habitat. **BARK** Smooth, brownish gray. **LEAF** Alternate, oblanceolate, smooth surface but dotted with tiny glands, margins untoothed or irregularly and bluntly toothed toward the tip. **FLOWER** Males and females on separate trees in short, spikelike catkins. **FRUIT** Fleshy, glistening drupe.

LEAVES AND FRUIT

1½–4¼ in (4–11 cm) long

dark red to black drupe

Alnus crispa

Green Alder

HEIGHT 10–26 ft (3–8 m)
TYPE Deciduous
OCCURRENCE E. North America

The bark of the green alder has some astringent qualities and has been used medicinally by American Indians. The aromatic young leaves are slightly sticky to the touch. **BARK** Reddish to grayish brown, smooth or slightly grooved. **LEAF** Alternate, ovate to broadly elliptic, toothed margins, smooth or slightly hairy beneath. **FLOWER** Males: pale yellowish green, in pendulous catkins; females: red, solitary, and small. **FRUIT** Woody, winged, conelike.

FRUIT

long stalks

Alnus glutinosa

European Alder

HEIGHT up to 80 ft (25 m)
TYPE Deciduous
OCCURRENCE Europe, W. Asia, N. Africa

Also known as the black alder, this water-loving tree is commonly seen along watersides and riverbanks, where it provides both erosion control and ornamental appeal. It has a straight trunk and a narrow crown. Its wood has been used extensively in constructing buildings near water because it does not rot when wet. It was also popular with clog-makers in Britain. Since the alder grows on relatively infertile soils, it is also used for site reclamation. **BARK** Smooth on young trees, becoming dark grayish black, fissured, and scaly. **LEAF** Alternate, usually obovate, green beneath, with coarsely double-toothed margins; smooth or with tufts of hairs in the vein axils; 5–10 pairs of lateral veins; young leaves and twigs sticky. **FLOWER** Males and females on same tree; males: reddish brown, in drooping catkins; females: red, solitary. **FRUIT** Woody, oval, conelike.

VENICE ON PILINGS

Built on islands in a lagoon of the Adriatic Sea between the 9th and 16th centuries, most of Venice is supported on pilings. These slender, sharpened poles were made from alder wood, which is ideal for the job because of its durability in water. The foundations of buildings in Venice consisted of oak wood planks and layers of marble placed over pilings.

LEAVES AND FRUIT

leaf 1½–3½ in
(4–9 cm) long

unripe fruit

male catkins
in clusters

FLOWERS

Alnus incana
Gray Alder

HEIGHT up to 65 ft (20 m)
TYPE Deciduous
OCCURRENCE N. and N.E. Europe,
North America, W. Asia

Also called black alder, this tree is found on flood plains and in mountain valleys. **BARK** Yellowish gray, smooth. **LEAF** Ovate, alternate, slightly lobed, double-toothed margins. **FLOWER** Borne separately on the same plant; males: reddish, in catkins, females: solitary, red, upright. **FRUIT** Woody, conelike.

fruit

male catkins

LEAVES, FLOWERS, AND FRUIT

Betula alleghaniensis
Yellow Birch

HEIGHT 80–100 ft (25–30 m)
TYPE Deciduous
OCCURRENCE C. and E. North America

About 75 percent of birch lumber comes from the yellow birch. **BARK** Silvery yellow-brown, peeling into ribbonlike strips. **LEAF** Alternate, ovate to oblong, double-toothed margins. **FLOWER** Borne on the same tree in catkins; males: yellow, drooping, females: reddish green, upright, cone-like. **FRUIT** Winged nutlets.

peels horizontally

large catkins

BARK   **MALE FLOWERS**

Betula lenta
Sweet Birch

HEIGHT 65–80 ft (20–25 m)
TYPE Deciduous
OCCURRENCE E. North America

This broadly spreading tree can be found in moist woods or on mountains. **BARK** Divided by fissures into large plates, does not peel. **LEAF** Alternate, sharply toothed margins, smooth or slightly hairy below; seven or more lateral veins. **FLOWER** Borne on the same tree, in catkins; males: yellow, drooping, females: green, upright, ovoid. **FRUIT** Winged nutlets borne in an oval, upright, conelike structure.

LEAVES

pointed tip

reddish brown

BARK

Betula utilis
Himalayan Birch

HEIGHT 55–115 ft (17–35 m)
TYPE Deciduous
OCCURRENCE Himalayas

The word "birch" is thought to have been derived from the Sanskrit word *bhurga*, "tree whose bark is used to write upon." The oldest surviving manuscripts, from Buddhist monasteries, date back 2,000 years. **BARK** Yellowish red-brown, peeling. **LEAF** Alternate, ovate to broadly elliptic, double-toothed margins. **FLOWER** Males and females borne on the same tree in catkins; males: yellow, drooping, females: green, upright. **FRUIT** Winged nutlets borne in an oval, upright, conelike structure.

conical to columnar crown

Paper Birch

HEIGHT up to 100 ft (30 m)
TYPE Deciduous
OCCURRENCE E. to W. North America

A fast-growing conical tree, the paper birch has resinous bark that is impervious to water and was used to make canoes and roofing for wigwams. **BARK** Creamy-white, peeling in thin layers to expose a pinkish orange layer beneath. **LEAF** Alternate, margins coarsely double-toothed, dark green above, often hairy on veins beneath. **FLOWER** Borne separately on the same tree, in drooping catkins; males: yellow, females: green. **FRUIT** Winged nutlets.

ovate leaves

numerous horizontal lenticels

green, drooping catkins

LEAVES AND FEMALE CATKINS   **BARK**

European White Birch

HEIGHT up to 65 ft (20 m)
TYPE Deciduous
OCCURRENCE Europe, W. and N. Asia

A short-lived pioneer species, the European white birch has a distinctive pendulous habit. **BARK** Smooth, pale yellow-brown, becoming white with age and developing dark, rough cracks. **LEAF** Alternate, ovate to triangular with coarsely double-toothed margins. **FLOWER** Borne in catkins on the same tree; males: yellow, drooping, females: green, upright, later pendulous, cylindrical. **FRUIT** Winged nutlets borne in catkins.

female catkin

double-toothed margins   **LEAVES AND FLOWER**

Carpinus betulus

European Hornbeam

HEIGHT up to 80 ft (25 m)
TYPE Deciduous
OCCURRENCE Europe, S.W. Asia

This tree has a fluted trunk and a broadly spreading habit. It is commonly planted as hedging or as a street tree. Its cultivars are the columnar 'Fastigiata', the pendulous 'Pendula', and 'Variegata' and 'Purpurea', which have variegated or purple leaves. **BARK** Smooth, gray, becoming slightly fissured with age. **LEAF** Alternate, ovate to oblong, double-toothed, 7–15 pairs of lateral veins, dark green above, downy beneath, usually turning yellow in fall. **FLOWER** In pendulous catkins on the same plant; males axillary, females at tips of shoots. **FRUIT** Nutlet at the base of a green, three-lobed bract, with 3–5 veins.

yellow-brown male catkins

green female catkins

FLOWERING SHOOT

Carpinus caroliniana

American Hornbeam

HEIGHT up to 40 ft (12 m)
TYPE Deciduous
OCCURRENCE E. North America, Mexico

Also called the blue beech, this tree has a fluted trunk. **BARK** Smooth, pale gray-brown, sometimes with dark horizontal bands. **LEAF** Alternate, ovate to oblong, 7–15 pairs of lateral veins, dark green above, downy on veins below, usually turning orange-red in fall. **FLOWER** In pendulous catkins on the same plant; males: yellowish, axillary, females: green, at tips of shoots. **FRUIT** Nutlet at the base of a green, three-lobed bract, usually toothed, with 5–7 veins.

double-toothed margin

LEAF

Corylus avellana

Hazelnut

HEIGHT up to 20 ft (6 m)
TYPE Deciduous
OCCURRENCE Europe

This shrubby, spreading tree often forms thickets. It has multiple stems and is known for its edible nuts, also called filberts. It has many cultivars, such as 'Contorta', the interesting horticultural corkscrew hazel cultivar, which has markedly twisted branches. There are also three rare cultivars—'Aurea', a yellow-leaved form, the cut-leaved 'Heterophylla', and the weeping 'Pendula'. **BARK** Smooth, copper brown, sometimes peeling in thin strips. **LEAF** Alternate, dark green, rounded to broadly obovate, double-toothed. **FLOWER** Males and females on the same plant; males: in long catkins, females: small, bud-like, with red stigmas. **FRUIT** Nut surrounded by a bractlike husk only slightly longer than the nut.

HAZEL COPPICES

The shoots of the hazelnut are often coppiced or cut back to encourage thick growth of its branches. They were once used to make hoops for barrels; they are still used to make woven fences, thatching spars, and hedges. The remains were bundled as "faggots" for fuel.

COPPICING

deeply lobed husk

to 4 in (10 cm) long

pale yellow catkins

NUTS

LEAVES

MALE FLOWERS

Corylus maxima
Giant Filbert

HEIGHT up to 33 ft (10 m)
TYPE Deciduous
OCCURRENCE S.E. Europe, W. Asia

This often shrublike tree usually has several main stems and a spreading habit. It is often grown in orchards (sometimes known as "plats") for its edible cobnuts. **BARK** Gray-brown, smooth, with horizontal lenticels. **LEAF** Alternate, broadly ovate to obovate, double-toothed, dark green, usually turning yellow in fall. **FLOWER** Males: in long, drooping yellow catkins; females: small, budlike, with red stigmas. **FRUIT** Softly hairy nut with a notched tip, in a husk.

pale brown shell
RIPE FRUIT
LEAF
to 4¾ in (12 cm) long
bractlike husk

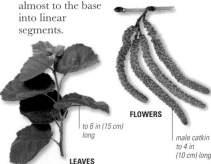

male catkin to 3¼ in (8 cm) long
FLOWERS
UNRIPE FRUIT

Corylus colurna
Turkish Hazel

HEIGHT up to 80 ft (25 m)
TYPE Deciduous
OCCURRENCE S.E. Europe, W. Asia

Widely planted as an ornamental in parks and gardens, this hazel is also useful as a street tree. It has a compact and conical head. It rarely sets fruit in northern latitudes. **BARK** Dark gray, corky, deeply furrowed. **LEAF** Alternate, ovate to broadly ovate, rarely obovate, double-toothed margins, dark green, usually turning yellow in fall. **FLOWER** Males and females on the same plant, appearing before the leaves; males: in long, drooping, pale yellow catkins; females: small, budlike, with red stigmas. **FRUIT** Edible nut surrounded by a bractlike husk, divided almost to the base into linear segments.

to 6 in (15 cm) long
FLOWERS
male catkin to 4 in (10 cm) long
LEAVES

Ostrya carpinifolia
Hop Hornbeam

HEIGHT up to 65 ft (20 m)
TYPE Deciduous
OCCURRENCE S. Europe, W. Asia

The wood of this tree is very hard and tough and has been used for handles, levers, and mallets. **BARK** Gray-brown, smooth when young, becoming vertically fissured and scaly. **LEAF** Alternate, ovate, with double-toothed margins, sparsely hairy on both sides, 12–15 pairs of lateral veins, usually turning yellow in fall. **FLOWER** Males and females on the same plant in pendulous catkins; males: yellow, axillary; females: green, at tips of shoots, tiny. **FRUIT** Drooping, conelike structure consisting of a nut within a creamy, bladderlike husk.

FRUIT AND LEAVES

Casuarina equisetifolia

Beefwood

HEIGHT 20–115 ft (6–35 m)
TYPE Evergreen
OCCURRENCE Myanmar, Malaysia, Indonesia,
Philippines, Papua New Guinea, Polynesia,
N. and N.E. Australia

STABILIZED SAND DUNES

Beefwood roots contain nitrogen-fixing bacteria, which enable it to flourish in soils that are too poor for other trees. As a result, it can be used to stabilize dunes and to control soil erosion. In exposed areas, it can also be used as windbreaks to protect crops.

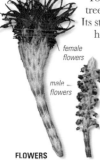

female flowers

male flowers

FLOWERS

Found on coastlines, this tree is sometimes invasive. Its stems resemble horsetails and the wood is an excellent source of fuel and charcoal. **BARK** Gray-brown to black, scaly, becoming fissured. **LEAF** Scalelike, tiny, 4–10 in each whorl, borne on green stems. **FLOWER** Males and females on the same tree; males: in cylindrical spikes at tips of twigs; females: in red-brown heads along branches. **FRUIT** Small, round, conelike nutlet, with winged seeds.

LEAVES

Carya illinoinensis

Pecan

HEIGHT 100–180 ft (30–55 m)
TYPE Deciduous
OCCURRENCE S. North America

Commercial cultivation of the pecan tree began by the end of the 19th century. It is now widely grown on plantations in the US, especially Texas, which has chosen it as its state tree. There are over 500 cultivars. **BARK** Pale gray-brown tinged with red, furrowed and deeply ridged, scaly surface.

FLOWERS — *yellow-green male catkins*

slightly curved at tips

green husk

LEAF **FRUIT**

LEAF Alternate, pinnate; 9–17 lanceolate, coarsely toothed leaflets. **FLOWER** Small and petalless; males in axillary pendulous catkins; females stalkless, in terminal spikes. **FRUIT** Reddish brown, ovoid-oblong, thin-shelled nut containing grooved, edible seeds.

CENTENNIAL NUTS

In 1846, an African American slave gardener from Louisiana successfully grafted a superior wild pecan to seedling pecan stocks. This increased the tree's productivity significantly and led to the development of the variety called "Centennial," from which the 500 current varieties originate.

PECANS

Juglans cinerea

Butternut

HEIGHT up to 100 ft (30 m)
TYPE Deciduous
OCCURRENCE E. and C. North America

Formerly used for paneling, butternut is seldom planted as an ornamental. In the wild, it is highly prone to butternut canker, a virulent fungal disease. **BARK** Gray, deeply fissured, with small scales on the ridges. **LEAF** Alternate, pinnate, with 11–17 oblong-lanceolate, coarsely toothed leaflets, hairy on both sides. **FLOWER** Small, petalless; males in axillary hanging catkins; females stalkless, in few-flowered spikes. **FRUIT** Egg-shaped nuts in clusters of 3–5, with sweet, oily seeds.

pointed green husk

unequal, rounded base

LEAVES

FRUIT

Juglans nigra

Black Walnut

HEIGHT up to 165 ft (50 m)
TYPE Deciduous
OCCURRENCE North America

This shade-intolerant tree secretes a substance that prevents vegetation from growing around it. Its timber is used for cabinets and veneers. **BARK** Dark gray-brown to blackish, with deep, scaly ridges. **LEAF** Alternate, pinnate, with 11–19 ovate-lanceolate, coarsely toothed leaflets. **FLOWER** Small, petalless; males in axillary catkins; females stalkless, in few-flowered spikes. **FRUIT** Spherical, ribbed nut, solitary or in pairs.

green husk

pointed tips

LEAVES WITH CATKINS

yellow-green male catkins

Juglans regia

English Walnut

HEIGHT up to 100 ft (30 m)
TYPE Deciduous
OCCURRENCE S.E. Europe,
Himalayas to China

The cultivation of the walnut dates back to 7000 BCE. It was introduced into Europe from Persia by the Romans. The first US plantations were established in 1867, and the main area of cultivation is now California. All parts of the fruit are utilized: the cracked shells are ground to form an industrial abrasive, and walnut oil extracted from the kernel is used as a salad oil. **BARK** Pale silvery gray, smooth, eventually becoming deeply fissured with age. **LEAF** Alternate, pinnate; 5–9 ovate to elliptic or obovate leaflets, with unequal, rounded bases. **FLOWER** Males and females on the same plant, both small and petalless; males: in axillary pendulous catkins, females: stalkless, on few-flowered spikes. **FRUIT** Round nut borne singly or in pairs, up to 2 in (5 cm) long, with an edible, sweet kernel.

MALE FLOWERS   catkins to 4 in (10 cm) long

FRUIT AND LEAFLETS

green husk of unripe fruit

leaflet to 18 in (45 cm) long

smooth, hard husk

MATURE FRUIT

Pterocarya fraxinifolia

Wingnut

HEIGHT 65–100 ft (20–30 m)
TYPE Deciduous
OCCURRENCE W. Asia, Caucasus

The wingnut has a very wide crown and grows best in moist soil near water. **BARK** Pale gray, smooth, becoming deeply furrowed with age. **LEAF** Alternate, pinnate; ovate to oblong-lanceolate, unstalked leaflets; sharply toothed. **FLOWER** Males and females on the same plant, both small and petalless; males in axillary pendulous catkins, females in very long, pendulous catkins. **FRUIT** Nut with two wings.

LEAVES AND FRUIT

11–25 leaflets

BARK

deep, interlacing ridges

winged fruit in hanging catkin

Carica papaya

Papaya

HEIGHT 6–33 ft (2–10 m)
TYPE Evergreen
OCCURRENCE West Indies, N. South America

A fast-growing tree with hollow stems, the papaya is widely cultivated throughout the tropics for its fruit. The unripe fruit, stems, and leaves produce a latex that contains the enzyme papain. This is used as a dietary supplement to aid digestion and as a meat tenderizer. **BARK** Greenish to gray-brown, smooth, with prominent leaf scars, and thin milky sap. **LEAF** Alternate, clustered at the stem tip, palmately divided into 7–11 lobes. **FLOWER** Males and females on separate trees, with pale

LUSCIOUS FRUIT

The papaya fruit has orange, yellow, or pink creamy, sweet flesh surrounding soft edible black seeds. In its native range, much of the delicate, perishable fruit is grown in home gardens and sold in local markets for fresh consumption, with little entering international trade. **DRIED FRUIT**

FRESH PAPAYA

The fruit needs to be harvested with care—scratching its skin releases latex, which stains the fruit.

yellow or pink petals; males in pendent panicles, females solitary or in few-flowered clusters. **FRUIT** Large ovoid-oblong, fleshy berry, with yellowish orange pulp and black seeds.

fruit weighs up to 22 lb (10 kg)

UNRIPE FRUIT

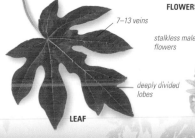

7–13 veins

FLOWERS

stalkless male flowers

deeply divided lobes

LEAF

Vasconcellea x heilbornii

Babaco

HEIGHT 3–7 ft (1–2 m)
TYPE Semi-evergreen
OCCURRENCE Ecuador, known only in cultivation

Also known as mountain papaya, this fast-growing treelike giant herb is thought to be a hybrid between two Andean papayas, *V. pubescens* and *V. stipulata*. **BARK** Greenish to gray-brown, smooth, with prominent leaf scars. **LEAF** Alternate, clustered at the stem tip, rounded, palmate, deeply divided and toothed, with 5–7 lobes, 1–7 veins and a long stalk. **FLOWER** Solitary, each on a pendulous stalk, with yellowish green petals, forming on the trunk during its growth phase. **FRUIT** Large torpedo-shaped green berry, yellow when ripe, borne on the stem; thin, edible skin, creamy flesh.

Moringa oleifera

Horseradish Tree

HEIGHT up to 33 ft (10 m)
TYPE Deciduous
OCCURRENCE N.W. India

European colonists in India used the root of this slender tree as a substitute for horseradish (not advisable as it contains toxic alkaloids, hence the common name). Widely cultivated in the tropics, its leaves, rich in vitamins and minerals, are used as a vegetable supplement. However, the immature green fruit is the most valued part of the plant and is prepared in a fashion similar to green beans. Oil derived from the seeds has been used for cooking, for lubrication, and in cosmetics. **BARK** Pale, smooth to slightly corky. **LEAF** Alternate, three-pinnate, with a terminal leaflet; leaflets ovate to elliptic or oblong, untoothed, finely hairy when young, turning smooth later. **FLOWER** White to cream, borne in large axillary, spreading panicles. **FRUIT** Long, pendulous capsule.

in 4–6 pairs

LEAFLETS

drooping branches

FRUIT

beanlike capsules

Bixa orellana

Annatto

HEIGHT 10–33 ft (3–10 m)
TYPE Evergreen
OCCURRENCE Tropical South America, S.E. Asia

Historically used for making body paint and fabric dye, this bushy tree is now used mainly as a food colorant for dairy products. **BARK** Pale to dark brown, later fissured. **LEAF** Alternate, in spirals, ovate, with a heart-shaped to blunt base. **FLOWER** Large terminal panicles, 5–7 obovate petals, usually pinkish. **FRUIT** Flattened, ellipsoidal capsule, with bristles, bright red when mature.

seeds in red-orange pulp

FRUIT

FLOWERS AND FRUIT

Cochlospermum religiosum

Silk Cotton Tree

HEIGHT up to 33 ft (10 m)
TYPE Deciduous
OCCURRENCE India, Myanmar, Thailand

Mostly found in dry monsoon areas, this small tree is also known as the buttercup tree. It is cultivated within its region for its abundant single yellow flowers, but it is uncommon outside its natural habitat. **BARK** Creamy gray and smooth. **LEAF** Alternate, palmate, with 3–5 divided lobes, softly hairy below, wavy margins. **FLOWER** Large, borne in terminal inflorescences on bare branches, with numerous stamens. **FRUIT** Large open capsule, with woolly seeds.

orange-red stamens

yellow petals

Bombax ceiba

Simul

HEIGHT up to 80 ft (25 m)
TYPE Deciduous
OCCURRENCE Sri Lanka, China, Malaysia, Australia

Often planted as a street tree, the simul is a blaze of color when in flower. **BARK** Grayish white. **LEAF** Alternate, palmate; 5–7 oblong-lanceolate, smooth leaflets. **FLOWER** Solitary, terminal, large, brilliant scarlet, with numerous stamens. **FRUIT** Woody capsule; seeds surrounded by fluffy hairs.

Baobab

Adansonia digitata

HEIGHT 33–80 ft (10–25 m)
TYPE Deciduous
OCCURRENCE Tropical Africa

The baobab, which can live for over 1,000 years, is a focus for myth: it is said that a devil uprooted the tree and replanted it upside down; spirits are linked with its night-opening flowers (the tree is pollinated by bats). The baobab has edible leaves, seeds, and pulp, and the inner bark is used to make rope. The massive trunk stores water, which can be tapped for drinking. **BARK** Grayish brown, tinged mauve, smooth. **LEAF** Alternate, digitate, with 5–7 elliptic-oblong to ovate leaflets that are hairy below when young. **FLOWER** Axillary, solitary, large, sweet-scented, with waxy and crinkled white to cream petals, numerous stamens. **FRUIT** Ovoid brown capsule, velvety hairy outside; black seeds.

Boab

Adansonia gregorii

HEIGHT 16–50 ft (5–15 m)
TYPE Deciduous
OCCURRENCE N.E. Australia
(Kimberley region)

The short trunk of this tree is enlarged and bottle-shaped, enabling it to store water. **BARK** Grayish brown, smooth. **LEAF** Alternate, with 3–7 elliptic to ovate or obovate leaflets. **FLOWER** Axillary, solitary, large, with oblong to spoon-shaped petals, white to cream, numerous stamens. **FRUIT** Brown capsule, velvety hairy surface, with kidney-shaped seeds.

spreading branches

Flame Tree

Brachychiton acerifolius

HEIGHT 115 ft (35 m)
TYPE Deciduous
OCCURRENCE E. Australia

Considered one of the most spectacular trees of Australia, this tree has bright coral-red flowers. **BARK** Gray, fissured or wrinkled. **LEAF** Alternate or whorled, ovate to lanceolate, sometimes with 3–5 lobes, especially in juvenile foliage. **FLOWER** Petalless, in large terminal panicles on leafless branches. **FRUIT** Dry, boat-shaped, woody follicle.

Ceiba speciosa

Floss Silk Tree

HEIGHT 50–75 ft (15–22 m)
TYPE Deciduous
OCCURRENCE South America (Brazil, N.E. Argentina), planted elsewhere in the tropics

Locally cultivated in South America before the arrival of the Europeans, this tree is characterized by a spiny, swollen trunk that can store water, and its green avocado-like fruit, which releases cotton-like fibers when ripe. This tree is often planted in the southern US as a street tree for its display of spectacular deep pink flowers. **BARK** Yellowish green, spiny, particularly when young. **LEAF** Alternate, digitate, with 5–7 narrowly elliptic leaflets.

FLOWER

purple streaks on flower base

FLOWER Deep pink, 2³/₄–4¹/₄ in (7–11 cm) long, with a streaked white to yellow base and oblong to spoon-shaped petals. **FRUIT** Large, woody, pear-shaped capsule; seeds in a mass of silky hairs.

LEAVES

large, glossy seeds

elliptic to lanceolate leaf

RIPE FRUIT

pyramidal spines

Durio zibethinus

Durian

HEIGHT 100–130 ft (30–40 m)
TYPE Evergreen
OCCURRENCE Sumatra, Borneo, cultivated elsewhere in S.E. Asia

The durian is famous—or notorious—for its fruits: though a delicacy, they are banned in hotels and on public transit because of their overpowering smell. **BARK** Gray to reddish brown, flaking irregularly. **LEAF** Alternate, smooth above, covered with hairs and silvery scales beneath. **FLOWER** In axillary clusters, with five yellowish white petals and five pale golden sepals. **FRUIT** Green to yellow, spherical capsule; seeds covered with creamy sweet flesh.

BAOBAB
Baobabs rise above the Madagascan forest canopy.
These majestic trees are a characteristic feature of
this island's landscape. Several baobab species have
been identified, but *Adansonia grandidieri* is perhaps
the best known.

Ceiba pentandra

Kapok

HEIGHT 60–230 ft (18–70 m)
TYPE Deciduous
OCCURRENCE South America, Africa

One of the tallest trees of the Amazon forests, kapok was held sacred by the ancient Mayas and many other native American tribes, probably because of its stature. Its base has pronounced exposed roots and is sometimes buttressed. The broad, pagoda-shaped crown is formed by superimposed branches arranged in groups of three. Kapok flowers, which bloom in the dry season from December to January, have a fetid, milky smell that attracts bats. The seeds, leaves, bark, and resin are used for various medicinal purposes. The tree is now cultivated in Southeast Asia and Africa. **BARK** Pale gray; with conical spines when young. **LEAF** Alternate, long-stalked, palmate, with 5–11 oblong-lanceolate leaflets. **FLOWER** Pink or off-white, in axillary clusters of 2–15. **FRUIT** Capsule; seeds embedded in a mass of woolly hairs (floss).

bell-shaped
flowers

FLOWERS

KAPOK FLOSS

The kapok was formerly cultivated for the floss of its fruit, mainly in Sri Lanka, Java, and the Philippines. The harvested fruit was opened and the seeds separated from the kapok floss, which was dried and then baled. This fiber has been used to stuff mattresses and as buoyancy material in life jackets. The oil from the seeds was used for soap-making.

FRUIT POD

Guazuma ulmifolia

Bastard Cedar

HEIGHT up to 65 ft (20 m)
TYPE Evergreen
OCCURRENCE South America

This tree has widely spreading, horizontal branches and is common in secondary forests. **BARK** Gray to gray-brown, rough. **LEAF** Alternate, in flattened rows, ovate to lanceolate, toothed. **FLOWER** In axillary panicles, with five greenish yellow petals. **FRUIT** Globose green capsule; black and honey-scented when ripe.

forked styles

curving petals

FLOWER

Lagunaria patersonia

Norfolk Island Hibiscus

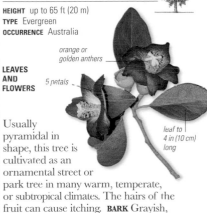

HEIGHT up to 65 ft (20 m)
TYPE Evergreen
OCCURRENCE Australia

orange or golden anthers

LEAVES AND FLOWERS

5 petals

leaf to 4 in (10 cm) long

Usually pyramidal in shape, this tree is cultivated as an ornamental street or park tree in many warm, temperate, or subtropical climates. The hairs of the fruit can cause itching. **BARK** Grayish, fissured lengthwise. **LEAF** Alternate, ovate to elliptic, densely scaly below. **FLOWER** Pink to rose-lilac, axillary, solitary. **FRUIT** Capsule lined with hairs.

Ochroma pyramidale

Balsa

HEIGHT up to 100 ft (30 m)
TYPE Evergreen
OCCURRENCE Tropical South America, West Indies

This tree has a straight trunk and a sparsely branched, spreading crown. It produces the lightest commercial wood in the world. Its flowers are pollinated by bats. **BARK** Grayish brown, smooth, porous. **LEAF** Alternate, rough, shallowly lobed and covered with reddish hairs. **FLOWER** Axillary, solitary; white to yellowish petals, numerous stamens. **FRUIT** Capsule that looks like a rabbit's foot.

ovate to circular

LEAVES AND FRUIT

FLOWER

flossy fruit covering

KAPOK

The spreading roots of a kapok tree (*Ceiba pentandra*) invade temple ruins at Angkor, Cambodia. Originally a native of South America, the kapok was sacred to the Mayans, who believed that the souls of the dead ascended to heaven via its branches.

Pachira aquatica

Shaving-Brush Tree

HEIGHT up to 65 ft (20 m)
TYPE Semi-evergreen
OCCURRENCE Tropical Mexico, Central and South America

Also known as the Guyana chestnut, this tree has branches in whorls, particularly when young. It is found along estuaries and lakesides and can be used as a hedge or for general planting. Its seeds, which resemble the European chestnut in flavor, can be toasted and ground to prepare a hot-chocolate-like beverage.
BARK Gray, slightly cracked lengthwise.
LEAF Alternate, palmate, with 4–7 smooth, elliptic to oblong-lanceolate leaflets.
FLOWER Axillary, solitary, yellow to creamy white petals, turning back to reveal numerous stamens, clustered in groups of about 15.
FRUIT Large, egg-shaped capsule, with edible seeds.

spreading habit

yellowish brown capsule

FRUIT

FLOWERS   pink-tipped stamens

petals 8–12 in (20–30 cm) long

Tilia americana

American Basswood

HEIGHT 80–130 ft (25–40 m)
TYPE Deciduous
OCCURRENCE E. North America

Often the dominant tree in the moist woods where it grows, American basswood has a broadly columnar to rounded crown. It is sometimes planted as a street tree. Its bark was widely used by American Indians for making rope and baskets.
BARK Brownish gray, deeply fissured with scaly ridges. **LEAF** Alternate, broadly ovate, coarsely toothed, with a heart-shaped base. **FLOWER** Pale yellow-green, in axillary or terminal, stalked clusters of up to ten flowers, fragrant.
FRUIT Woody, rounded drupe, four-ribbed, covered with gray-brown hairs.

LEAF

Tilia cordata

Little-Leaf Linden

HEIGHT up to 100 ft (30 m)
TYPE Deciduous
OCCURRENCE Europe, W. Asia

This tall tree has a somewhat pyramidal crown. Its wood is soft and can be worked with ease. **BARK** Gray-brown, smooth when young; dark gray, ridged at maturity. **LEAF** Alternate, ovate to rounded, glossy green above, waxy beneath, with sharply toothed margins. **FLOWER** Axillary or terminal, stalked clusters of up to ten flowers, pale green bracts at base, fragrant. **FRUIT** Woody, spherical nutlike drupe, smooth.

pale yellow-green flowers

LEAVES AND FLOWERS

broadly columnar habit

Tilia x europaea

Common Linden

HEIGHT up to 130 ft (40 m)
TYPE Deciduous
OCCURRENCE Europe

The common linden is rare as a natural hybrid and is usually cultivated. Its trunk often has burs, usually with numerous suckers at the base. This is the commonly planted "lime tree" in European parks and streets. **BARK** Gray-brown, smooth when young; dark gray, ridged at maturity. **LEAF** Alternate, broadly ovate, glossy green above, tufts of hairs beneath. **FLOWER** Pale yellow-green, with pale green bracts at base, fragrant, in axillary or terminal, stalked clusters of up to ten. **FRUIT** Woody, rounded nutlike drupe, faintly ribbed, covered with gray-brown hairs.

toothed leaf edges

LEAVES WITH FRUIT

nutlets

silvery underside of leaf

pendulous fruit

sharply toothed leaf margins

broadly columnar crown

Tilia tomentosa

Silver Linden

HEIGHT up to 100 ft (30 m)
TYPE Deciduous
OCCURRENCE S.E. Europe, S.W. Asia

The flowers of this tree are inconspicuous but exceptionally fragrant. They are used to make linden tea (tisane), which helps to induce sweating and to counter colds and fevers. The flowers are picked when fully fragrant and then dried. This and other *Tilia* species are popular with beekeepers for honey production. **BARK** Gray, with a network of shallow ridges and furrows. **LEAF** Alternate, broadly ovate to rounded, slightly lobed, green and slightly hairy above, covered with silvery hairs beneath. **FLOWER** Pale yellow-green, with a pale green bract beneath, in axillary or terminal, stalked clusters of up to ten. **FRUIT** Egg-shaped, warty nutlike drupe.

Triplochiton scleroxylon

Obeche

HEIGHT up to 215 ft (65 m)
TYPE Deciduous
OCCURRENCE Tropical W. Africa
(from Guinea to Cameroon)

This species accounts for almost half the timber produced in West Africa. Its trunk is straight, but sometimes fluted in old trees. **BARK** Gray to orange-brown, becoming scaly. **LEAF** Alternate, broadly ovate to triangular, lobed to about one-third of the length, with 5–7 lobes. **FLOWER** In short panicles, somewhat saucer-shaped, with white petals that are red-purple at the base. **FRUIT** Up to five winged carpels.

Theobroma cacao

Cocoa

HEIGHT up to 33 ft (10 m)
TYPE Evergreen to semi-deciduous
OCCURRENCE S. Mexico, Central America, cultivated in W. Africa

Cultivated in tropical regions for its seeds—the cocoa "beans" used to make cocoa and chocolate—this tree has a low, spreading crown. The seeds of the fruit pod are scooped out, fermented, and dried, and then shipped to chocolate-producing countries for shelling, roasting, and processing. **BARK** Dark brown, rough, fissured. **LEAF** Alternate, large, elliptic to oblong, pendulous **FLOWER** Pink to white, with petals that are hood-shaped at the base and spreading sepals; borne singly or in groups on the trunk and branches at the same time as the fruit. **FRUIT** Ovoid-oblong, yellow to reddish purple pod, five-celled, furrowed, with numerous reddish brown seeds embedded in a whitish, sweetish, buttery pulp.

"BITTER WATER"

The word "chocolate" derives from the Mayan *xocolatl*, which means "bitter water." Christopher Columbus brought cocoa beans to Europe from America, but it was only in 1875 that milk chocolate was invented by Swiss chemist Henri Nestlé.

COCOA POD

CHOCOLATE

TRUNK

small white flowers on trunk

UNRIPE FRUIT

untoothed margin

LEAVES

wrinkled pod

Jam-Tree

Muntingia calabura

HEIGHT up to 40 ft (12 m)
TYPE Evergreen
OCCURRENCE Mexico, Caribbean, South America, introduced in S.E. Asia

prominent yellow stamens

5 petals

SOLITARY FLOWER

Also known as the Jamaican cherry, this tree was introduced into Asia during the time of the Spanish Empire and was transported on the Acapulco–Manila galleon route. It has an umbrella-shaped crown and widely spreading, horizontal, drooping branches. Its twigs are covered with sticky, glandular red hairs. The sweet berries can be eaten fresh or made into jam. The bark can be made into ropes, and the flowers are used in traditional medicine. **BARK** Pale brownish gray, smooth, fibrous. **LEAF** Alternate, ovate-lanceolate, dark green above, covered with sticky hairs beneath that radiate from the center; asymmetrical base, three veins. **FLOWER** White, borne in axillary groups of 1–5. **FRUIT** Dull red fleshy berry, with numerous tiny seeds.

toothed margin

LEAVES

⅜–½ in (1–1.25 cm) wide

UNRIPE FRUIT

Thingwa

Hopea odorata

HEIGHT up to 150 ft (45 m)
TYPE Evergreen
OCCURRENCE S.E. Asia

Mainly grown for its strong timber, this tree is also planted as an ornamental and shade tree. **BARK** Dark brown or black, cracks into small pieces. **LEAF** Alternate, 4–8 in (10–20 cm) long, tapering at the tip. **FLOWER** Small, with five pinkish to white petals, hairy on both sides, in branched terminal or axillary panicles. **FRUIT** Single-seeded, round nut.

Chengal

Neobalanocarpus heimii

HEIGHT up to 110 ft (33 m)
TYPE Evergreen
OCCURRENCE Thailand, Malaysia

The heavy, durable timber of this tree used to be the best-known in Malaysia. **BARK** Grayish, flaky. **LEAF** Leathery, lanceolate to crescent-shaped, with an unequal base, tip tapers to a long, blunt point. **FLOWER** Pale greenish yellow with 15 stamens, borne in terminal or axillary panicles. **FRUIT** Oblong to cylindrical, shiny nut, with a short point at the tip.

Shorea robusta

Sal

HEIGHT up to 115 ft (35 m)
TYPE Evergreen
OCCURRENCE Myanmar, India, Nepal

This tree has a straight, cylindrical trunk. Younger trees have a pointed habit, which becomes more rounded with age. Although an evergreen, the tree sheds nearly all its leaves in dry areas, between February and April. Sal provides very good-quality, durable timber, which is much sought-after for construction, especially for purposes that require strength with flexibility, such as railroad ties and house- and bridge-building. The tree is revered by Buddhists—it is said that the Buddha meditated in a grove of sal trees. **BARK** Dark brown, with deep longitudinal furrows in mature trees. **LEAF** Tough, shiny leaves, 4–10 in (10–25 cm) long with a rounded base, oval-oblong in shape, ending in a blunt point, 10–12 pairs of secondary veins. **FLOWER** Yellowish, inner petals orange, calyx and petals are covered with white down on the outside; borne in large axillary or terminal, racemose panicles. **FRUIT** Winged nut; seeds may germinate on the tree.

MORE THAN TIMBER

Like many tropical tree species, the sal is used for far more than timber. The seeds of the tree are used for oil, and the oilcake is used to feed livestock. The leaves can also be used for cattle feed. The tree yields a white, aromatic resin when tapped, which is burned as incense during religious ceremonies. It is also used for caulking boats and ships and in paints and varnishes. The resin has medicinal uses.

LEAF HARVEST

glossy foliage

FLOWERING BRANCHES

conspicuous flowers

Shorea albida

Alan

HEIGHT 130 ft (40 m)
TYPE Evergreen
OCCURRENCE N.W. Borneo

This tree occurs on peat swamps, the largest trees growing at the edges and the smallest in the center. The intermediate trees are an important source of red meranti timber. **BARK** Grayish, deeply fissured. **LEAF** Oblong-elliptic, tip tapers to a long point, leathery; 16–20 pairs of slender, secondary veins. **FLOWER** Borne in terminal or axillary, doubly branched panicles up to 7 in (18 cm) long; branchlets carry up to three flowers, with cream petals and 20–25 stamens. **FRUIT** Egg-shaped nuts, ³⁄₈ in (1.2 cm) long, covered in grayish-buff hairs.

Shorea javanica

Damar

HEIGHT up to 110 ft (33 m)
TYPE Semi-evergreen
OCCURRENCE Sumatra

This tree is grown in plantations in southern Sumatra. The timber is valued for plywood production, which is its most important use. The tree is also used for its high-quality, clear resin—known as "damar." The damar trees begin their production of resin after 20 years, yielding it for about 30 years before dying some time between 50 and 60 years of age. On average, a tree will yield some 100 lb (50 kg) per year. In dry areas, it sheds nearly all its leaves between February and April. Its branchlets are covered with a tawny down. **BARK** Reddish, rough. **LEAF** Oblong-elliptic to ovate, tip tapers to a long blunt point, leathery; 19–25 pairs of very slender, secondary veins, midrib slender above. **FLOWER** In terminal or axillary, single-branched panicles up to 5½ in (14 cm) long, about three flowers, each with white petals and 15 stamens, on a branchlet. **FRUIT** Egg-shaped nut up to ½ in (1.4 cm) long and ³⁄₈ in (1 cm) wide, covered in tawny-brown down, with a prominent point at tip.

Dryobalanops aromatica

Kapur

HEIGHT up to 110 ft (33 m)
TYPE Evergreen
OCCURRENCE Malaya, Borneo, Sumatra

A gigantic tree, often with a trunk over 6½ ft (2 m) wide, kapur is an important source of timber and camphor. **BARK** Reddish, flaky. **LEAF** Dark green, waxy, leathery, triangular to heart-shaped. **FLOWER** In panicles, white petals in rosette, about 30 stamens. **FRUIT** Smooth nut.

glossy green foliage

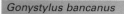

Aquilaria malaccensis

Agarwood

HEIGHT up to 150 ft (45 m)
TYPE Evergreen
OCCURRENCE S. and S.E. Asia

This tree yields the world's most valuable incense. Its bark produces strong fibers that are used for making rope and cloth. **BARK** Whitish, smooth, cracking irregularly. **LEAF** Elliptic-oblong to oblong-lanceolate, with pointed tip. **FLOWER** Green to yellow, in groups of 1–3 umbels, each with about ten flowers. **FRUIT** Hairy, spherical capsule.

Gonystylus bancanus

Ramin

HEIGHT up to 165 ft (50 m)
TYPE Evergreen
OCCURRENCE Malaysia, Indonesia

The ramin grows in freshwater swamps and seasonally flooding forests. It is highly valued for its timber. **BARK** Dark brown, shallowly fissured. **LEAF** Alternate, often folded, leathery, elliptic, oblong, or rounded. **FLOWER** In clusters, covered with yellowish down, with 13–20 petals. **FRUIT** Rough, spherical capsule.

Acer campestre

Hedge Maple

HEIGHT 20–33 ft (6–10 m)
TYPE Deciduous
OCCURRENCE Europe, N. Africa, W. Asia

The hedge maple occurs in broad-leaved woodlands and is common in hedgerows. In rare cases, it can grow up to 90 ft (28 m). In Europe, it is sometimes planted as a shade or street tree. **BARK** Gray-brown, scaly or fissured. **LEAF** Opposite, palmate, 3–5 lobes; the stalk yields sap **FLOWER** Green, in small, erect clusters. **FRUIT** Winged keys, arranged in pairs.

winged fruit

LEAVES AND FRUIT

leaves divided halfway

Acer negundo

Box Elder

HEIGHT 50–65 ft (15–20 m)
TYPE Deciduous
OCCURRENCE S.E. Canada, E. US

Also called the Manitoba maple, this tree grows along the banks of streams and lakes and on swampy ground. Its wood is soft and weak and has been used as an inferior timber. In Europe, it is often used for windbreaks and street plantings. **BARK** Pale to light brown, scaly, furrowed with age. **LEAF** Opposite, pinnate with 3–7 ovate leaflets. **FLOWER** Males and females on separate trees; yellow-green, in drooping clusters. **FRUIT** Winged keys, arranged in pairs.

winged keys

FRUIT

Acer palmatum

Japanese Maple

HEIGHT 26–40 ft (8–12 m)
TYPE Deciduous
OCCURRENCE Japan, China, Korea

Long cultivated in Japan, the Japanese maple was introduced into Europe in 1820. This tree has a graceful and spreading habit and slender shoots that end in small, paired buds. It is commonly planted in gardens for its fall colors. **BARK** Gray-brown, with pale and longitudinal

stripes, which are variable in some cultivars. **LEAF** Opposite, palmate, with 5–9, deep, taper-pointed lobes. **FLOWER** Small, purple, arranged in small and upright clusters. **FRUIT** Winged keys, arranged in pairs.

LEAVES AND FRUIT

finely pointed leaf lobes

red, winged fruit

MEDLEY OF COLORS

The Japanese maple has more than 500 cultivars. They differ in the depth of division of the leaf lobes—these are themselves dissected sometimes, or narrowly linear—and in the leaf color, which ranges from green to purple to golden or variegated. There is also a dwarf group, which is popular for bonsai.

Acer pseudoplatanus

Sycamore Maple

HEIGHT 65–100 ft (20–30 m)
TYPE Deciduous
OCCURRENCE Europe, N. Africa, W. Asia

The sycamore maple is an invasive maple with a broad, spreading crown, colonizing open areas. Control of invasive populations is possible by selecting only male trees. **BARK** Gray-brown, smooth, flaking into irregular plates in older trees. **LEAF** Opposite, palmate, with five deep, coarsely toothed lobes, heart-shaped at the base, dark green above, paler beneath. **FLOWER** Green, arranged in small pendulous clusters from the slender shoots. **FRUIT** Winged keys, arranged in pairs, up to 1 in (2.5 cm) long.

LEAVES AND FLOWERS

leaf to 3–6 in (7.5–15 cm) wide

clustered winged fruit

FRUIT

pendulous flowers

Acer rubrum

Red Maple

HEIGHT up to 80 ft (25 m)
TYPE Deciduous
OCCURRENCE North America (N.E. United States, S.E. Canada)

Growing in diverse habitats and climates, the red maple is one of the species that account for the striking red fall colors of North American forests. **BARK** Pale gray and smooth, with plate-like scales on mature trees. **LEAF** Opposite, with three shallow and sharply toothed lobes. **FLOWER** Dull yellowish red to bright yellow, on long-stalked clusters, appearing before the leaves. **FRUIT** Winged keys, in pairs.

pointed, toothed lobes

red-brown shoots

FALL FOLIAGE

Acer saccharum

Sugar Maple

HEIGHT 100–120 ft (30–36 m)
TYPE Deciduous
OCCURRENCE N.E. US, S.E. Canada

This large, fast-growing tree provides abundant shade and beautiful fall foliage, and is an excellent tree for parks and large yards. It is an important timber tree, as well as the source of maple syrup and sugar. It takes about 40 gallons of sap to make one gallon of syrup. **BARK** Gray-brown, smooth or slightly fissured, becoming darker, deeply furrowed, and scaly on older trees. **LEAF** Opposite, with 3–5 shallow lobes and conspicuous veins, deep matt green, turning yellow to orange or red in fall. **FLOWER** Small, greenish yellow, in unstalked clusters hanging from long stems, appearing with or slightly before the leaves;

males and females on the same tree or separate trees. **FRUIT** Winged keys arranged in pairs, 1 in (2.5 cm) long, in clusters, turning brown when mature in fall.

FRUIT

flower to ³⁄₁₆ in (5 mm) long

FLOWER CLUSTERS

fruit to 1 in (2.5 cm) long

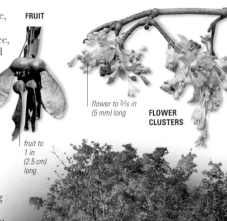

leaf to 5 in (13 cm) long

LEAF

deep fissures

BARK

SWEET SYRUP

In the past, gashes were made in the bark of the tree and the sap collected in birch buckets, poured into hollowed out tree stumps, and then evaporated by adding hot stones, to make maple syrup. Today, the sap is tapped directly through plastic tubing that runs into a central storage tank.

PANCAKES WITH SYRUP

Aesculus hippocastanum

Horse Chestnut

HEIGHT up to 130 ft (40 m)
TYPE Deciduous
OCCURRENCE Native to the Balkans, naturalized throughout Europe

The common name of this tree is derived from the horseshoe-shaped leaf scars that can be seen below the sticky terminal buds. The large seeds (sometimes known as conkers) are inedible. **BARK** Dark brown, flaking into plates. **LEAF** Opposite, digitate, with 5–7 obovate leaflets, each with a narrow triangular base, sparsely hairy

below, with toothed margins. **FLOWER** In columnar, upright panicles, with 4–5 creamy white petals veined pink to red at the base. **FRUIT** Green, spherical capsule, with glossy brown seeds.

smooth seed

unstalked leaflets

spiny husk

FRUIT   LEAF

LEAVES AND FLOWERS

Blighia sapida

Ackee

HEIGHT up to 33 ft (10 m)
TYPE Evergreen
OCCURRENCE W. Africa

If not prepared correctly, the fruit of the ackee is highly poisonous. The national fruit of Jamaica, it is named after Captain Bligh, who collected samples in Jamaica and sent them to London's Kew Gardens. **BARK** Gray, smooth to slightly rough. **LEAF** Alternate, pinnate with 3–5 pairs of elliptic leaflets, no terminal leaflet, smooth above, hairy

below. **FLOWER** White, fragrant, borne in racemes. **FRUIT** Leathery to fleshy three-valved capsule, opening to reveal three dark brown, poisonous seeds; large white, fleshy, edible aril, which is attached to the fruit by a red or pink membrane.

dense spreading branches

RIPE FRUIT   *red tinged with yellow*

JAPANESE MAPLE
A favorite among horticulturists and garden designers, the Japanese maple (*Acer palmatum*) is valued for its delicate foliage and brilliant fall colors. The subspecies shown here, *A. palmatum dissectum*, is a variety with deeply divided leaves

Dimocarpus longan

Longan

HEIGHT up to 130 ft (40 m)
TYPE Evergreen
OCCURRENCE S. China, S.E. Asia

Although the longan is a tropical fruit that is best eaten fresh, there is a considerable canning industry for the fruit because they retain their flavor better than the lychee or rambutan. The fruit can be dried, either whole or after removal of the outer skin, and is used to prepare a refreshing drink. The seeds are high in saponin (a soaplike compound) and can be used for shampoos. **BARK** Smooth, becoming slightly flaky. **LEAF** Alternate, pinnate, without a terminal leaflet; 4–10 elliptic to ovate-oblong, untoothed leaflets, glossy green above, gray-green beneath, minutely hairy. **FLOWER** Yellow-brown, smooth to densely woolly, borne in a terminal inflorescence. **FRUIT** Smooth to warty, spherical to oval fleshy drupe, with a sticky, translucent white aril.

dense, dark green foliage

drooping clusters of yellow-brown fruit

FRUIT

Koelreuteria paniculata

UNRIPE FRUIT

triangular, 3-sided capsule

Golden Rain

HEIGHT up to 40 ft (12 m)
TYPE Deciduous
OCCURRENCE China

Planted as an ornamental for its yellow flowers, bladderlike fruit, and yellow fall color, this tree has a broadly spreading crown. In China, the flowers have been used as a yellow dye and are a component in a traditional medicine. **BARK** Gray-brown, fissured into scaly ridges. **LEAF** Alternate, ovate to ovate-oblong, smooth above, with irregularly toothed margins. **FLOWER** Numerous, small, yellow with red center, in terminal panicles. **FRUIT** Bladder-like capsule, green, tinged red, ripening to brown.

conical panicle

7–14 leaflets

LEAVES AND FLOWERS

Litchi chinensis

Lychee

HEIGHT up to 100 ft (30 m)
TYPE Evergreen
OCCURRENCE S. China to N. Vietnam, cultivated in N. Thailand, Australia, India, Madagascar, Mauritius, Réunion, South Africa

The lychee tree was cultivated as early as 1500 BCE. The crop has spread very slowly to new areas due to its exacting

to 2 in (5 cm) long

FRUIT

climatic requirements. It can be grown in many areas but fails to set fruit unless the conditions are ideal. Today, fresh lychees are available in European markets; the canned product has long been exported. **BARK** Gray, smooth. **LEAF** Alternate, pinnate without a terminal leaflet; leaflets in 2–4 pairs, elliptic- to ovate-lanceolate, glossy deep green above, waxy beneath. **FLOWER** Borne in large branched, terminal clusters, numerous, petalless, with golden, hairy calyx. **FRUIT** Showy, spherical to ovate, fleshy capsule in loose, pendent clusters, usually reddish when mature; seeds covered with a fleshy, edible aril.

TRUNK AND BRANCHES

Nephelium lappaceum

Rambutan

HEIGHT 33–80 ft (10–25 m)
TYPE Evergreen
OCCURRENCE Cultivated in S.E. Asia from Sri Lanka to Papua New Guinea

The rambutan thrives in the humid tropics, and its fruit is usually eaten fresh locally. Thailand is one of the major producers of the fruit, followed by Malaysia, Indonesia, and the Philippines. Young shoots are used to make green dye for silk already dyed yellow. **BARK** Gray to brown, smooth, with white flecks. **LEAF** Alternate, pinnate; 2–4 pairs of ovate to obovate, untoothed leaflets. **FLOWER** Yellowish green to white, small, petalless, in clusters; males and females on separate trees. **FRUIT** Oval to spherical, strawberry red, rose pink, or yellowish capsule; translucent white to pinkish, fleshy edible aril.

glossy, deep green leaflets

loose, pendent clusters of fruit

FRUIT AND LEAVES

Boswellia sacra

Frankincense

HEIGHT up to 16 ft (5 m)
TYPE Deciduous
OCCURRENCE Arabian Peninsula

A small tree with a trunk that is often branched at the base, the frankincense tree is known for its aromatic resin, which is used as incense. Historically, it was worth its weight in gold, and most famously it was one of the gifts offered to Christ by the three Magi, who carried it, along with gold and myrrh, to Bethlehem. In ancient Egypt, the first female pharaoh, Queen Hatshepsut, found living frankincense trees in the Land of Punt (now Somalia) and planted them in the grounds of the Temple of Karnak. **BARK** Papery, peeling. **LEAF** Alternate, pinnate, with a terminal leaflet; 6–8 pairs of obovate-oblong leaflets, hairy above and below, margins with small rounded teeth. **FLOWER** Small, white to pink, borne in axillary racemes at the ends of branches. **FRUIT** Small green drupe.

TREE

egg-shaped drupe

FRUIT

flowers in racemes

FRUIT

leaf clusters at ends of branches

FLOWERING BRANCHES

white to reddish bark

SACRED FRAGRANCE

Frankincense was burned in religious rites in ancient Egypt and Rome and in Jewish tabernacles; it is still used in Catholic and Coptic churches. At the height of trade, some 3,000 tons were used annually. Today, world production is about 500 tons.

FRANKINCENSE RESIN

Gumbo Limbo

HEIGHT 16–65 ft (5–20 m)
TYPE Deciduous
OCCURRENCE United States (S. Florida),
West Indies, Mexico to Venezuela

Found in coastal mangroves, this tree,
also known as the tourist tree, has a
thick trunk and massive, spreading
branches. Commonly used as a living
fence, it has been planted as a street tree
in coastal towns and as an ornamental.
The trunk yields resin and the bark,
formerly used as a medicine for gout,
is used to make glue, varnish, and incense.
BARK Reddish brown to copper-colored,
smooth. **LEAF** Alternate, pinnate, with
a terminal leaflet; 3–7 ovate-oblong
leaflets, dark green above, paler below.
FLOWER Cream, males and females borne
on separate trees in terminal and lateral
narrow clusters; males about twice as
long as the females.
FRUIT Red, three-
sided, angular drupe-
like capsule, splitting
into three valves to
release the bony seeds.

peeling in papery flakes

MATURE BARK

Myrrh

HEIGHT 6–12 ft (2–4 m)
TYPE Deciduous
OCCURRENCE Arabian
Peninsula, Horn of Africa

These small trees or shrubs have knotted
and spiny branches. Myrrh resin came
from Arabia along the "incense road" in
long camel trains to Egypt, Rome, and
farther west. About 10,000 camel
loads were transported annually on
this trade route. Myrrh was used as
an incense, for embalming, and as a
medicine. It is still used in Chinese
traditional medicine. **BARK** Green to pale
brown, peeling, papery; exudes a grayish
resin. **LEAF** Alternate, trifoliate, with a
well-developed, obovate to elliptic terminal
leaflet; small, poorly developed lateral
leaflets. **FLOWER** Yellow-green to white,
borne at the ends of short lateral
branches. **FRUIT** Smooth drupe,
containing a hard stone.

spiny
branches

Anacardium occidentale

Cashew

HEIGHT 15–40 ft (4–12 m)
TYPE Evergreen
OCCURRENCE N.E. Brazil, introduced
in India, S.E. Asia, Africa

kidney-shaped
nuts

prominent veins

The cashew tree is widely cultivated in
the tropics for its nut. The Portuguese
brought the cashew nut to India from
Brazil in the 16th century, from where it
was introduced to Africa. Vietnam has
emerged as its leading producer today.
BARK Gray to brown, smooth, fissured
with age; exudes sap that turns black
on exposure. **LEAF** Alternate, obovate
to obovate-oblong,
untoothed margin.

FLOWER Borne in a
terminal panicle, with
yellow-green to pinkish
petals. **FRUIT** Nut at the end
of a fleshy, fruitlike stalk.

LEAVES

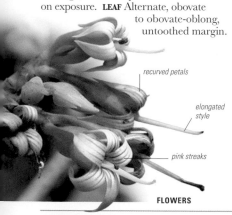

recurved petals

elongated
style

pink streaks

FLOWERS

Gluta renghas

Renghas

HEIGHT up to 165 ft (50 m)
TYPE Evergreen
OCCURRENCE Malaysia, Indonesia, Philippines,
Papua New Guinea

Found in swamp forests, this tree has a
dense crown and its trunk is sometimes
buttressed. It yields a reddish timber with
a beautiful grain, but this is rarely utilized
because felling and processing of the
wood can cause allergic reactions. The
seeds can be eaten after being roasted.
BARK Pale brown, becoming grayish with
age; exudes black, resinous, irritant sap.
LEAF Alternate, leathery, elliptic to oblong
or oblanceolate. **FLOWER** White, fragrant,
in axillary panicles.
FRUIT Spherical,
pinkish brown,
fleshy drupe.

scaly surface

BARK

Harpephyllum caffrum

Kaffir Plum

HEIGHT 20–50 ft (6–15 m)
TYPE Evergreen
OCCURRENCE S. and E. Africa

The name of this tree is derived from its place of origin, Kaffraria, now part of Eastern Cape, South Africa. It has a small, compact, and roundish crown. An ornamental shade tree, it is planted as a street tree in South African towns and cities. Its fruit is used to make jams and jellies, and can also be fermented into a wine. **BARK** Silvery white to brown, with raised ridges or cracked segments. **LEAF** Alternate, pinnate; 4–8 pairs of sickle-shaped leaflets, with wavy or untoothed margins. **FLOWER** Whitish green, males and females on separate trees, borne in panicles near ends of branches. **FRUIT** Plumlike drupe, red when ripe, edible, with a sour taste.

LEAVES

Mangifera indica

Mango

HEIGHT 33–150 ft (10–45 m)
TYPE Evergreen
OCCURRENCE Known only in cultivation

Mangoes have been in cultivation for over a thousand years. There are over 1,000 cultivars, with some 500 of these in India alone. They are divided into two types: the Indian type with a single embryo per seed, and those with multiple embryos, mostly from Southeast Asia. In India, the unripe fruit is made into pickles and chutney. It is also dried and powdered to be used as a spice or as a meat tenderizer. **BARK** Grayish brown, smooth or with thin fissures, becoming darker, rough, scaly or furrowed with age. **LEAF** Alternate, leathery, usually narrowly elliptic to lanceolate, often with wavy margins. **FLOWER** Greenish yellow, in terminal panicles. **FRUIT** Fleshy, often fibrous drupe, sometimes with a turpentine flavor.

RIPE FRUIT

yellowish green to reddish skin

dense crown

yellow to orange flesh

glossy green above

LEAF ROSETTE

slender stalks

Mastic

Pistacia lentiscus

HEIGHT 8–12 ft (2.4–3.6 m)
TYPE Evergreen
OCCURRENCE Mediterranean region

Also known as Chios mastic, this low, spreading tree usually has a crooked trunk. Only one variety (*Pistacia lentiscus* var. *chia*), grown on the Greek island of Chios, yields mastic resin, the original chewing resin used as a breath freshener. The resin is also used in water pipes, coffee, Turkish delight, and for medicinal purposes. **BARK** Pale gray-brown, turns dark gray-brown and rough, with large

TREE IN BLOSSOM

scaly plates. **LEAF** Alternate, pinnate; 4–10 oblong-lanceolate leaflets. **FLOWER** Males and females on separate trees, yellowish white with red stamens and stigmas. **FRUIT** Spherical, bright red drupe, ripening to black.

LEAFLETS

flower to 1¼ in (3 cm) long

to 1¼ in (3 cm) long

fruit in clusters

LEAVES, FLOWERS, AND FRUIT

FLOWER CLUSTER

Pistachio

Pistacia vera

HEIGHT up to 33 ft (10 m)
TYPE Deciduous
OCCURRENCE C. Asia, Afghanistan, Iran, Turkey

leaflet 2–4 in (5–10 cm) long

Probably the earliest known cultivated tree, possibly dating back to 6,000 BCE, the pistachio is a small tree, known for its edible nutlike fruit. It is said that the Queen of Sheba reserved the harvest of the best pistachio trees for herself, and carried pistachios as a gift for King Solomon in 950 BCE. **BARK** Gray-brown to russet, smooth, becoming rough. **LEAF** Alternate, trifoliate or pinnate with a terminal leaflet; 1–3 pairs of large, hairy, ovate to broadly lanceolate leaflets. **FLOWER** Males and females borne on separate trees; small, petalless, greenish brown, in panicles. **FRUIT** Edible, one-seeded drupe.

LEAVES AND FRUIT

PISTACHIO NUTS

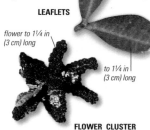

Pleiogynium timoriense

Burdekin Plum

HEIGHT 65–120 ft (20–36 m)
TYPE Semi-evergreen
OCCURRENCE Pacific Islands, Papua New Guinea, Australia

A spreading rainforest tree, the Burdekin plum tree is known for its fleshy fruit. Marketed as "bush tucker," the fruit tends to be exceedingly acid and needs to be

stored for several days to become soft and mellow. It is usually stewed or made into jams and jellies. **BARK** Dark gray or gray-brown, fissured, flaky. **LEAF** Alternate, pinnate with a terminal leaflet, glossy dark green. **FLOWER** Greenish yellow, small, in many-flowered, axillary panicles; males and females on separate trees. **FRUIT** Egg-shaped, edible drupe, dark purple when ripe, with a large single seed.

Schinus molle

Pepper Tree

HEIGHT 15–50 ft (5–15 m)
TYPE Evergreen
OCCURRENCE South America

Widely cultivated in dry subtropical areas, this tree has slender, drooping branches. It is often invasive in open wasteland. Its fruit was once used to make pink peppercorns. **BARK** Gray and smooth when young, turning yellowish brown, rough, and scaly. **LEAF** Alternate, pinnate with a terminal leaflet; leaflets lanceolate to linear-lanceolate, smooth to slightly toothed. **FLOWER** Yellowish white, small; males and females on separate trees, in axillary clusters at the tips of branches. **FRUIT** Lavender to pink drupes.

19–41 leaflets

small, spherical fruit

LEAVES AND FRUIT

Spondias dulcis

Ambarella

HEIGHT 20–60 ft (6–18 m)
TYPE Deciduous/Evergreen
OCCURRENCE Pacific Islands, S.E. Asia, introduced in West Indies

NEW LEAVES

The sour fruit of this tree is stewed and used in preserves, pickles, and sambal. It tastes of apples and pineapples, and has a pungent, resinous aroma. **BARK** Grayish to reddish brown, becoming fissured. **LEAF** Alternate, pinnate with a terminal leaflet; leaflets elliptic to obovate-oblong, with smooth or scalloped margins. **FLOWER** Cream to white, small, in terminal panicles; males and females on same tree. **FRUIT** Oval, thick-skinned drupes in clusters, containing yellow pulp.

9–25 leaflets

UNRIPE FRUIT

Ailanthus altissima

Tree of Heaven

HEIGHT 50–65 ft (15–20 m)
TYPE Deciduous
OCCURRENCE N. China, widely cultivated

This fast-growing tree has a rounded crown. Philip Miller (1691–1771), a noted English gardener, was the first to raise it from seeds sent to London from China. **BARK** Gray, finely fissured, becoming darker and rougher with age. **LEAF** Alternate, pinnate with a terminal leaflet, dark green; leaflets 13–31, ovate, finely hairy, untoothed or with 1–3 teeth at the base, bearing glands. **FLOWER** Small, greenish, males and females usually on separate trees, borne in terminal panicles; males with a fetid scent. **FRUIT** Flattened winged seed up to 1½ in (4 cm) long, green at first, turning yellow-brown tinged with red.

FOLIAGE AND FLOWERS

notch near base of leaflets

winged fruit

LEAVES AND FRUIT

AN ORNAMENTAL WEED

Following its discovery by the West, this tree was planted widely in Europe. It was noted that silkworms produced a high-quality thread when fed on its leaves instead of the mulberry's. In 1784, it was introduced into the United States by William Hamilton. A century later, biologists realized that it had invaded and colonized large waste areas in the southern US.

Leitneria floridana

Corkwood

HEIGHT up to 20 ft (6 m)
TYPE Deciduous
OCCURRENCE S.E. United States

Considered an endangered tree, only one species of the corkwood can be found in scattered coastal and riverine floodplains of Missouri, Arkansas (where it is locally common), Florida, Texas, and in Georgia along the Altamaha River. This tree has spreading branches and a loose, open crown. **BARK** Dark gray, tinged with brown, divided by shallow fissures. **LEAF** Alternate, elliptic to elliptic-lanceolate, bright green above, covered with soft hairs beneath, on reddish stems. **FLOWER** Inconspicuous catkins on separate plants; both male and female catkins cylindrical; females upright and shorter. **FRUIT** Oblong, compressed, one-seeded, dry drupe.

Azadirachta indica

Neem

HEIGHT up to 50 ft (16 m)
TYPE Evergreen/Semi-evergreen
OCCURRENCE N.W. India, Myanmar,
cultivated in tropical Asia and Africa

The people of India have long been aware of the medical properties of the neem. These are recorded in early Sanskrit writings and are embedded in Ayurvedic medicine. Neem research was part of the upsurge of nationalistic sentiment started by Mahatma Gandhi. Often referred to as "the village pharmacy" tree, the neem's parts are used to treat diseases caused by fungi, viruses, and bacteria. Traditionally, neem seeds were used as an insect repellent and neem cake was spread on the soil as a fertilizer. **BARK** Red-brown to grayish, becoming fissured and flaky with age. **LEAF** Alternate, pinnate with or without a terminal leaflet; 4–7 pairs of sickle-shaped to lanceolate leaflets, with sharply toothed margins; two pairs of glands at base of leaf stalk. **FLOWER** Borne in axillary inflorescences, white, petals softly hairy on both sides, sweetly scented. **FRUIT** Single-seeded drupe, turning yellow when ripe.

NATURAL INSECTICIDE

Extracted from the kernel of the neem fruit, neem oil has valuable pesticidal and medicinal properties. Research has identified a compound in neem oil that works as an antifeedant, suggesting that the oil could have a great future as a selective, non-toxic insecticide. Its use as an environmentally safe alternative to synthetic insecticides and pesticides now draws interest from industrialized countries. The oil is also used in medicinal products for an array of blood, digestive, skin, and immune system disorders.

NEEM OIL

fleshy covering

to ⅜ in (1 cm) long

SEED

UNRIPE FRUIT

⅜–¾ in (1.2–2 cm) long

Cedrela odorata

Spanish Cedar

HEIGHT 40–100 ft (12–30 m)
TYPE Deciduous
OCCURRENCE West Indies,
South America

The Spanish cedar is a fast-growing
species, usually with a rounded crown.
It is an important avenue and shade
tree in its native region and in Africa,
where it is cultivated. It is also used as
a shade tree in coffee and cocoa
plantations. The wood of the tree has
a strong aromatic odor and is resistant
to insects. It is an important timber for
furniture-making, especially for the
manufacture of chests, and wardrobes.
BARK Gray to brown, thick, becoming
rough and furrowed. **LEAF** Alternate,
pinnate, without a terminal leaflet.

10–30 leaflets

LEAVES

FLOWER Numerous, borne in terminal
panicles, small, with yellow-green
staminal tube. **FRUIT** Woody capsule,
with winged seeds.

CEDAR WOOD FOR CIGAR BOXES

Cigars were originally packed in chests containing
about 10,000 cigars. The bankers H. Upmann started
shipping cigars in cedar boxes for their directors in
London. They continued to use this packaging when
they changed to the cigar business, and it became
standard for all major brands, because cedar wood
helps to prevent cigars from drying out. Today, the
wood is specially grown for the purpose.

CEDAR-LINED CIGAR BOX

Khaya senegalensis

Bisselon

HEIGHT up to 100 ft (30 m)
TYPE Evergreen
OCCURRENCE Africa

This tree is also called the African mahogany. It was one of the first African mahoganies to be exported to Europe, but today, due to its relatively small size and low weight, it is seldom exported. The bark contains compounds that are used for medicinal and veterinary purposes. **BARK** Gray, scaly. **LEAF** Alternate, pinnate; pale green leaflets. **FLOWER** In drooping, axillary panicles, creamy petals and staminal tube, with red disk. **FRUIT** Four-valved, woody capsule with winged seeds.

bark exudes red sap

knobbly surface

TRUNK   **BARK**

Dysoxylum fraserianum

Australian Rosewood

HEIGHT 40–80 ft (12–25 m)
TYPE Evergreen
OCCURRENCE Australia (New South Wales, Queensland)

A common rainforest tree, the Australian rosewood is also planted as an ornamental in large parks, including the Sydney Botanical Gardens. It was named after Charles Fraser, who was the first superintendent of the Gardens. Large and fast-growing, the tree has a dense, leafy, spreading crown and a large, buttressed trunk. It needs moist soil to thrive. The wood is reddish and has a delicate perfume that is similar to roses. It has been used for carving, furniture, and cabinet-making. **BARK** Pale brown to yellowish gray, scaly. **LEAF** Alternate, pinnate without a terminal leaflet; 4–12 elliptic to obovate leaflets. **FLOWER** Cream to white, fragrant, in terminal and lateral panicles. **FRUIT** Cream tinged with pink, four-celled capsule, containing one or two seeds with a reddish aril.

Chukrasia tabularis

Yinma

HEIGHT up to 130 ft (40 m)
TYPE Deciduous
OCCURRENCE S. and S.E. Asia.

The yinma has a fluted and buttressed trunk and its timber is valued for making furniture. **BARK** Dark brown, fissured. **LEAF** Alternate, pinnate, with ovate to oblong leaflets. **FLOWER** Fragrant, creamy green to yellowish white, in axillary clusters. **FRUIT** Woody capsule.

6–12 leaflets   **LEAVES**

Lansium domesticum

Langsat

HEIGHT up to 100 ft (30 m)
TYPE Evergreen
OCCURRENCE Thailand, Malaya, Sumatra, Java, Borneo

The langsat is a complex and variable species with wild and cultivated forms. There are two major varieties: langsat, slender trees bearing oval fruit, and duku, spreading trees bearing rounded fruit. **BARK** Pale reddish brown or with fawn blotches, slightly furrowed and scaly. **LEAF** Alternate, pinnate with a terminal leaflet; 2–4 pairs of ovate-elliptic to oblong leaflets, slightly hairy beneath. **FLOWER** Borne in racemes on the branches or trunk, with greenish yellow petals and staminal tube. **FRUIT** Oval or globose berry, pale yellow to brown, skin sometimes exuding latex.

FRUIT

1–2 in (2.5–5 cm) wide

Lovoa trichilioides

Nigerian Golden Walnut

HEIGHT up to 150 ft (45 m)
TYPE Evergreen
OCCURRENCE S. to S.W. Africa

This well-known timber tree is found in lowland rainforest, but is also grown on plantations. **BARK** Smooth, with large irregular flaking pieces. **LEAF** Pinnate, without terminal leaflet; leaflets elliptic in six pairs, rounded or shortly pointed at the base. **FLOWER** Greenish white, with four sepals and petals, borne in large panicles. **FRUIT** Black or purplish black pendulous capsule, containing winged seeds.

FLOWER PANICLES

Sandoricum koetjape

Santol

HEIGHT up to 150 ft (45 m)
TYPE Evergreen
OCCURRENCE Cambodia, Laos, Malaya, (naturalized in Malaysia, Indonesia, Molucca Islands, Mauritius, Philippines, India)

Besides being valued for its fruit, this low-branched species is prized for its timber. **BARK** Pale. **LEAF** Spirally arranged, with three elliptic to oval leaflets, 8–10 in (20–25 cm) long, blunt at the base. **FLOWER** Borne in stalked panicles, with five greenish, yellowish, or pinkish yellow petals. **FRUIT** Oval to round drupe, containing milky fluid, 3–5 brown seeds in white translucent pulp.

pointed tip

wrinkled base of fruit

seed ¾ in (2 cm) long

SEED

LEAFLET

Melia azedarach

Chinaberry

HEIGHT up to 130 ft (40 m)
TYPE Deciduous
OCCURRENCE Sri Lanka, India, China, S.E. Asia, Australia

Widely cultivated in tropical areas, this tree has a fluted trunk when mature. Forms of the chinaberry have been in cultivation for some 2,500 years. There are two groups of cultivars: the Chinese group, which has larger fruit, and the Indian cultivars. **BARK** Gray-brown, smooth, with lenticels, becoming lightly fissured. **LEAF** Alternate, usually bipinnate, with a terminal leaflet; 7–11 ovate to elliptic leaflets, dark green above, pale green, often sparsely hairy beneath. **FLOWER** Borne in axillary clusters, with white to lilac petals and staminal tube, densely hairy inside and sweetly scented. **FRUIT** Ovoid, plum-shaped drupe, yellow-brown when ripe; poisonous.

FLOWERS

Swietenia macrophylla

Baywood

HEIGHT up to 150 ft (45 m)
TYPE Evergreen/Deciduous
OCCURRENCE S. Mexico, Central and South America

Baywood is the most valuable timber tree in tropical Central and South America. Also known as Honduras mahogany, its wood is fairly lightweight and strong, with a medium and uniform texture. It takes an excellent polish and is resistant to decay.
BARK Pale brown, rough, deeply fissured.
LEAF Alternate, pinnate without a terminal leaflet, slender yellow-green axis ending in a narrow point; 3–6 pairs of unequal-sided leaflets, 2¼–6 in (6–15 cm) long.
FLOWER Small, greenish yellow, short-stalked, in panicles, 4–6 in (10–15 cm) long, five petals, ten brown stamens, fragrant. **FRUIT** Seeded capsule, erect, oval, 4¼–7 in (11–18 cm) long, 3 in (7.5 cm) wide, on long, stout stalks.

over ⅜ in (1 cm) thick

BARK

Swietenia mahagoni

Mahogany

HEIGHT 40–50 ft (12–16 m)
TYPE Deciduous
OCCURRENCE US (S. Florida), Bahamas, Antilles, Haiti, Jamaica

With its buttressed trunk and spreading crown, this tree has been prized since the 16th century, when its timber was first shipped to Europe. Most natural stands of mahogany were felled long ago. Today,

FRUIT AND LEAVES

the largest living specimen is believed to be in Florida's Everglades National Park.
BARK Gray to dark reddish brown, smooth to slightly fissured, becoming scaly.
LEAF Alternate, pinnate without a terminal leaflet, untoothed.
FLOWER Greenish yellow, in panicles.
FRUIT Woody capsule, stalked, upright, with winged seeds.

open capsule

oblong fruit   **FRUIT**

FLOWERS

greenish yellow fused stamens

Toona ciliata

Toon

HEIGHT up to 180 ft (55 m)
TYPE Deciduous
OCCURRENCE India, S. China, S.E. Asia
Malaysia, E. Australia

Also known as the red cedar, this tall tree has a cylindrical, sometimes buttressed, trunk. It grows in subtropical rainforest and scrubby areas, often bordering rivers and streams. Its wood is highly valued for cabinet-making, and it has been virtually logged out in its range due to extensive exploitation of its timber. In Australia, it used to be felled before conversion of areas to agricultural land, but the remaining forests where it occurs are now in a World Heritage site. In the past, its flowers were used as a source of red and yellow dyes for silk, cotton, and wool. The tree has been used medicinally, particularly as an astringent and a tonic. **BARK** Grayish white to brown, usually fissured and flaking. **LEAF** Alternate, pinnate, with up to 20 ovate-lanceolate to lanceolate leaflets, smooth to sparsely hairy. **FLOWER** In large terminal panicles, white to creamy white staminal tube, fragrant. **FRUIT** Brown capsule, divides into five segments when dry.

FLOWERS

5 petals

creamy white
flowers

open
capsule

FRUIT

LEAVES AND FLOWERS

Xylocarpus granatum

Cannonball Mahogany

HEIGHT up to 65 ft (20 m)
TYPE Semi-evergreen
OCCURRENCE E. Africa, S.E. Asia, Tonga

The wood of this tree was once used for boat-building. Its bark is used for making dyes and medicines and its roots also have medicinal properties. **BARK** Pale to yellow-brown, smooth, scaling in irregular flakes. **LEAF** Alternate, pinnate; leaflets in 1–3 pairs, with rounded tips. **FLOWER** In axillary white to pink clusters. **FRUIT** Spherical, hanging capsule.

elliptic to obovate
LEAFLETS

thinly branched buttresses

Calodendrum capense

Cape Chestnut

HEIGHT up to 65 ft (20 m)
TYPE Deciduous, rarely evergreen
OCCURRENCE South Africa to Tanzania and Ethiopia

An ornamental with a dense, compact, and rounded crown, this shade tree is suitable for planting in parks and streets. **BARK** Gray, smooth, mottled, and streaky.

LEAF Opposite, smooth, with untoothed edges. **FLOWER** In open terminal panicles, with five narrow petals, five pale pink stamens. **FRUIT** Woody, five-lobed, rough capsule.

ovate-oblong to elliptic leaves

pale pink flowers
LEAVES AND FLOWERS

Chloroxylon swietenia

Satinwood

HEIGHT up to 105 ft (32 m)
TYPE Deciduous
OCCURRENCE Madagascar, Sri Lanka, S. India

Satinwood grows in the dry, interior forests of its native range. It has hard, heavy, yellowish wood that polishes well. Its timber was once an important

Sri Lankan export. **BARK** Yellowish gray, deeply fissured. **LEAF** Pinnate, equal on both sides, up to $9\frac{1}{2}$ in (24 cm) long, 10–20 pairs of oblong leaflets. **FLOWER** Tiny, white, about $\frac{3}{16}$ in (7 mm) wide, on pyramidal racemes up to 6 in (15 cm) long, often produced when the tree is leafless. **FRUIT** Capsule, up to $1\frac{1}{4}$ in (3 cm) long, oblong-ovoid, three-celled, each cell containing about four flat, winged seeds.

Citrus x aurantium

Bitter Orange

HEIGHT up to 33 ft (10 m)
TYPE Evergreen
OCCURRENCE China, Vietnam

The bitter or Seville orange has a round crown and its seedlings are often covered with spines. It is believed to have originally grown in the area of the China–Vietnam border, and its long history of cultivation brought it through Arabia and into southern Europe by the 11th–12th centuries. The Spanish introduced it and the more widely cultivated sweet orange (*Citrus sinensis*) into South America and Mexico in the mid-1500s. Its fragrant white flowers are the

thick-skinned
unripe fruit

finely toothed
edges

FRUIT AND LEAVES

VERSATILE CITRUS

The bitter orange is used as a rootstock for other citrus trees, in herbal remedies, and to make marmalade. It is also planted as an ornamental, especially in the Mediterranean region.

ORNAMENTAL PLANTING

source of neroli oil. **BARK** Green to grayish brown. **LEAF** Alternate, ovate to ovate-oblong, smooth, with narrowly winged stalks. **FLOWER** White, fragrant, solitary or in short axillary racemes. **FRUIT** Spherical, greenish yellow to bright orange.

Citrus x aurantiifolia

Lime

HEIGHT up to 16 ft (5 m)
TYPE Evergreen
OCCURRENCE Known only in cultivation

winged stalks

The lime tree has irregular, drooping branches and spiny twigs. A native of India, it was brought by the Arabs to Africa and the Middle East. It spread to Europe during the Crusades

LEAVES AND FRUIT

and was later taken to the Caribbean and Mexico following the Spanish conquest. The juice from the fruit is used in cooking, soft drinks, pickles, and for medicinal purposes. Its extracts and essential oils are used in aromatherapy, and in perfumes and cleansing products. **BARK** Green to grayish brown. **LEAF** Alternate, elliptic to ovate-oblong, with finely toothed margins. **FLOWER** White, up to ten, on short axillary racemes. **FRUIT** Ovoid to globose, with a thin skin.

FRUIT

greenish yellow skin

greenish pulp

Citrus x limon

Lemon

HEIGHT 10–20 ft (3–6 m)
TYPE Evergreen
OCCURRENCE Known only in cultivation

Unpalatable as a fresh fruit due to its acidic taste, lemon is mostly consumed in cooking and in drinks. **BARK** Green to grayish brown. **LEAF** Alternate, elliptic-ovate to oblong, with toothed margins, on winged stalks. **FLOWER** Axillary; solitary or in clusters of 2–3. **FRUIT** Ovoid, greenish to golden yellow, with thick and rough skin.

white flowers
elliptic-oblong leaves

LEAVES AND FLOWERS

FRUIT

Citrus reticulata

Tangerine

HEIGHT 10–20 ft (3–6 m)
TYPE Evergreen
OCCURRENCE S.E. Asia, S. Europe, Brazil, S.E. United States

The tangerine was probably brought into cultivation in tropical Southeast Asia. It is one of the major parent species that gave rise to the remaining hybrid *Citrus*. **BARK** Green to grayish brown. **LEAF** Alternate, elliptic to lanceolate, on winged stalks. **FLOWER** White, solitary or in clusters of 2–3. **FRUIT** Rounded, with thin skin, indented on top.

LEAVES AND FRUIT

toothed edges

bright orange skin

FLOWER

Flindersia australis

Crow's Ash

HEIGHT 50–130 ft (15–40 m)
TYPE Evergreen/Semi-evergreen
OCCURRENCE E. Australia

The Crow's ash or Australian teak has a dense, spreading crown. It is an excellent urban shade tree. Its timber is yellow-brown. **BARK** Gray to dark brown, smooth, becoming scaly with rounded flakes. **LEAF** Alternate, pinnate, with a terminal leaflet; 3–13 elliptic to narrowly ovate leaflets, aromatic when crushed. **FLOWER** White to cream, in terminal panicles. **FRUIT** Woody five-valved capsule, covered with short, blunt prickles.

Limonia acidissima

Wood Apple

HEIGHT up to 23 ft (7 m)
TYPE Deciduous
OCCURRENCE S. Asia

The wood apple grows in the dry areas of its native habitat. Its fruit is a favorite of elephants. **BARK** Pale gray or whitish; branchlets with straight spines that are up to 1½ in (4 cm) long. **LEAF** Pinnate, with one terminal leaflet; 2–3 pairs of opposite, obovate, stalkless leaflets. **FLOWER** White, green, or reddish purple, with small petals and 7–12 stamens, numerous, on axillary clusters, often from leafless nodes. **FRUIT** Round, woody, many-seeded fruit, with sticky pulp.

Flindersia brayleyana

Queensland Maple

HEIGHT 80–115 ft (25–35 m)
TYPE Evergreen
OCCURRENCE Australia (Queensland)

boat-shaped valve

FRUIT POD

This tree is valued for its easily workable pinkish wood that is used for cabinet-making and indoor fittings. In Australia, it is planted as an ornamental. **BARK** Gray, flaky. **LEAF** Opposite, pinnate with a terminal leaflet; 3–10 broadly elliptic leaflets. **FLOWER** White to cream, borne in terminal panicles. **FRUIT** Woody capsule, covered with short, blunt prickles, splitting into five valves.

Zanthoxylum simulans

Flatspine Prickly Ash

HEIGHT up to 20 ft (6 m)
TYPE Deciduous
OCCURRENCE China

This tree is found in mountain woods and thickets. Its leaves are aromatic when crushed. **BARK** Gray with conical knobs. **LEAF** Pinnate; up to 11 ovate, toothed leaflets. **FLOWER** Small, green, in clusters up to 2 in (5 cm) wide. **FRUIT** Round, warty, green, ripens to red.

glossy green leaflet

red-stalked fruit

LEAVES AND FRUIT

Zanthoxylum piperitum

Sichuan Pepper

HEIGHT up to 33 ft (10 m)
TYPE Deciduous
OCCURRENCE China, Japan, Korea

The fruit of this tree is used for flavoring and seasoning food. **BARK** Yellowish brown, smooth to shallowly fissured.

LEAF Alternate, pinnate with a terminal leaflet; usually 9–17, ovate to elliptic-lanceolate, toothed leaflets. **FLOWER** Greenish, in terminal clusters; males and females on separate trees. **FRUIT** Globose follicle, greenish, ripening to brown, with black seeds.

Cornus kousa

Kousa Dogwood

HEIGHT 10–50 ft (3–15 m)
TYPE Deciduous
OCCURRENCE China, Japan, Korea

This tree has a columnar habit. Its foliage turns red in fall. **BARK** Grayish to red-brown. **LEAF** Opposite, dark green above, waxy and downy beneath. **FLOWER** Yellowish green, in dense heads on long stalks. **FRUIT** Red, fleshy drupe.

FRUIT AND LEAVES

strawberry-like fruit   ovate to ovate-elliptic leaves

Cornus mas

Cornelian Cherry

HEIGHT up to 25 ft (8 m)
TYPE Deciduous
OCCURRENCE C. and S. Europe, S.W. Asia

Cultivated in the past for its edible fruit, which has a plumlike flavor, this tree is now usually planted as a winter-flowering ornamental. It has numerous cultivars. **BARK** Dark brown, scaly. **LEAF** Opposite, ovate to elliptic, hairy on both sides. **FLOWER** Yellow, appearing before leaves. **FRUIT** Bright red, round drupe.

FLOWERS   short flower clusters

Cornus nuttalli

Pacific Dogwood

HEIGHT up to 65 ft (20 m)
TYPE Deciduous
OCCURRENCE W. North America

The flower of this tree is the floral emblem of British Columbia. **BARK** Gray, smooth, becoming scaly with age. **LEAF** Opposite, elliptic to obovate, dark green. **FLOWER** In clusters, with creamy white bracts. **FRUIT** Edible red drupe.

small and yellowish green   **FLOWERS**

Davidia involucrata

Handkerchief Tree

HEIGHT up to 65 ft (20 m)
TYPE Deciduous
OCCURRENCE China

Also called dove tree, the genus is named after Father Armand David, a French missionary, who was the first to report in 1869 that this tree had white flowers "fluttering like doves." During the decades that followed, French and British plant-hunters tried to introduce the tree into Europe. The form most grown today was raised in French nurseries at the end of the 19th century. **BARK** Orange-brown, peeling vertically in small flakes. **LEAF** Alternate, broadly ovate, heart-shaped base, smooth above, downy beneath. **FLOWER** Terminal, on short spur shoots, in small heads, surrounded by two asymmetrical white bracts. **FRUIT** Green with a purple bloom, solitary, usually pear-shaped.

FLOWER CLUSTERS

large white bracts

toothed leaf margin

FOLIAGE

Nyssa sylvatica

Blackgum

HEIGHT up to 80 ft (25 m)
TYPE Deciduous
OCCURRENCE E. North America

The blackgum, also called tupelo, has a pyramidal crown and drooping branches. It is planted as an ornamental and street tree due to its red fall color. It is also popular for environmental planting. **BARK** Dark gray, vertically ridged, breaking into irregular scales. **LEAF** Alternate, dark glossy green above, slightly hairy beneath. **FLOWER** Axillary, greenish, in stalked heads; males and females on same or separate trees. **FRUIT** Ovoid, blue drupe.

ovate to elliptic

LEAVES

Fouquieria columnaris

Boojum Tree

HEIGHT up to 60 ft (18 m)
TYPE Deciduous
OCCURRENCE Mexico (Baja California)

This strange-looking tree has a succulent main stem that has been often compared to an upside-down green carrot. It was given its unusual name by plant explorer Godfrey Sykes in 1923, after a fictitious character in a Lewis Carroll book. Its tall, gently tapering trunk has bristles with short branches, armed with spines. On older trees, the main trunk splits into two or more stems near the top. The tree grows on rocky hillsides, alluvial plains, and in deserts. **BARK** Pale yellow-green, tough, smooth but dimpled with twig scars. **LEAF** Alternate, obovate, fleshy, smooth. **FLOWER** Creamy yellow, tubular, borne on spikelike clusters. **FRUIT** Pale brown capsule, with three valves that curve backward after opening.

thin secondary branches

FLOWERING BRANCHES

flowers in clusters

BOOJUM BOOSTERS

Trees of the Fouquieriacene family are pollinated by a variety of insects. One species, *E. splendens*, was thought to be pollinated by hummingbirds, but these are now known to feed on the nectar without carrying pollen between plants.

HUMMINGBIRD

Camellia sinensis

Tea

HEIGHT 33–50 ft (10–15 m)
TYPE Evergreen
OCCURRENCE China, N. India

TEA HARVESTING

Tea leaves are harvested every 7–15 days, depending on the development of the tender shoots. Slow-developing leaves give a better flavor. They are dried to make green, black, or oolong teas.

PICKING TEA

The tea plant is the source of the world's most popular beverage. Under cultivation, it is trimmed and kept as low bushes or hedges. The use of tea was originally restricted to China and Japan. The Dutch introduced it to Europe and dominated the trade for more than a century before yielding to the British. In 1823, the first wild tea plant was discovered in Assam, India. On January 10, 1839, the first samples of Assam tea were auctioned in London, a historic event that determined the future course of tea cultivation all over the world. Today, more tea is produced from Assam plants than from the Chinese type. It is fermented to give black tea as opposed to Chinese unfermented green tea. **BARK** Gray, rough. **LEAF** Alternate, leathery, lanceolate to elliptic, slightly hairy when young, becoming smooth. **FLOWER** White, large, axillary, solitary, with 5–7 petals and numerous yellow stamens. **FRUIT** Capsule that splits open when seeds ripen.

FLOWER AND FRUIT

glossy surface

LEAVES

Franklinia alatamaha

Franklin Tree

HEIGHT up to 16–24 ft (5–7 m)
TYPE Deciduous
OCCURRENCE North America

Discovered in Georgia in 1765, this tree
was named after Benjamin Franklin. It
was last seen in the wild in 1803 and is
now known only in cultivation. The tree
has a dense, rounded crown. **BARK** Dark
brown, smooth. **LEAF** Alternate, obovate,
finely toothed, dark green above, paler
with fine hairs beneath. **FLOWER** Axillary,
solitary, large, with five white petals.
FRUIT Spherical, dry, woody capsule.

LEAVES AND FLOWER   *numerous yellow stamens*

Diospyros ebenum

Ebony

HEIGHT up to 100 ft (30 m)
TYPE Evergreen
OCCURRENCE S. India, Sri Lanka

This tree has nearly uniform black wood,
the densest and darkest of the Indian-
Asian ebony timbers. It is slow-growing
and has a buttressed, sometimes fluted
trunk. **BARK** Black to gray-black, flaking in
small rectangular pieces. **LEAF** Alternate,
elliptic to ovate-oblong. **FLOWER** Males and
females on separate trees; males: yellowish,
with white corolla, borne in clusters of
3–5; females: yellowish white, solitary.
FRUIT Large, spherical to ovoid berry.

Diospyros quaesita

Calamander

HEIGHT up to 115 ft (35 m)
TYPE Evergreen
OCCURRENCE Sri Lanka

Calamander timber is black, with brown
bands. It is valued for its durability and
ornamental value, but the tree is now
rare because of its slow growth and
irregular flowering period. **BARK** Black,
very rough, peeling to reveal a brown
layer. **LEAF** Alternate, 3¼–7 in (8–18 cm)
long, leathery, elliptic-oblong to
lanceolate. **FLOWER** Males: yellow, in small
clusters; females: yellowish white to white,
solitary. **FRUIT** Spherical berry.

Diospyros kaki

Kaki

HEIGHT up to 90 ft (27 m)
TYPE Deciduous
OCCURRENCE China, cultivated in Japan

Also called Sharon fruit, the kaki has a short, crooked trunk and a dense crown. It has over 1,000 cultivars. Its fruits are of two types. The astringent type, with high levels of soluble tannins, cannot be eaten until fully ripe and is best grown in cooler regions. The non-astringent type needs hot summers. **BARK** Grayish brown, scaly, and divided into square plates.

FRUIT *yellow to orange coloration*

LEAF Alternate, leathery, ovate to elliptic or rounded, dark green above, pale green and hairy beneath, at least on the veins.
FLOWER Males and females on separate trees; males: yellowish or red, with white corollas, borne in clusters of 3–5; females: yellowish white, solitary.
FRUIT Large, spherical to ovoid berry, with a large, persistent calyx.

untoothed margins **LEAVES**

Diospyros virginiana

Persimmon

HEIGHT up to 50–65 ft (15–20 m)
TYPE Deciduous
OCCURRENCE E. United States

Often planted as an ornamental, this tree has a broadly spreading crown. Its ripe fruit is pulpy and can be fermented to make persimmon beer. **BARK** Dark brown-gray to black, with square, scaly, thick plates. **LEAF** Alternate, leathery, ovate-oblong to elliptic. **FLOWER** Males and females on separate trees, both yellowish white and bell-shaped; males in clusters of 3–5; females solitary. **FRUIT** Large, spherical to ovoid, yellow to orange berry.

persistent calyx

FRUIT *smooth surface* **LEAF**

Halesia carolina

Carolina Silverbell

HEIGHT up to 40 ft (12 m)
TYPE Deciduous
OCCURRENCE S.E. United States

The Carolina silverbell is a small ornamental that provides a spectacular display of flowers in spring. Its trunk is short or multi-stemmed and its crown is rounded.
BARK Reddish brown, scaly.
LEAF Alternate, elliptic to ovate-oblong, thinly hairy on both sides, with finely toothed margins and a long-pointed tip.
FLOWER White, with bell-shaped corolla, borne in clusters of 3–5 at the nodes on old wood. **FRUIT** Pear-shaped, four-winged, green drupe.

bell-shaped flowers

FLOWERING SHOOT

Styrax officinalis

Snowbell

HEIGHT up to 23 ft (7 m)
TYPE Deciduous
OCCURRENCE Mediterranean region

Resin from the bark of this tree was once used by the Sumerians in ointments. **BARK** Gray-brown, becoming vertically fissured. **LEAF** Alternate, with whitish, star-shaped hairs. **FLOWER** White, with yellow anthers, in axillary, drooping clusters. **FRUIT** Greenish yellow, ovoid drupe.

LEAVES AND FLOWERS

ovate leaves

white petals

Couroupita guianensis

Cannonball Tree

HEIGHT up to 100 ft (30 m)
TYPE Evergreen/Deciduous
OCCURRENCE Tropical South America

The flowers of this narrow-crowned tree have an unusual sweet scent and are pollinated by bats. **BARK** Brown, smooth, becoming slightly fissured. **LEAF** Alternate, elliptic to oblong or obovate, smooth, except for veins below. **FLOWER** Six reddish-tinged sepals, six pinkish to orange-red petals; only one flower opens at a time. **FRUIT** Large, brown capsule.

curved disk at center

FLOWER

spherical capsule   **RIPE FRUIT**

Bertholletia excelsa

Brazil Nut

HEIGHT up to 165 ft (50 m)
TYPE Deciduous
OCCURRENCE Tropical South America

This tall tree has large woody fruit. **BARK** Gray-brown, fissured. **LEAF** Alternate, leathery, smooth, with smooth or wavy margins. **FLOWER** Pale yellow to white, in axillary spikes or terminal panicles. **FRUIT** Capsule with 10–25 seeds (nuts).

FRUIT

hard, woody shell

longitudinally fissured bark

Chrysophyllum cainito

Star Apple

HEIGHT up to 100 ft (30 m)
TYPE Evergreen
OCCURRENCE West Indies, cultivated in tropical America, S.E. Asia, Africa

This tall tree has a broad and dense crown. **BARK** Brown, rough, and fissured. **LEAF** Alternate, oblong to obovate, dark green above, brown beneath. **FLOWER** Yellowish to purple-white, borne in axillary clusters. **FRUIT** Egg-shaped to spherical berry, with thick rind.

LEAVES, FRUIT, AND FLOWERS

fruit 2–4 in (5–10 cm) wide

densely hairy undersides

small flowers

Argania spinosa

Argan

HEIGHT up to 33 ft (10 m)
TYPE Evergreen
OCCURRENCE Morocco

This tree has a dense, wide crown. It is valued for the oil that is extracted from its nuts. **BARK** Gray to yellow-brown, cracked, and divided in small plates. **LEAF** Alternate, usually in clusters, lanceolate-oblong. **FLOWER** Greenish white, in axillary clusters. **FRUIT** Green to brown, ovoid berry with 1–3 seeds.

yellow stamens

FLOWERS

Manilkara bidentata

Bulletwood

HEIGHT up to 110 ft (33 m)
TYPE Evergreen
OCCURRENCE N. South America, West Indies

The timber of the bulletwood is hard, heavy, and durable. It is used for cabinet-making and to make violin bows. The tree was also tapped or felled for its latex, which was the source of balata gum. **BARK** Brown, thick, fissured and scaly; pink inner bark. **LEAF** Alternate, dark green, elliptic, to 9 in (23 cm) long, often covered in a black mold. **FLOWER** Small, fragrant, whitish, bell-shaped, in clusters of 3–10. **FRUIT** Smooth berry, with sticky pulp and one shiny, blackish seed.

Palaquium gutta

Gutta Percha

HEIGHT up to 150 ft (45 m)
TYPE Evergreen
OCCURRENCE Malay Peninsula, Sumatra, Borneo

This tree has a columnar trunk, usually with small buttresses. Its flowers smell of burned sugar. Its latex was once used for wire insulation but has been replaced by synthetics. It is now used for dental fillings. **BARK** Grayish brown, fissured. **LEAF** Alternate, obovate-ovate to elliptic, dark green above, golden brown with fine silky hairs beneath. **FLOWER** Pale green, in axillary clusters. **FRUIT** Green, globose to egg-shaped, finely hairy nut.

Manilkara zapota

Sapodilla

HEIGHT 16–65 ft (5–20 m)
TYPE Evergreen
OCCURRENCE Mexico, West Indies, tropical Central America

Sapodilla is grown for its edible fruit. The tree's latex, called "chicle," was used in the past as the first chewing gum. **BARK** Dark brown, rough. **LEAF** Alternate, ovate-elliptic to oblong-lanceolate, parallel veins. **FLOWER** Solitary, in leaf axils. **FRUIT** Reddish to yellow-brown berry.

yellow-brown flesh

shiny black seeds

FRUIT

Abiu

HEIGHT 33–115 ft (10–35 m)
TYPE Evergreen
OCCURRENCE Tropical South America

This tree has a pyramidal or rounded crown. It is mostly grown in home gardens. **BARK** Gray-brown, with white latex. **LEAF** Alternate, variable shape, usually smooth. **FLOWER** White to pale yellow, solitary or in clusters of 2–5, fragrant. **FRUIT** Round to ovoid yellow berry.

LEAVES

Sapote

HEIGHT 25–65 ft (7–20 m)
TYPE Evergreen/Semi-evergreen
OCCURRENCE Mexico, Central America, South America, S.E. Asia

This tree has a narrow or spreading crown with thick branches. **BARK** Reddish brown. **LEAF** Alternate, obovate, dark green above, pale green to pale brown beneath. **FLOWER** White to pale yellow, in clusters of 6–15 in axils of fallen leaves. **FRUIT** Dark brown, globose berry with soft, pink to red flesh, sweetish taste.

FRUIT AND FOLIAGE

Canistel

HEIGHT 26–65 ft (8–20 m)
TYPE Evergreen
OCCURRENCE Mexico

Grown for its fruit, this tree has been introduced into tropical South America, the Philippines, and the Seychelles. **BARK** Dark gray-brown, furrowed. **LEAF** Alternate, obovate-elliptic, smooth. **FLOWER** White to pale yellow, solitary or in clusters. **FRUIT** Yellow berry.

LEAVES AND FRUIT

smooth skin

Miraculous Berry

HEIGHT up to 10 ft (3 m)
TYPE Evergreen
OCCURRENCE W. Africa

An unusual trait of this tree's fruit is that it can make bitter or sour food taste sweet. **BARK** Fibrous. **LEAF** Alternate, obovate to oblanceolate, smooth, in clusters. **FLOWER** White, small, in axillary clusters. **FRUIT** Small, single-seeded, bright red berry.

LEAVES AND FRUIT

elongated leaves

oval berry

Arbutus menziesii

Madrone

HEIGHT up to 130 ft (40 m)
TYPE Evergreen
OCCURRENCE Canada (British Columbia),
US (California, Oregon, Washington)

A highly ornamental horticultural
species, this tree is prized for its peeling
bark, showy flowers, and brightly colored
fruit. It is named after Archibald
Menzies, a Scottish botanist and surgeon,
who was the first to discover it, in 1792.
BARK Red-brown, smooth, peeling,
becoming fissured with age; green when
freshly exposed. **LEAF** Alternate, smooth
or slightly downy when young, dark
green above, dull or waxy beneath.
FLOWER White or tinged pink, borne in
large, broad, upright, terminal panicles.
FRUIT Orange-red, rough and warty,
berrylike drupe, with mealy flesh.

small, urn-shaped flowers

BARK

elliptic to obovate leaves

FLOWERS AND LEAVES

Arbutus unedo

**FLOWERS AND
LEAVES**

Strawberry Tree

HEIGHT up to 40 ft (12 m)
TYPE Evergreen
OCCURRENCE S.W. Ireland,
Mediterranean region

The strawberry tree grows mostly in
thickets and woodland in rocky places.
The fruit is edible but not tasty. It has a
very high sugar content and sometimes
ferments on the tree. In several
Mediterranean countries, it is used
to make wines and liqueurs. The
strawberry tree is incorporated in the
heraldic emblem of the Spanish city of
Madrid, with a bear stretching out to eat
the fruit of the tree. **BARK** Red-brown,
not peeling but shredding into strips.
LEAF Alternate, elliptic to oblong or
obovate, smooth, dark glossy green above,
paler beneath. **FLOWER** Small, white or
tinged pink, borne in drooping terminal
clusters. **FRUIT** Orange-red, spherical
drupe, with mealy flesh.

*leaf to 4 in
(10 cm)
long*

*rough, warty
skin*

urn-shaped flowers

*rough, fissured
surface*

FRUIT   **BARK**

Rhododendron

Rhododendron arboreum

HEIGHT up to 50 ft (15 m)
TYPE Evergreen
OCCURRENCE S.W. China, Himalayas, Sri Lanka

This species was the first rhododendron to be introduced to Europe from the Himalayas. It is broadly columnar in shape. **BARK** Red-brown, rough, and shredding. **LEAF** Alternate, oblong to lanceolate, glossy dark green above, silvery to rusty brown beneath; poisonous. **FLOWER** Red, pink, or white, bell-shaped, in dense terminal clusters of up to 20. **FRUIT** Brown woody capsule, with numerous tiny seeds.

pointed tip

LEAVES

Assyrian Plum

Cordia myxa

HEIGHT 10–50 ft (3–15 m)
TYPE Deciduous/Semi-evergreen
OCCURRENCE N. Africa, India, S.E. Asia, Australia

Widely cultivated, this tree often has a crooked trunk. **BARK** Gray-brown to blackish, shallowly fissured. **LEAF** Alternate, smooth to hairy below. **FLOWER** White, in cymes. **FRUIT** Brownish yellow, oval drupe.

FOLIAGE

Spanish Elm

Cordia alliodora

HEIGHT up to 65 ft (20 m)
TYPE Evergreen/Semi-deciduous
OCCURRENCE Tropical South America, West Indies

Spanish elm wood is in great demand for boat decks, cabinetry, veneers, flooring, and paneling. Its flowers, fruit, and leaves are used medicinally. **BARK** Gray to brown, becoming rough and fissured. **LEAF** Alternate, elliptic-oblong, smooth or with scattered hairs. **FLOWER** Small, white, in terminal panicles. **FRUIT** Oblong nutlet.

branches in horizontal layers

Wigandia

Wigandia caracasana

HEIGHT up to 12 ft (3.6 m)
TYPE Evergreen
OCCURRENCE South America

Wigandia is a coarse shrub and is sometimes grown as an ornamental because of its large, showy leaves and violet flowers. However, its leaves and stem have stinging hairs, which can cause severe allergic reactions. It is considered a noxious weed in Australia. **BARK** Green-brown. **LEAF** Alternate, ovate, toothed, long-stalked, with glandular stinging hairs. **FLOWER** Purple-blue petals, bell-shaped, in large terminal cymes. **FRUIT** Capsule that splits open on ripening.

Eucommia ulmoides

Hardy Rubber Tree

rounded to spreading habit

HEIGHT up to 65 ft (20 m)
TYPE Deciduous
OCCURRENCE C. China

Very rare in the wild, this tree is widely cultivated in China for medicinal use and as a street tree. It produces latex, but is not exploited for rubber. **BARK** Gray-brown, rough. **LEAF** Alternate, usually elliptic, smooth. **FLOWER** Greenish brown, axillary; males in clusters; females solitary; on separate trees. **FRUIT** Elliptic to oblong, winged nut.

densely toothed margins

LEAVES

MALE FLOWERS

Cinchona calisaya

Quinine

HEIGHT up to 80 ft (25 m)
TYPE Evergreen
OCCURRENCE South America

This tropical tree is the primary source of the antimalarial drug quinine, which is found in its bark. **BARK** Gray-brown, vertically and horizontally fissured. **LEAF** Opposite, elliptic to oblong or ovate or obovate, smooth above, smooth to downy beneath. **FLOWER** White to pink, fragrant; in terminal panicles, short- and long-styled on separate trees. **FRUIT** Ovate-oblong capsule.

large glossy leaves

smooth margins

FOLIAGE

FLOWERS AND BUDS

Coffea arabica

Arabica Coffee

HEIGHT 13–16 ft (4–5 m)
TYPE Evergreen
OCCURRENCE Ethiopia, cultivated in tropical regions

FLOWERS

5-lobed flowers

There are probably at least 25 species of coffee growing wild, all indigenous to tropical Africa, especially Ethiopia. All species of arabica coffee are woody, ranging from small shrubs to large trees, and have horizontal branches in opposite pairs. This species accounts for 74 percent of world production of coffee.
BARK Brown, with fine vertical fissures.
LEAF Opposite, glossy dark green, ovate to elliptic, smooth. **FLOWER** Borne in clusters of 5–20 in leaf axils, with five white petals, fragrant. **FRUIT** Ovoid berry, about $1/2$ in (1.25 cm) long; green ripening to yellow and then red, black when dried, with two seeds.

berry ripens to red

COFFEE ON THE GO

Coffee was transported to the Arabian Peninsula around 600 CE, and the custom of coffee-drinking then spread throughout the Ottoman Empire. Coffee houses opened in Vienna in 1555 and in England in 1650. It was not until the 1690s that the Dutch introduced coffee into Java. A plant from Java was sent to Amsterdam, where it set fruit. Coffee plants were then sent to Paris and Surinam.

COFFEE BEANS

Coffea canephora

Robusta Coffee

HEIGHT up to 33 ft (10 m)
TYPE Evergreen
OCCURRENCE W. Africa

An important species planted in Africa and Asia, this tree has long, drooping branches. Once chewed as a stimulant, the coffee beans are now used exclusively for the production of instant coffee, or sometimes blended with arabica coffee. **BARK** Brown, with fine vertical fissures. **LEAF** Opposite, glossy dark green, often toothed or wavy margins, oblong-elliptic. **FLOWER** Borne in clusters of 5–20 in leaf axils, with 6–8 white petals. **FRUIT** Red, ovoid berry.

berry ¾–1 in (1.8–2.5 cm) long

FRUIT

Neolamarckia cadamba

Kadam

HEIGHT 80–150 ft (25–45 m)
TYPE Deciduous
OCCURRENCE India, China, S.E. Asia

The kadam tree occurs in many of the Hindu writings about Lord Krishna. **BARK** Pale brown, smooth, becoming gray-brown, fissured, ridged, and flaky. **LEAF** Opposite, elliptic, smooth, with narrowly triangular terminal stipules. **FLOWER** Numerous, in round heads, at ends of short side twigs. **FRUIT** Greenish capsule, turning brown, in spherical heads.

FLOWER HEAD

yellowish white flowers

Alstonia scholaris

Dita

HEIGHT up to 130 ft (40 m)
TYPE Evergreen
OCCURRENCE India, S. China, S.E Asia, tropical Australia

Often seen in parks and along streets, this tree has a distinctive pagoda-like crown. Its wood was once used to make writing tablets. **BARK** Gray; exudes white sap. **LEAF** In whorls of 4–10, with many lateral veins. **FLOWER** White, with overlapping lobes, in terminal or axillary inflorescences. **FRUIT** Long, paired follicles.

elliptic to obovate

LEAVES

Dyera costulata

Jelutong

HEIGHT up to 260 ft (80 m)
TYPE Deciduous
OCCURRENCE S. Thailand, Malay Peninsula, Sumatra, Borneo, Sulawesi

The wood of this tree is commonly used to make pencils, picture frames, and cabinets. **BARK** Gray to brown, mottled. **LEAF** Arranged in whorls of 5–8, usually at the ends of the twigs, elliptic to obovate. **FLOWER** Axillary inflorescences, with small, white corollas. **FRUIT** Long, paired follicles, containing ellipsoidal seeds.

FOLIAGE

Frangipani
Plumeria rubra

HEIGHT up to 33 ft (10 m)
TYPE Deciduous
OCCURRENCE Mexico, South America

This tree with fragrant flowers is central to Mayan creation myths. **BARK** Pale green to pale brown, smooth; exudes white latex. **LEAF** Alternate, elliptic, with pointed tips. **FLOWER** Large, in terminal clusters. **FRUIT** Gray-green, oblong follicles.

FLOWERS IN BLOOM   *pink-yellow lobes*

Serpentine Root
Rauvolfia serpentina

HEIGHT up to 10 ft (3 m)
TYPE Evergreen
OCCURRENCE Sri Lanka, India, China, Malay Peninsula

This medicinal tree is usually unbranched. It contains the alkaloid reserpine, which is used in some medicinal drugs. **BARK** Thin, yellowish green. **LEAF** Elliptic to obovate, in whorls of up to three, near tips of stems. **FLOWER** White or tinged with purple, with overlapping lobes, in terminal and lateral cymes. **FRUIT** Oval, orange ripening to purple-black, paired drupes.

untoothed edges

red stalks

LEAVES AND FLOWERS

Crepe Jasmine
Tabernaemontana divaricata

HEIGHT up to 16 ft (5 m)
TYPE Evergreen
OCCURRENCE Myanmar, Thailand, India

Widely cultivated in the tropics as an ornamental, this tree contains alkaloids that also make it a useful medicinal plant. Its flowers exude an intense, penetrating perfume. All parts of this tree are poisonous. **BARK** Green to pale brown. **LEAF** Opposite, elliptic. **FLOWER** White, in terminal inflorescences of 1–8; ovoid buds. **FRUIT** Oval follicles in pairs.

pointed leaf tip   *5 petals*

FLOWER AND LEAVES

Iboga
Tabernanthe iboga

HEIGHT up to 6 ft (2 m)
TYPE Evergreen
OCCURRENCE W. Africa, Gabon, Cameroon

The iboga has an upright and branching trunk. Its leaves, seeds, and root bark contain alkaloids, including a psychoactive compound, ibogaine, which is illegal in some countries, such as the US. Known as the "Tree of Life," the Iboga tree has been used for hundreds of years as a source of stimulant and aphrodisiac preparations by people living in its native habitat. Extracts from the tree have been used experimentally to treat impotence and to break drug addiction. **BARK** Green to pale brown; exudes white latex. **LEAF** Opposite, dark green, elliptic to ovate or oblanceolate, smooth and untoothed. **FLOWER** White corollas, spotted with pink; in axillary clusters of up to 12. **FRUIT** Oval, orange-red.

Brugmansia x candida

Angel's Trumpet

HEIGHT 5–16 ft (1.5–5 m)
TYPE Evergreen
OCCURRENCE Peru

Often planted in gardens, this species is a hybrid of *B. aurea* and *B. versicolor*. It includes numerous cultivars, some with double flowers. All parts of the plant are highly toxic. It has spectacular flowers that are sweetly scented, particularly in the evenings. Angel's trumpet can be grown in frost-free Mediterranean or subtropical climates. **BARK** Grayish, thin. **LEAF** Alternate, up to 16 in (40 cm) long, with soft hairs.

FLOWER Solitary, white, pink, to yellow, up to 24 in (60 cm) long, with recurved petals. **FRUIT** Green, ovoid to spindle-shaped, pendulous capsule.

ovate leaves

FLOWERS AND LEAVES

trumpet-shaped flower

Solanum betaceum

Tree Tomato

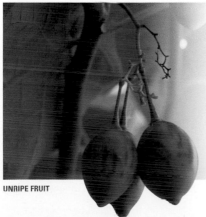

UNRIPE FRUIT

HEIGHT 6–25 ft (2–8 m)
TYPE Evergreen
OCCURRENCE South America, Africa, S.E. Asia, New Zealand

The commercial production of this tree's fruit is restricted to New Zealand, where it began in 1920. Internationally, the trade remains on a small scale. **BARK** Greenish brown, thin. **LEAF** Alternate, ovate, heart-shaped base, with soft hairs. **FLOWER** Bell-shaped, fragrant, pink to pale blue, in axillary clusters. **FRUIT** Ovoid, smooth, purplish red to orange-red or yellow berry.

Fraxinus excelsior

European Ash

HEIGHT up to 150 ft (45 m)
TYPE Deciduous
OCCURRENCE Europe, W. Asia

A broadly columnar, tall tree, European ash has a spherical to round crown and is commonly found on limestone in moist woods and on riverbanks. **BARK** Gray-brown and smooth, becoming ridged and furrowed. **LEAF** Opposite, pinnate with a terminal leaflet; 7–15 ovate-oblong to lanceolate leaflets, dark green above, hairy beneath on the midrib, toothed margins. **FLOWER** Small, purplish, with sepals and petals absent, in short, axillary clusters, opening from black buds before the leaves appear. **FRUIT** Winged key, glossy green turning pale brown, in hanging clusters.

tapered tip

winged fruit in drooping clusters

LEAVES AND FRUIT

flowers in dense clusters

FLOWERS

ELASTIC ASH WOOD

The wood of European ash is known for its strength and flexibility; it is easily bent when steamed or seasoned. Once used to make shafts and wheel rims for carriages and wagons, it is now used to make sturdy baskets, oars, and agricultural implements.

BASKET

Fraxinus ornus

Manna Ash

HEIGHT up to 65 ft (20 m)
TYPE Deciduous
OCCURRENCE S. Europe, S.W. Asia

Also called flowering ash for its showy flower clusters, this tree has a round crown and a broadly spreading habit. In Sicily, the tree is tapped to form "manna" from the solidified sap. This contains high concentrations of mannitol, a sugar that can be used as a sweetener by people with diabetes. **BARK** Gray, smooth. **LEAF** Opposite, pinnate with a terminal leaflet; 5–9 ovate to lanceolate leaflets, dark green above, hairy beneath on the midrib, sharply toothed margins, and distinctly stalked lateral leaflets. **FLOWER** White, small, with four slender petals, borne before the leaves, in short, fluffy axillary clusters. **FRUIT** Green lanceolate key, ripening to pale brown, with a flattened wing, hanging in clusters.

pointed leaflets

flowers in conical clusters

FLOWERING BRANCHES

Fraxinus pennsylvanica

Green Ash

HEIGHT up to 80 ft (25 m)
TYPE Deciduous
OCCURRENCE N. and C. United States

Often planted as an ornamental, this fast-growing tree has a broadly columnar shape. **BARK** Gray-brown, with interlacing ridges. **LEAF** Opposite, pinnate with a terminal leaflet; 5–9 ovate to lanceolate leaflets, green above, hairy beneath on the midrib. **FLOWER** Greenish purple, petalless, small; males and females borne on separate trees, in short clusters. **FRUIT** Green winged key, ripening to pale brown.

tapered tips

slightly furrowed

LEAVES

BARK

Olea europaea

Olive

HEIGHT up to 50 ft (15 m)
TYPE Evergreen
OCCURRENCE Middle East, Mediterranean region, N. Africa

white flowers in clusters

gray-green leaves

fruit to 1½ in (4 cm) long

FRUIT

LEAVES AND FLOWERS

OLIVES AND THEIR OIL

Olive trees are grown throughout the Mediterranean region for their edible fruit. Harvested in late summer, olives are pickled in brine to remove bitter chemicals, or pressed to extract their oil.

OLIVE OIL

PICKING OLIVES

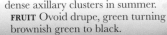

The wild olive is a small, bushy plant, but cultivated trees have a typical gnarled trunk. It grows best in a warm climate and tolerates periods of drought. It is a long-lived species; individual trees can survive for up to 500 years. Probably domesticated by the Minoans around 2500 BCE, the olive was spread throughout the Mediterranean region by the Greeks and Romans. Franciscan missionaries brought olive trees to California from Mexico in the 1700s.

BARK Gray, furrowed, sometimes peeling.
LEAF Opposite, lanceolate, or ovate (wild trees), gray-green above, paler beneath due to small silvery scales. **FLOWER** White, fragrant, small, four-toothed, borne in dense axillary clusters in summer.
FRUIT Ovoid drupe, green turning brownish green to black.

Myoporum acuminatum

Boobialla

HEIGHT 6–25 ft (2–8 m)
TYPE Evergreen
OCCURRENCE Australia (New South Wales, Queensland)

A species that grows on sandy soil and rocky sites, this broad-crowned tree can be used for hedging and street planting, particularly in coastal areas, as it is resistant to saline spray. **BARK** Gray-brown, deeply fissured. **LEAF** Alternate, toothed near tip. **FLOWER** White, with purple spots, in axillary inflorescences of 3–8. **FRUIT** Ovoid, purple or purple-black drupe.

elliptic leaves

pointed tip

FOLIAGE

Catalpa bignonioides

Southern Catalpa

HEIGHT up to 60 ft (18 m)
TYPE Deciduous
OCCURRENCE S.E. US, naturalized elsewhere

This bean tree is much branched, with a spreading habit and a round crown. It is frequently used as an ornamental. **BARK** Pale brown tinged with red, with irregular scales. **LEAF** Opposite or in threes, unlobed or shallowly lobed. **FLOWER** Large; white corollas with two lobes, frilled at the margin, with rows of yellow spots and many purple spots. **FRUIT** Beanlike, pendulous pod.

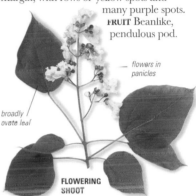

flowers in panicles

broadly ovate leaf

FLOWERING SHOOT

Crescentia cujete

Calabash Tree

HEIGHT up to 40 ft (12 m)
TYPE Evergreen
OCCURRENCE West Indies, tropical South America

The calabash tree has dense, tiered, spreading branches with a broad crown and a relatively short trunk. Its fruits are dried and polished to make utensils and musical instruments. **BARK** Whitish to silver gray, rough. **LEAF** Alternately arranged in clusters on short shoots, oblanceolate to obovate, tapering at the base. **FLOWER** Yellow-green, with purple markings, large, cup-shaped, solitary or in clusters, usually borne on the trunk; night-flowering. **FRUIT** Large, round gourd; hard shell.

5–12 in (12–30 cm) wide

FRUIT

Jacaranda

HEIGHT 16–50 ft (5–15 m)
TYPE Deciduous
OCCURRENCE Argentina, Bolivia

Its striking display of flowers makes this tree a popular ornamental for streets and parks. **BARK** Pale brown, rough and fissured with age. **LEAF** Opposite, bipinnate; 13–41 small, smooth or downy leaflets. **FLOWER** Purplish blue, in terminal panicles. **FRUIT** Oval pod; winged seeds.

FLOWERS

tubular corolla

Sausage Tree

HEIGHT 33–50 ft (10–15 m)
TYPE Deciduous
OCCURRENCE Tropical Africa

The flowers of this tree are pollinated by nectar-eating bats; it rarely fruits in their absence. **BARK** Pale brown, rough, often cracked. **LEAF** Opposite, pinnate, with

drooping panicle

gray-green capsule

FRUIT

3–6 pairs of elliptic to lanceolate leaflets. **FLOWER** Red to purplish, bell-shaped. **FRUIT** Pendulous, sausage-shaped capsule.

Midnight Horror

HEIGHT 16–65 ft (5–20 m)
TYPE Evergreen/Semi-deciduous
OCCURRENCE India, E. Asia

The night-blooming flowers of this tree have a harsh, musty smell that attracts pollinating bats. **BARK** Pale gray-brown, smooth or finely cracked. **LEAF** Opposite, pinnate, with 3–4 ovate to oblong leaflets, clustered at ends of branches. **FLOWER** Large, trumpet-shaped, reddish purple outside, yellow to cream inside, in terminal clusters. **FRUIT** Long, pendent woody capsule.

slender crown

WINGED SEED

Spathodea nilotica

Flame Tree

HEIGHT up to 60 ft (18 m)
TYPE Evergreen
OCCURRENCE Tropical Africa

upright pods — The flame tree is grown for its shade and color. It is used for fire-resistant landscaping, as its wood is difficult to burn. **BARK** Pale gray and warty. **LEAF** Opposite, pinnate; 11–15 pairs of oval to ovate leaflets, hairy beneath. **FLOWER** Large, bell-shaped, red-orange, with yellow edges, in racemes. **FRUIT** Greenish brown pods; numerous papery seeds.

terminal leaflet

LEAVES AND FLOWERS

Tabebuia chrysantha

Yellow Trumpet Tree

HEIGHT up to 80 ft (25 m)
TYPE Deciduous
OCCURRENCE Mexico, Central America, Venezuela

This is the national tree of Venezuela. **BARK** Pale to dark gray and scaly. **LEAF** Palmate, with 5–7 stalked, oval to oblong leaflets. **FLOWER** Golden yellow, trumpet-shaped, in terminal panicles. **FRUIT** Hairy capsule.

Tabebuia impetiginosa

Pink Trumpet Tree

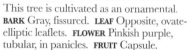

HEIGHT up to 65 ft (20 m)
TYPE Deciduous
OCCURRENCE South America

This tree is cultivated as an ornamental. **BARK** Gray, fissured. **LEAF** Opposite, ovate-elliptic leaflets. **FLOWER** Pinkish purple, tubular, in panicles. **FRUIT** Capsule.

Tabebuia serratifolia

Yellow Poui

HEIGHT up to 150 ft (45 m)
TYPE Deciduous
OCCURRENCE Tropical Central and South America

The showy flowers of the yellow poui bloom when the tree has no leaves. Its hard, durable timber has been used for marine and naval construction, bridges, flooring, and furniture. It is also planted as an ornamental and street tree in South America, but is now rare in the wild due to overexploitation. **BARK** Pale brown to gray, fissured, scaly. **LEAF** Opposite, pinnate with one terminal leaflet; five ovate-oblong to elliptic, toothed leaflets. **FLOWER** Yellow, tubular, in terminal and lateral clusters. **FRUIT** Long capsule, with winged seeds.

Citharexylum spinosum

Fiddlewood

HEIGHT up to 50 ft (15 m)
TYPE Deciduous/Evergreen
OCCURRENCE Caribbean, N. South America

A popular ornamental and street tree in tropical and subtropical areas, fiddlewood has hard and durable wood that was historically used for tools. It was called "bois fidèle" or faithful tree by the French, which was corrupted to "fiddlewood" in English. Despite the name *spinosum*, the tree bears no spines. Where the tree is deciduous, the leaves turn orange before falling. **BARK** Pale brown, becoming scaly, with longitudinal thin strips. **LEAF** Opposite or in whorls of three, ovate to oblong or elliptic. **FLOWER** White, small, tubular, borne in axillary and terminal, spikelike inflorescences. **FRUIT** Oblong drupe, borne on pendulous stalks, red, turning black, containing four seeds.

irregular crown

Gmelina arborea

Gumhar

HEIGHT up to 65 ft (20 m)
TYPE Deciduous
OCCURRENCE India to S. China, Malay Peninsula, Indonesia

This broad-crowned, fast-growing tree is grown in plantations for its wood. **BARK** Pale ashy gray to grayish yellow, smooth. **LEAF** Opposite, broadly ovate, with brownish hairs beneath. **FLOWER** In axillary clusters, with five unequal lobes: upper two curved backward, next two forward-pointing and orange-red, bottom lobe lemon yellow. **FRUIT** Oblong to obovoid, yellowish green, fleshy drupe.

Premna serratifolia

Headache Tree

HEIGHT up to 16 ft (5 m)
TYPE Evergreen
OCCURRENCE S. and S.E. Asia, Australia, Pacific Islands

Used occasionally for living fence poles and garden stakes, this tree is valued for its tolerance to salt spray and saline soil. **BARK** Yellowish brown with vertical furrows, soft, thin, flaky. **LEAF** Opposite, oblong to broadly ovate, sometimes hairy along veins. **FLOWER** Greenish white petals, forming a short, hairy tube, with two unequal lobes, scented, in terminal compound corymbs. **FRUIT** Round, bluish black, fleshy drupe, 1 1/4–2 1/4 in (3–6 mm) wide.

Tectona grandis

Teak

HEIGHT up to 165 ft (50 m)
TYPE Deciduous
OCCURRENCE Asia: India to Thailand, Cambodia, Vietnam, Laos, Java

One of the best-known tropical hardwood species, teak has been exploited for its durable and versatile wood for hundreds of years. British colonists in India and Burma (now Myanmar), and Dutch colonists in Indonesia, established teak plantations to provide a ready supply of timber for ship-building, general construction, and fine furniture. The tree takes up to 60 years to mature and can be exceptionally long-lived. There are two contenders for the oldest teak tree, both about 154 ft (47 m) tall; one in Palghat district, Kerala, India with a girth of 21 ft (6.42 m) and the other in Uttaradit province, Thailand, with a girth of 32 ft (9.57 m), estimated to be more than 1,000 years old. The trunk of the teak tree is fluted. **BARK** Pale brown, thin, flaky in narrow, vertical strips.

FRUIT

papery calyx

LEAF Opposite, large, ovate to broadly obovate, rough above, soft hairs beneath. **FLOWER** White, with a small, funnel-shaped corolla, the calyx densely covered with brown hairs, numerous, borne in terminal and lateral, wide pyramidal inflorescences, at the ends of shoots. **FRUIT** Thin, inflated calyx surrounding a stone containing four cavities, each with one seed.

LEAVES

12–20 in (30–50 cm) long

TEAK WOOD FURNITURE

The dark brown wood of the teak tree has a distinct grain, dries with little degradation, and is easily worked with hand or power tools. The untreated wood weathers well, resists rot, and is not attacked by termites. These properties make it one of the most valuable woods for furniture-making.

TEAK WOOD CHAIR

Paulownia tomentosa

Princess Tree

HEIGHT up to 65 ft (20 m)
TYPE Deciduous
OCCURRENCE China, cultivated in Korea, Japan, North America, Europe

Also known as the empress tree, after Anna Paulovna, queen of William II of the Netherlands, this tree was first planted in Jardin des Plantes, Paris, in 1834. It was introduced into North America a few years later and naturalized. Centuries ago, the tree was cultivated in Japan, where it was traditionally valued, particularly for making the stringed

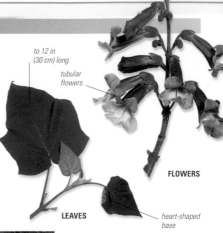

to 12 in (30 cm) long

tubular flowers

FLOWERS

LEAVES

heart-shaped base

instrument called the "koto." **BARK** Brown-gray, smooth, visible lenticels when young, splitting lengthwise with age. **LEAF** Opposite, ovate, 3–5 lobes, hairy, untoothed or lobed margins. **FLOWER** Bell-shaped, large, pale purple with darker spots, yellow stripes inside, in terminal panicles. **FRUIT** Woody, ovoid capsule, up to 2 in (5 cm) long, hairy, ripening from green to brown.

RIPE FRUIT

ovoid capsule

Paulownia x taiwaniana

Paulownia

HEIGHT up to 65 ft (20 m)
TYPE Deciduous
OCCURRENCE Island of Taiwan

This tree is a natural hybrid between *P. fortunei* and *P. kawakami*. It grows quickly and is cultivated mainly for its fine, light timber. It can also be pruned to supply leaves and flowers as fodder for livestock.

It is highly ornamental with masses of sweetly scented, trumpet-shaped flowers in spring. **BARK** Grayish, rough. **LEAF** Opposite, ovate, thin, 4–12 in (10–30 cm) long, with 3–5 lobes, pointed tip. **FLOWER** Petals 2–2¼ in (5–6 cm) long, pale purple with deep violet spots on yellow "throat"; in terminal, pyramidal panicles. **FRUIT** Woody capsule, oblong-ovoid, 1½–1¾ in (3.5–4.5 cm) long.

Ilex aquifolium

English Holly

HEIGHT up to 65 ft (20 m)
TYPE Evergreen
OCCURRENCE Europe, W. Asia

The holly has been cultivated since ancient times. There are numerous cultivars with variations in the density of prickles, in patterns of variegation, and the color of berries. Its glossy leaves also vary in shape. Its wood is heavy and fine-grained and has been used for inlay work in furniture, chess pieces, and printing blocks. **BARK** Pale gray, smooth.
LEAF Alternate, ovate to elliptic, wavy margins with spines.
FLOWER Small, white, sometimes purple-tinged, fragrant; males and females on separate trees, borne in axillary clusters.
FRUIT Berry, usually shiny bright red, but yellow in some cultivars; poisonous.

FESTIVE WREATH

In ancient Rome, the festival of Saturnalia took place during the winter solstice. It was a time of high spirits and gift-giving, which included sending sprigs of holly to friends. Some pagan peoples brought holly indoors to ward off evil spirits. Gradually, these traditions were absorbed into Christianity, and the holly became associated with Christmas.

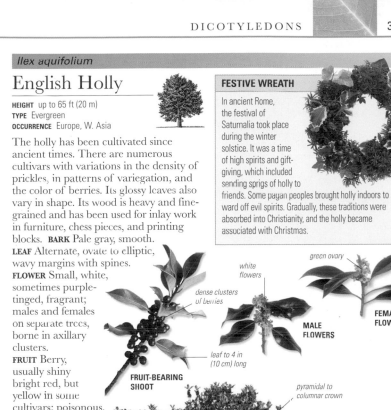

green ovary

white flowers

dense clusters of berries

MALE FLOWERS

FEMALE FLOWERS

leaf to 4 in (10 cm) long

FRUIT-BEARING SHOOT

pyramidal to columnar crown

Ilex paraguariensis

Maté

HEIGHT up to 65 ft (20 m)
TYPE Evergreen
OCCURRENCE South America

The first maté plantations were founded by the Jesuits in 1650 CE. Today, Argentina accounts for about 45 percent of the total crop. A tall, multi-stemmed bush in the wild, Maté is pruned to 10–20 ft (3–6 m) in cultivation to stimulate growth and to make the leaves easier to pick. The leaves are used to make a tea-like drink. **BARK** Gray-brown, smooth. **LEAF** Alternate, obovate, leathery. **FLOWER** Axillary; males in clusters of 3–11; females 1–3, on separate trees. **FRUIT** Reddish to black, spherical drupe.

LEAVES

toothed margins

white flowers

FLOWERS AND FRUIT

unripe fruit

MATÉ TEA

Maté is traditionally drunk from a gourd with a metal straw that has a filter to strain out leaf fragments. The bottom of the gourd is filled with burned or toasted leaves and hot water. Burned sugar, lemon juice, and/or milk are used to flavor the tea.

TEA

GOURD AND STRAW

Pseudopanax crassifolius

Lancewood

HEIGHT 20–60 ft (6–18 m)
TYPE Evergreen
OCCURRENCE New Zealand

The crown of this tree is rounded at maturity and its juvenile foliage differs from adult leaves. **BARK** Grayish, smooth. **LEAF** Juveniles: very long, linear, toothed; adults: oblanceolate, smooth, toothed. **FLOWER** Greenish, in terminal umbels; males with five petals; females petalless. **FRUIT** Globose, black, fleshy drupe.

Schefflera actinophylla

Umbrella Tree

HEIGHT 16–40 ft (5–12 m)
TYPE Evergreen
OCCURRENCE Papua New Guinea, tropical Australia

This tree is so named because of its compound leaves that form an umbrella-shaped rosette. **BARK** Gray, smooth. **LEAF** Alternate, digitate, with 5–16 elliptic to obovate, smooth leaflets. **FLOWER** Bright red, stalkless, clustered on straight branches. **FRUIT** Purple-black drupe.

Steganotaenia araliacea

Carrot Tree

HEIGHT 10–16 ft (3–5 m)
TYPE Deciduous
OCCURRENCE S.W. and C. Africa

All parts of this tree smell strongly of carrots, hence its common name. **BARK** Pale greenish gray, papery and peeling. **LEAF** Alternate, drooping, crowded at the ends of branches; pinnate

with ovate, deeply toothed leaflets and a terminal leaflet. **FLOWER** Tiny, white to yellow, in compound umbels. **FRUIT** Small, flat, ovate to pear-shaped, with three prominent ribs.

TREE IN LEAFLESS PHASE

Pittosporum undulatum

Cheesewood

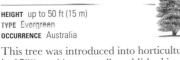

HEIGHT up to 50 ft (15 m)
TYPE Evergreen
OCCURRENCE Australia

This tree was introduced into horticulture in 1789, and is now well established in cultivation. It is commonly used for hedges and windbreaks. However, it can be very invasive in scrubland. **BARK** Dark gray, smooth. **LEAF** Alternate, ovate to elliptic or lanceolate, clustered at ends of branches, aromatic when crushed. **FLOWER** White, turning yellow, borne in short terminal panicles. **FRUIT** Globose capsule, with red-brown seeds.

LEAF AND FLOWER   *wavy margins*   *flowers in short clusters*

Pittosporum tobira

Tobira

HEIGHT 16–20 ft (5–6 m)
TYPE Evergreen
OCCURRENCE China, Japan

Widely cultivated in areas with a Mediterranean climate, this species is sometimes used as a low hedge or as a small ornamental tree. It has a rounded crown. **BARK** Dark gray, smooth. **LEAF** Alternate, oblanceolate to obovate, leathery, sometimes curved back, aromatic when crushed. **FLOWER** White, turning yellow, in short terminal panicles, fragrant. **FRUIT** Globose capsule with red-brown seeds.

white petals

glossy leaves

FLOWERS AND LEAVES

Sambucus canadensis

Elderberry

HEIGHT up to 16 ft (5 m)
TYPE Deciduous
OCCURRENCE North America

The fruit of this tree has more Vitamin C per unit weight than oranges or tomatoes. **BARK** Pale yellowish brown, soft, spongy, fissured. **LEAF** Opposite, pinnate with a terminal leaflet; 5–7 lanceolate to elliptic, toothed leaflets, smooth or slightly hairy beneath. **FLOWER** Creamy white, numerous, in flat, terminal panicles. **FRUIT** Small, berrylike drupe, 3–5 nutlets.

FRUIT   *dark purple drupes*

Sambucus nigra

Elderberry

HEIGHT up to 32 ft (10 m)
TYPE Deciduous
OCCURRENCE Europe

BRANCHLET

pointed leaflets

flowers with broad flattened heads

CORDIALS AND WINES

Both the flowers and fruit of the elder tree are used to make wine. Elder fruit is also used to make jellies and the flowers to make a non-alcoholic cordial. The use of elder flowers for this purpose has greatly increased in the last 25 years. An estimated 100 tons of wild flowers are harvested annually in Britain for cordial-making. Elder is also used to make medicinal herbal remedies.

DRIED FLOWERS AND INFUSION

The European black elderberry is common in damp woods and wasteland. It often grows around farm buildings and along walls, where its seeds are scattered in bird droppings. Elderberry grows rapidly, and its branches form a dense, shrubby growth. Many cultivated forms have been bred, with different leaf colors and forms, as well as ones with colored flowers or larger fruit. **BARK** Pale yellowish brown, soft, spongy, fissured.

LEAF Opposite, pinnate with a terminal leaflet; 5–7 ovate to elliptic leaflets, slightly hairy beneath, sharply toothed; exuding a foul odor when crushed. **FLOWER** Creamy white, strongly fragrant, numerous, borne in terminal flat panicles. **FRUIT** Berrylike, purple-black drupe, with 3–5 one-seeded nutlets.

broadly columnar to rounded head

FRUIT

drupe to ¼ in (6 mm) wide

Lobelia giberroa
Giant Lobelia

HEIGHT up to 32 ft (10 m)
TYPE Evergreen
OCCURRENCE Kenya

One of the strange herbaceous plants of African mountains that have developed a treelike habit, this species has a hollow stem. There are also related species that are stemless. **BARK** Brownish, not highly developed. **LEAF** In rosettes, alternate, oblanceolate, hairy, with toothed margins. **FLOWER** Green with mauve stamens, borne in a long terminal inflorescence. **FRUIT** Capsule.

LEAFY ROSETTE

sparsely branched stems

Montanoa quadrangularis
Arboloco

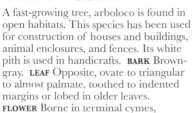

HEIGHT up to 65 ft (20 m)
TYPE Evergreen
OCCURRENCE Colombia, Venezuela

A fast-growing tree, arboloco is found in open habitats. This species has been used for construction of houses and buildings, animal enclosures, and fences. Its white pith is used in handicrafts. **BARK** Brown-gray. **LEAF** Opposite, ovate to triangular to almost palmate, toothed to indented margins or lobed in older leaves. **FLOWER** Borne in terminal cymes, numerous, daisylike with white ray florets and yellow central disk. **FRUIT** Head of brown-black seeds.

Dendrosenecio johnstonii
Giant Groundsel

HEIGHT 16–32 ft (5–10 m)
TYPE Evergreen
OCCURRENCE E. African mountains

The giant groundsel grows around Mount Kilimanjaro in northern Tanzania, in a belt of alpine grassland, shrubs, and bogs. This gigantic, odd-looking plant has treelike characteristics. Its sparsely branched stems terminate in large rosettes of leaves. These are densely furred as protection against the intense light and harsh climatic conditions in its mountainous habitat. The old, dead leaves act as a screen around its trunk. **BARK** Brownish, not highly developed. **LEAF** In rosettes, broadly ovate to elliptic, hairy, with toothed margins. **FLOWER** Borne in terminal inflorescences, numerous, to 3 ft (1 m) long, daisylike with white ray florets and yellow central disk. **FRUIT** Head of brown-black achenes.

leaf-clad stems

EUROPEAN BLACK ELDER
The structure of the flowerheads of the European
black elder tree (*Sambucus nigra*) is clearly seen
here. The buds eventually open as fragrant greenish
white and pink blossoms. The elder is a common
inhabitant of damp woodlands throughout Europe.

Glossary

A number of specialist botanical and scientific terms have been used in this book. Use this glossary to obtain a concise definition of these terms. Terms in italic type are defined elsewhere in the glossary.

ACHENE A small, dry and hard, one-seeded fruit that does not split open for seed distribution.

ALTERNATE Describes leaves that are borne singly at each node, in two vertical rows, on either side of an axis. (See Leaf Arrangements, p.347.)

ANTHER Part of the *stamen* that releases pollen; usually borne on a filament.

ARIL Coat that covers some seeds; often fleshy and brightly colored.

AXIL Upper angle between a part of a plant and the stem that bears it.

AXILLARY Borne in an *axil*, usually referring to flowers.

BIPINNATE A compound leaf arrangement (see p.347) in which the *leaflets* are themselves *pinnate*.

BRACT Modified leaf at the base of a flower or flower head. A bract may be small and scalelike, or large and petal-like, or it may resemble normal foliage.

BRACTEOLE Secondary *bract* sheathing a flower in an *inflorescence*.

BURR *1.* Prickly, spiny, or hooked fruit, seed head, or flower head. *2.* Woody outgrowth on the trunk of some trees.

BUTTRESS Trunk base that is fluted or swollen, giving stability to a tree in shallow soil conditions.

CALYX (*pl.* calyces) Collective name for *sepals*, joined or separate, that form the outer whorl of the *perianth*.

CAPSULE A type of dry fruit that splits open to disperse ripe seed.

CARPEL Female flower part consisting of a *style*, a *stigma*, and an *ovary*.

CATKIN A type of *inflorescence*, usually pendulous, in which scalelike *bracts* and tiny, often petalless flowers are arranged in a *spike*.

CLONE A genetically identical group of plants derived from one individual by vegetative reproduction.

LEAF SHAPES

Leaves occur in a great variety of shapes, and a selection of the most common types is shown below. Some leaves do not match one of these shapes exactly and may be a combination of two.

These shapes apply to both simple leaves, which are undivided, and compound leaves, which are divided into two or more component parts, each of which is known as a leaflet.

NEEDLELIKE   LINEAR   ROUNDED   OBLONG   ELLIPTIC

HEART-SHAPED   OVATE   OBOVATE   LANCEOLATE   OBLANCEOLATE

COLUMNAR A tree shape that is taller than broad, with parallel sides. (see Tree Habit, p.348.)

CONE The seed-bearing structure of conifer trees.

COROLLA *1.* Collective name for petals. *2.* Inner whorl of *perianth* segments in some monocotyledons.

CORYMB Broad, flat-topped or domed *inflorescence* of stalked flowers or flower heads arising at different levels on alternate sides of an axis. (See Flower Arrangements, p.346.)

CULTIVAR Contraction of "cultivated variety." A cultivated plant that retains distinct characteristics when propagated.

CYME Branched *inflorescence* with each axis ending in a flower. (See Flower Arrangements, p.346.)

DECIDUOUS A tree that loses its leaves and remains leafless for some months of the year, usually in winter (temperate zones) or the dry season (tropical zones).

DIGITATE A *palmate* compound leaf divided into five *leaflets* arising from a single basal point. (See Compound Leaf Arrangements, p.347.)

DRUPE A type of fruit consisting of one or several hard seeds (stones) surrounded by a fleshy outer covering.

ELLIPTIC A flat leaf shape that is broadest at the center, tapering toward each end. (See Leaf Shapes, facing page.)

ENDOCARP The hard outer covering of the seed of a succulent fruit.

ENDOSPERM Specialized food store within the fertilized seed of angiosperms (flowering plants) that nourishes the embryo during germination.

EVERGREEN A tree that bears leaves throughout the year.

FOLLICLE Dry fruit, formed from a single *carpel,* that splits along one side to release one or more seeds.

HABIT The overall shape of a tree. (See Tree Habit, p.348.)

FLOWER PARTS

Most flowers are made up of petals, sepals, and the male and/or female flower parts (some flowers are exclusively male or female). The main distinction is between those that have distinct sepals and petals (advanced) and those that do not (primitive).

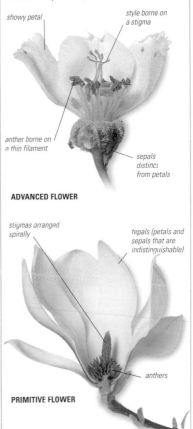

showy petal

style borne on a stigma

anther borne on a thin filament

sepals distinct from petals

ADVANCED FLOWER

stigmas arranged spirally

tepals (petals and sepals that are indistinguishable)

anthers

PRIMITIVE FLOWER

HERITAGE TREE A tree of considerable age that has some important cultural or historical significance.

HYBRID Naturally or artificially produced offspring of genetically distinct parents of different species. Hybrids show new characteristics.

INFLORESCENCE Arrangement of flowers around a single axis.

LANCEOLATE Leaf that is broadest below the center, tapering to a narrow tip. (See Leaf Shapes, p.344.)

FLOWER ARRANGEMENTS

Flowers are arranged on a single stem either singly or in groups called inflorescences. Groups of flowers are displayed in a characteristic pattern around the stem—a descriptive feature and a means of identification. The most common types of inflorescences are shown here.

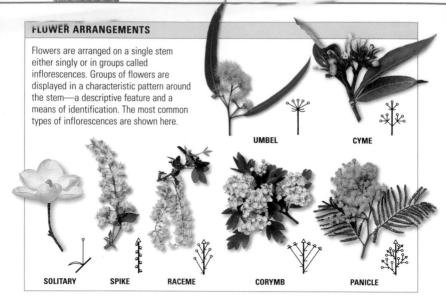

UMBEL

CYME

SOLITARY   **SPIKE**   **RACEME**   **CORYMB**   **PANICLE**

LATERAL *1.* Located on or to the side of an axis. *2.* Side shoot arising from the stem of a plant.

LEAFLET Single division of a compound leaf. Also known as a pinna.

BARK TYPES

As the trunk of a tree grows, the bark has to crack or peel to accommodate its increasing girth. Every species has a distinctive bark texture; some examples are shown here.

SMOOTH IN EARLY YEARS

IRREGULAR PLATES

RIDGED AND FISSURED

VERTICAL PEELING

HORIZONTAL PEELING

ROUGH FLAKING

LENTICEL Raised pore on the surface of bark or some fruits that provides access for air to the inner tissues.

MESOCARP The soft, fleshy, middle portion of the wall of a succulent fruit between the skin and the hard layer.

MIDRIB Primary (usually central) vein running from the stalk to the tip of a leaf or leaflet. Also called midvein.

NATIVE A species that occurs naturally in a particular region, as opposed to one that has been introduced.

NATURALIZED A non-native species that has become established in the wild in a region where it was introduced.

NODE Point on a stem, sometimes swollen, at which leaves, leaf buds, and shoots arise.

OBLANCEOLATE Leaf shape that is broadest above the center, tapering to a narrow basal point. Also called inversely lance-shaped. (See Leaf Shapes, p.344.)

OBLONG Describes a leaf shape with two sides of roughly equal length. (See Leaf Shapes, p.344.)

OBLONG-ELLIPTIC Describes a leaf shape that is oblong with ends that are round.

OBOVATE A leaf shape that is egg-shaped in outline and broadest above the middle. (See Leaf Shapes, p.344.)

OIL DOTS The tiny reservoirs that occur on the surfaces of leaves of some trees, known for their aromatic oils; sometimes visible as black spots.

OPPOSITE A leaf arrangement in which the leaves are borne in pairs at each *node*, in the same place but on opposite sides of an axis. (See Simple Leaf Arrangements, right.)

OVARY Female flower part that contains the ovules, which develop into seeds (see also *carpel*).

OVATE Describes a leaf shape that is broadest below the middle. (See Leaf Shapes, p.344.)

OVOID Describes a solid form that is broadest below the middle; usually refers to a fruit.

PALMATE A compound leaf that is fully divided into *leaflets* arising from a single basal point. (See Compound Leaf Arrangements, right.)

PANICLE A branched *raceme*. (See Flower Arrangements, facing page.)

PEALIKE Describes a flower with an erect standard petal, two lateral wing petals, and two lower, keeled petals enclosing the stamens and *pistil*.

SIMPLE LEAF ARRANGEMENTS

Simple leaves are not divided into secondary units. They are arranged in one of two patterns: opposite (paired on either side of the stem) or alternate (in a staggered arrangement).

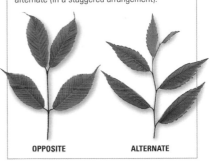

OPPOSITE   ALTERNATE

COMPOUND LEAF ARRANGEMENTS

Leaves that are divided into individual leaflets are known as compound leaves. Leaflets may be arranged symmetrically around the tip of the stem or along its length.

PINNATE   PALMATE

LEAF MARGINS

The lamina, or leaf blade, of both simple and compound leaves may have a smooth edge (entire) or it may be shaped with indentations. The individual pattern is particular to each species of tree and can serve as an identification feature. As shown below, the indentations may be toothed, lobed, or wavy, but in addition there are also other less common variations.

ENTIRE   TOOTHED   LOBED   WAVY

PEDICEL The stalk supporting a flower, flower head, or fruit.

PERIANTH Collective term for the petals and *calyx*.

PERICARP The part of the fruit that encloses the seed.

PINNATE A compound leaf arrangement in which the *leaflets* (pinnae) are arranged either alternately or in opposite pairs on a central axis. (See Compound Leaf Arrangements, p.347.)

PIONEER SPECIES Species that are usually the first to colonize inhospitable sites and cleared ground, leading the way for other vegetation. They improve soil quality and protect land from erosion.

PISTIL Female reproductive organ of a flower, composed of one or several fused or separate *carpels*.

RACEME *Inflorescence* of stalked flowers radiating from a single, unbranched axis, with the youngest flowers near the tip. (See Flower Arrangements, p.346.)

SEMI-DECIDUOUS OR SEMI-EVERGREEN A tree that loses its leaves for only a short period during the year or that sheds a proportion of its leaves periodically but is never entirely leafless.

SEPAL One of the usually green parts of an advanced flower outside the petals. (See Flower Parts, p.345.)

SPIKE An *inflorescence* in which stalkless flowers are arranged on an unbranched axis. (See Flower Arrangements, p.346.)

STAMEN Male part of a flower, usually composed of an *anther* borne on a filament.

STAMINAL TUBE A structure formed from joined *stamens*.

STIGMA Female part of a flower found at the tip of the *pistil* that receives pollen. (See Flower Parts, p.345.)

STIPULE Leaflike or bractlike structure borne, usually in pairs, at the point where a leaf-stalk arises from a stem.

STYLE Female part of flower connecting the *ovary* and the *stigma*. (See Flower Parts, p.345.)

SUCKER *1*. Shoot that arises below the soil level, usually from the roots rather than from the stem or crown of the plant. *2*. Shoot that arises from the stock of a grafted or budded plant.

SYNCARP An aggregate or multiple fruit that is produced from fused *pistils*; the individual fruits join together in a mass and grow together to form a single fruit.

TEPAL The term that is given to the *sepals* and petals when they are indistinguishable from one another, as in the case of primitive angiosperms. (See Flower Parts, p.345.)

TERMINAL A term that describes the position at the end of a stem or shoot.

UMBEL Flat- or round-topped *inflorescence* in which numerous stalked flowers are borne in a terminal position from a single point. (See also Flower Arrangements, p.346.)

TREE HABIT

A tree's shape is species-specific and can help in identification. However, habit can vary depending on age and habitat and other external features such as climate. For example, a tree growing in the open will differ greatly in shape compared to one of the same species growing in dense forest.

CONICAL   **SHRUBLIKE**

SPREADING

COLUMNAR

Tree Families

Refer to this alphabetical list to find out which tree families and genera are represented in this book and on which page(s) their species can be found.

Adoxaceae *Sambucus* (pp.339–40). **Amaranthaceae** *Charpentiera; Haloxylon* (p.148). **Anacardiaceae** *Anacardium; Gluta; Harpephyllum; Mangifera; Pistacia; Pleiogynium; Schinus; Spondias* (pp.296–9). **Annonaceae** *Annona; Asimina; Cananga; Polyalthia* (pp.116–8). **Apocynaceae** *Alstonia; Dyera; Plumeria; Rauvolfia; Tabernaemontana; Tabernanthe* (pp.325–6). **Aquifoliaceae** *Ilex* (pp.337–8). **Araucariaceae** *Agathis; Araucaria* (pp.92–3). **Araliaceae** *Pseudopanax; Schefflera* (p.338). **Asparagaceae** *Cordyline; Dracaena; Yucca* (pp.126–7). **Asphodelaceae** *Aloe* (pp.125–6). **Betulaceae** *Alnus; Betula; Carpinus; Corylus; Ostrya* (pp.257–62). **Bignoniaceae** *Catalpa; Crescentia; Jacaranda; Kigelia; Oroxylum; Spathodea; Tabebuia* (pp.331–3). **Bixaceae** *Bixa; Cochlospermum* (p.269). **Boraginaceae** *Cordia; Wigandia* (p.322). **Burseraceae** *Boswellia; Bursera; Commiphora* (pp.294–5). **Buxaceae** *Buxus* (p.145). **Cactaceae** *Carnegiea* (p.149). **Campanulaceae** *Lobelia* (p.341). **Canellaceae** *Canella* (p.113). **Cannabaceae** *Celtis* (p.229). **Caricaceae** *Carica, Vasconcellea* (pp.267–8). **Caryocaraceae** *Caryocar* (p.179). **Casuarinaceae** *Casuarina* (p.263). **Cercidiphyllaceae** *Cercidiphyllum* (p.153). **Chrysobalanaceae** *Chrysobalanus; Parinari* (pp.167–8). **Combretaceae** *Terminalia* (p.153). **Compositae** *Dendrosenecio; Montanoa* (p.341). **Cornaceae** *Cornus; Davidia; Nyssa* (pp.310–11). **Cucurbitaceae** *Dendrosicyos* (p.242). **Cunoniaceae** *Davidsonia* (p.184). **Cupressaceae** *Calocedrus; Chamaecyparis; Cryptomeria; Cunninghamia;* x *Cupressocyparis; Cupressus; Juniperus; Metasequoia; Platycladus; Sequoia; Sequoiadendron; Taxodium; Tetraclinis; Thuja; Thujopsis; Xanthocyparis* (pp.99–104). **Cycadaceae** *Cycas* (p.69). **Dicksoniaceae** *Dicksonia* (p.65). **Dipterocarpaceae** *Dryobalanops; Hopea; Neobalanocarpus; Shorea* (pp.282–4). **Ebenaceae** *Diospyros* (pp.316–7). **Ericaceae** *Arbutus; Rhododendron* (pp.321–2). **Erythroxylaceae** *Erythroxylum* (p.181). **Eucommiaceae** *Eucommia* (p.323). **Euphorbiaceae** *Aleurites; Baccaurea; Euphorbia; Hevea; Mallotus; Vernicia* (pp.177–9). **Fagaceae** *Castanea; Chrysolepis ; Fagus; Quercus* (pp.243–55). **Fouquieriaceae** *Fouquieria* (p.314). **Ginkgoaceae** *Ginkgo* (p.71). **Guttiferae** *Calophyllum; Garcinia* (p.180). **Hamamelidaceae** *Liquidambar; Parrotia* (p.154). **Juglandaceae** *Carya ; Juglans; Pterocarya* (pp.264–6). **Labiatae** *Gmelina; Premna; Tectona* (pp.334–5). **Lauraceae** *Chlorocardium; Cinnamomum; Endiandra; Eusideroxylon; Laurus; Persea; Sassafras; Umbellularia* (pp.118–22). **Lecythidaceae** *Bertholletia; Couroupita* (p.318). **Leguminosae** *Acacia; Albizia; Amherstia; Bauhinia; Butea; Cassia; Castanospermum; Ceratonia; Cercis; Colophospermum; Colvillea; Cynometra; Dalbergia; Delonix; Dipteryx; Erythrina; Falcataria; Gleditsia; Gymnocladus; Inocarpus; Koompassia; Laburnum; Leucaena; Parkia; Peltogyne; Peltophorum; Pericopsis; Prosopis; Pterocarpus;*

Robinia; Samanea; Sophora; Tamarindus (pp.185–209). **Loranthaceae** *Nuytsia* (p.152). **Lythraceae** *Lawsonia* (p.153). **Magnoliaceae** *Liriodendron; Magnolia* (p.114). **Malvaceae** *Adansonia; Bombax; Brachychiton; Ceiba; Durio; Guazuma; Lagunaria; Ochroma; Pachira; Theobroma; Tilia; Triplochiton* (pp.269–81). **Melastomataceae** *Tibouchina* (p.167). **Meliaceae** *Azadirachta; Cedrela; Chukrasia; Dysoxylum; Khaya; Lansium; Lovoa; Melia; Sandoricum; Swietenia; Toona; Xylocarpus* (pp.301–8). **Moraceae** *Antiaris; Artocarpus; Broussonetia; Ficus; Maclura; Milicia; Morus* (pp.230–41). **Moringaceae** *Moringa* (p.268). **Muntingiaceae** *Muntingia* (p.282). **Musaceae** *Ravenala* (p.140). **Myricaceae** *Morella* (p.256). **Myristicaceae** *Myristica* (p.114). **Myrtaceae** *Corymbia; Eucalyptus; Eugenia; Melaleuca; Metrosideros; Psidium; Syzygium* (pp.153–67). **Nothofagaceae** *Nothofagus* (p.243). **Oleaceae** *Fraxinus; Olea* (pp.328–30). **Oxalidaceae** *Averrhoa* (p.184). **Palmae** *Areca; Arenga; Borassus; Caryota; Ceroxylon; Cocos; Copernicia; Corypha; Elaeis; Hyphaene; Jubaea; Lodoicea; Metroxylon; Phoenix; Raphia; Roystonea; Trachycarpus; Washingtonia* (pp.127–40). **Pandanaceae** *Pandanus* (p.124). **Paulowniaceae** *Paulownia* (p.336). **Phytolaccaceae** *Phytolacca* (p.152). **Pinaceae** *Abies; Cedrus; Larix; Phyllocladus; Picea; Pinus; Pseudotsuga; Tsuga* (pp.76–91). **Pittosporaceae** *Pittosporum* (p.339). **Platanaceae** *Platanus* (pp.144–5). **Podocarpaceae** *Podocarpus* (pp.96–7). **Polygonaceae** *Triplaris* (p.148). **Proteaceae** *Grevillea; Macadamia* (pp.142–3). **Quillajaceae** *Quillaja* (p.184). **Rhamnaceae** *Hovenia; Ziziphus* (pp.225–6). **Rhizophoraceae** *Rhizophora* (p.181). **Rosaceae** *Crataegus; Cydonia; Eriobotrya; Malus; Prunus; Pyrus; Sorbus* (pp.210–25). **Rubiaceae** *Cinchona; Coffea; Neolamarckia* (pp.323–5). **Rutaceae** *Calodendrum; Chloroxylon; Citrus; Flindersia; Limonia; Zanthoxylum* (pp.308–12). **Salicaceae** *Pangium; Populus; Salix* (pp.291–2). **Santalaceae** *Santalum* (pp.152–3). **Sapindaceae** *Acer; Aesculus; Blighia; Dimocarpus; Koelreuteria; Litchi; Nephelium* (pp.285–93). **Sapotaceae** *Argania; Chrysophyllum; Manilkara; Palaquium; Pouteria; Synsepalum* (pp.318–20). **Schisandraceae** *Illicium* (p.112). **Sciadopityaceae** *Sciadopitys* (p.97). **Scrophulariaceae** *Myoporum* (p.331). **Simaroubaceae** *Ailanthus; Leitneria* (p.300). **Solanaceae** *Brugmansia; Solanum* (p.327). **Staphyleaceae** *Staphylea* (p.154). **Styraceae** *Halesia; Styrax* (pp.317–318). **Taxaceae** *Cephalotaxus; Taxus; Torreya* (pp.97–9). **Theaceae** *Camellia; Franklinia* (pp.315–6). **Thymelaeaceae** *Aquilaria; Gonystylus* (p.285). **Ulmaceae** *Trema; Ulmus; Zelkova* (pp.226–9). **Umbelliferae** *Steganotaenia* (p.339). **Urticaceae** *Cecropia; Dendrocnide; Musanga* (p.242). **Verbenaceae** *Citharexylum* (p.334). **Winteraceae** *Drimys* (p.113). **Xanthorrhoeaceae** *Kingia; Xanthorrhoea* (pp.124–5).

Index